CONTENT

Acknowledgements 4

About the Author 5

Glossary & Abbreviations 6

Maps 7

Introduction 9

Chapter 1   Overview 10

Chapter 2   The Bombers 13

Chapter 3   The Opponents: Fighters and AA Guns 19

Chapter 4   The Allies Strike Back 25

Chapter 5   The End of the Beginning 35

Chapter 6   A Turning of the Tide, and the Dutch arrive 42

Chapter 7   Bigger, Better and Faster 54

Chapter 8   The Catalinas arrive; the Allies Apply Pressure 62

Chapter 9   A New Wing and New Aircraft 71

Chapter 10 Trading Hudsons for Beauforts – and the Black Cats fly 83

Chapter 11 The Americans and the Dutch depart; Lucky 13 returns 93

Chapter 12 No. 2 Squadron operations and the RAAF's heavies take over 104

Chapter 13 The RAAF heavies move forward 117

Chapter 14 The Cats fly to China, and the war's end 123

Conclusion 132

Appendix 1   No.18 NEI Squadron and its Australian roots by Elmer Mesman 133

Appendix 2   Flying in RAAF Bombers – Brian Winspear's Story 138

Main Sources 149

Index of Names 152

ACKNOWLEDGEMENTS

Special thanks, in alphabetical order, to:

Bob Alford, Aviation Historian, whose research contributed much of the historical data

Kaylene Anderson, as always

Members of the Facebook group Children of 18 Squadron NEI-RAAF

Michael Claringbould for his assistance, aircraft profiles and the front cover artwork

Linda Fazldeen AM for proofreading

Group Captain David Fredericks, Director History and Heritage Services, RAAF

Elmer Mesman, for his contribution (Appendix 1)

Gosewinus F van Oorschot, author

Bob Livingstone for proofreading and B-24 photos

Dr Peter Williams, Military Historian, for his insights and perceptive comments

Brian Winspear AM for his contribution (Appendix 2)

Sharon Yang, Royal Australian Air Force

In the USA: the staff of Maxwell-Gunter Air Force Base, the New York Public Library, and the Library of Congress in Washington DC.

The author acknowledges the contribution of the Northern Territory Government, whose NT History Awards sponsored research in the USA.

To Richard and Sarah

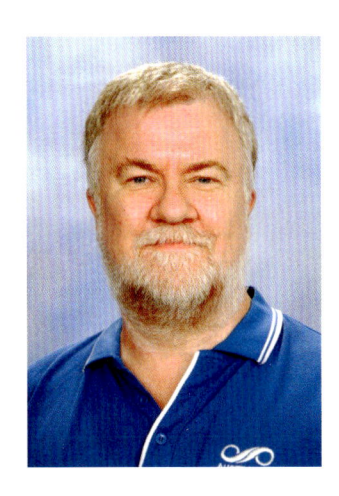

ABOUT THE AUTHOR

Dr Tom Lewis, OAM, is one of Australia's foremost military historians and the author of twenty books. Tom is a former naval officer, where he was an intelligence analyst and an instructor at the RAN College; and a high school teacher in three states.

Other books by the author:

Attack on Sydney – a commemoration of the 80th anniversary of the midget submarine raid on Sydney in 1942 (Big Sky, 2022)

Australia Remembers 4 – the Bombing of Darwin (Big Sky, 2022) – a book for young people, suitable for upper primary/lower secondary. (Big Sky, 2022)

Eagles over Darwin (Avonmore Books, 2021)

Atomic Salvation. How the A-Bomb Attacks Saved the Lives of 32 Million People. (Big Sky, 2020)

Darwin Bombed! A Young Person's Guide to the Japanese attacks of 19 February 1942 (Avonmore Books, 2020)

The Empire Strikes South (Avonmore Books, 2017)

Honour Denied – Teddy Sheean A Tasmanian Hero (Avonmore Books, 2016)

Carrier Attack Darwin 1942 (with Peter Ingman, Avonmore Books, 2013)

Lethality in Combat (Big Sky, 2012)

The Submarine Six (Avonmore Books, 2011)

Darwin's Submarine I-124 (Avonmore Books, 2010)

Zero Hour in Broome (with Peter Ingman, Avonmore Books, 2010)

Captain Hec Waller: A Memorial Book (co-author, 2008)

10 Shipwrecks of the Northern Territory (co-author, 2007)

Australian Naval Leaders (RAN College, 2006)

By Derwent Divided (Tall Stories, 2000)

A War at Home (Tall Stories, 1999 & multiple reprints)

Darwin Sayonara (Boolarong, 1999)

Sensuikan I-124 (Tall Stories, 1997)

Wrecks in Darwin Waters (Turton & Armstrong, 1992)

GLOSSARY & ABBREVIATIONS

(Japanese terms in italics)

BG	Bombardment Group (USAAF)
BS	Bombardment Squadron (USAAF)
CRTC	Combat Replacement Training Center
Dokuritsu Chutai	Independent *chutai* (or Independent Squadrons), often reconnaissance units (JAAF).
FG	Fighter Group (USAAF)
HMAS	His Majesty's Australian Ship
IJN	Imperial Japanese Navy
JAAF	Japanese Army Air Force
Kokutai	An IJN air group, consisting of between three to six *chutai*
Ku	Abbreviation of *Kokutai*
LAC	Leading Aircraftman
NEI	Netherlands East Indies
NWA	North-West Area
OTU	Operational Training Unit
POW	Prisoner of War
PRU	Photographic Reconnaissance Unit
RAAF	Royal Australian Air Force
RAF	Royal Air Force
RCAF	Royal Canadian Air Force
RCM	Radar Countermeasures
Sentai	An abbreviation of Japanese *hiko sentai* defining a JAAF flying regiment.
SWPA	South West Pacific Area
US	United States
USAAF	United States Army Air Force
USN	United States Navy
USS	United States Ship
VHF	Very High Frequency
WAG	Wireless Air Gunner

A map showing the RAAF North West Area (NWA) of Australia and the Japanese-occupied Netherlands East Indies. Many of the locations mentioned in the text are localised and it is not possible to show them on a map of this scale. However, most of the attacks by Hudsons or B-25s were against Timor as well as targets in the Kai, Aru and Tanimbar island groups. The introduction of B-24s enabled more distant targets throughout the NEI to be attacked. Late in the war the use of newly constructed airfields at Truscott and Corunna Downs in Western Australia enabled very long range strikes against targets in Java and Borneo.

Key airfields used by bombers in the NWA. At the outbreak of war, the only two military airfields were located at Darwin and Batchelor, with small civilian airstrips in other centres. During 1942-43 a vast construction effort resulted in many airfields being built along the Stuart Highway which was the overland supply route between Darwin and southern Australia. The key airfields used by bombers were Hughes, McDonald, Fenton and Long. The last Japanese attack on Darwin was in November 1943, following which RAAF Darwin became the key operational base during the final year of the war. Milingimbi and Drysdale Mission were two fairly basic airfields to the east and west of Darwin used as forward bases from 1942, while new airfields were built at Gove in Arnhem Land and Truscott and Corunna Downs in Western Australia. Darwin and Grote Eylandt were the home of pre-war flying boat bases, and both locations saw use by RAAF Catalinas during the war.

INTRODUCTION

The purpose of this book is to detail Allied bomber operations flown from northern Australia during the period March 1942 to August 1945, or specifically from the North-West Area (NWA). The NWA was an RAAF command zone comprising the Northern Territory and the north of Western Australia.

During that time Australia was part of General Douglas MacArthur's wider South West Pacific Area (SWPA) command, and the vast majority of combat operations took place in the New Guinea theatre. From September 1942 these were the responsibility of the US Fifth Air Force, which assumed operational command of RAAF units in that theatre. The subsequent New Guinea campaign was both complex and wide ranging, with a vast array of USAAF and RAAF squadrons seeing service there.

However, the Fifth Air Force did not generally have operational command over units on the Australian mainland, which remained under RAAF control. So a lesser-known air campaign was fought between Japanese air units in the Netherlands East Indies (NEI) and Allied units in the NWA, centred on the northern town of Darwin. In recent years several books have focused on the defensive efforts by Allied fighter units over Darwin, but works describing Allied bomber operations taking the fight to the Japanese from the same area have been sparse.

Probably the best work is Bob Alford's *Darwin's Air War*, first published in 1991 and followed by a larger second edition ten years later. This provides an excellent general overview of the campaign, both defensive and offensive, but understandably lacks detail in certain areas.

Hence the purpose of this book, partly inspired by my friendship with RAAF bomber crewman Brian Winspear. Brian experienced the bombing of the Darwin RAAF base on 19 February 1942 after flying Hudsons from Timor during the NEI campaign. He later served with Vengeance and Beaufort squadrons, and his full story is told in Appendix 2.

Indeed, the offensive campaign from the NWA commenced with two understrength Hudson squadrons taking the fight to Japanese forces in nearby Timor in 1942, aided occasionally by USAAF B-17s, B-25s and B-26s. They were later joined by a Dutch B-25 unit, which gave a unique flavour to NWA operations. From 1943 USAAF B-24s added a new dimension to the fight, as their long endurance could reach deep into the NEI. Other RAAF types to see offensive service in the NWA were Vengeances (very briefly), Beauforts, Venturas, B-24s, B-25s and Catalina flying boats. The last type waged an important mining campaign against Japanese held ports in the NEI and later to the Philippines and beyond.

Generally, the NWA and New Guinea campaigns are distinct. However, there was some blurring due to the operations of certain units, namely those with long endurance that operated B-24s and Catalinas. Hence some New Guinea missions are also mentioned in this narrative as they concern units primarily operating in the NWA.

I trust this book brings to life this little-known campaign for a current generation of readers and serves to remind us of the sacrifice of so many brave airmen all those years ago.

Dr Tom Lewis OAM
Canberra, Australia
October 2022

CHAPTER 1
OVERVIEW

When the Pacific War began in December 1941, Australia had been at war for over two years since September 1939. Australian troops had been sent overseas as part of the overall British Empire war effort and had seen combat in the European and the Mediterranean theatres. Defence measures in Australia itself were largely confined to measures to protect against German U-Boats and surface raiders. It was one of the latter, the *Kormoran*, which sunk the cruiser HMAS *Sydney* off the West Australian coast in November 1941. In the main, however, the island continent had been left out of the conflict and found itself largely unprepared for the Pacific War.

In January 1942 the initial attacks on Australia were by submarines. Four Japanese 80-man boats laid mines and then lay in wait with their torpedoes. On 20 January, they launched an unsuccessful attack against a small convoy entering the northern port of Darwin. Subsequently one of the submarines, the *I-124*, got into a fight with a corvette, HMAS *Deloraine*. The Australian ship was the victor, and the other three submarines fled.

One month later, the Japanese had their revenge. Four Japanese aircraft carriers, veterans of the Pearl Harbor strike, launched 188 bombers and fighters against Darwin. At the time the RAAF had not a single fighter aircraft in service in Australia, and a handful of USAAF P-40 fighters that just happened to be present were easily accounted for. The raid pulverised Darwin, killing 236 people, sinking 11 ships, and destroying 30 aircraft.

Australia's citizens, who had largely felt insulated from the war, were stunned by the news of the raid. It came just four days after the shock of the fall of the British bastion of Singapore, through which Australian defence policy had rested. The following weeks were dark times indeed, as a Japanese invasion appeared certain.

Fortunately, Australia was not alone. It had fought in an alliance with British, Dutch and American forces to defend the islands to its north. Following the surrender of the Netherlands East Indies in early March 1942, some of these forces had been evacuated to Australia. Among them were two battered USAAF heavy bomber units, the 7th and 19th Bombardment Groups, equipped with B-17 Flying Fortresses and LB-30 Liberators.

Interestingly, in late 1941 the commander of the (US) Far East Air Force in the Philippines, Major General Lewis Brereton, had foreseen the need to withdraw to Australia and to prepare bases there. In this respect he made reference to the commander of US forces in the Philippines, General Douglas MacArthur:

> …MacArthur was far sighted. Never at any time did he fail to realize that, if a campaign in the Philippines was unsuccessful, it would be essential … to provide … defense of Northern Australia, the Dutch East Indies and the Malay Peninsula.

This followed a 22 November report to the US Army's Chief of Staff, General George C Marshall, by Major General Dwight D Eisenhower. The future leader of the D-Day operation said:

> …our base must be Australia and we must start at once to expand it and secure our communications to it. In the last we dare not fail.

Hence the use of northern Australia by US air units had been foreseen before the start of the Pacific War. Some work had been completed in surveying Australian airfields and positioning supplies of 100 octane aviation fuel as used by US aircraft. In September 1941 just prior to the outbreak of war, 19th Bombardment Group B-17s flying to the Philippines from the US had used Australian bases including Darwin. After much of the Far East Air Force was destroyed during Japanese attacks on the first days of the war, on 20 December some of these same B-17s were sent back to the relative safety of Batchelor, south of Darwin.

Two days later the 19th BG launched its first attack from Australian soil. At 1033 on 22 December nine B-17s took off from Batchelor, bound for the Gulf of Davao in the Philippines and a strike on Japanese shipping timed for sunset. Under the command of Captain Cecil Combs, each B-17 carried four 500-pound bombs.

Arriving over the Gulf of Davao they bombed a Japanese convoy of seven ships before flying onto Del Monte to refuel and rearm. Then came a strike on Japanese forces landing at Lingayen Gulf on Luzon. The following morning only six B-17s were ready to fly. Shortly after take-off one aircraft, developed engine trouble and aborted, while another also aborted with engine trouble and flew on to Batchelor.

The other aircraft released their bombs over the target. However, overcast conditions prevented any damage assessment. The remaining three serviceable machines left Del Monte and bombed the Japanese in the Gulf of Davao before returning to Batchelor. At Del Monte, the remaining unserviceable B-17 had been repaired and flown to Batchelor after unsuccessfully bombing Japanese forces at Cotabato on Mindanao. Hence, all nine aircraft had returned to Batchelor by the evening of 23 December.

The following day the 19th BG's status report showed that of the 14 aircraft available at Batchelor there were:

Three B-17s on mission. Four here in commission. Seven here out of commission.

Those three aircraft listed as "on mission" had departed Batchelor on 24 December and flown to Del Monte to attack Davao. While taxiing to the runway one bomber blew a tyre and aborted. The remaining pair took off, flown by Lieutenant George Schaetzel and Lieutenant Alvin J Mueller. Over Davao they were met with anti-aircraft fire before being attacked by No. 3 *Kokutai* A6M2 Zeros.

During the combat the B-17s were repeatedly fired at. Both bombers made it back to Batchelor albeit damaged (they were subsequently declared unrepairable). On Schaetzel's aircraft Staff Sergeant James Cannon had been killed and another man wounded, while two gunners in Mueller's crew were also wounded. Cannon was buried in grave 112 at Darwin's Gardens Cemetery the following day.

In the meantime, discussions had focussed on Darwin becoming the headquarters for the Far East Air Force. However, its facilities were almost non-existent. Instead, the 19th BG was ordered to operate alongside Dutch forces in the Netherlands East Indies. On 31 December the serviceable B-17s (mostly older model B-17Ds) took off from Batchelor bound for Java where the aircraft found themselves at the forefront of efforts to stem the Japanese advance.

The 19th BG was soon joined by elements of the 7th Bombardment Group operating a mix of B-17s and LB-30 Liberators which had made the long flight from the US. After a brief but fiercely fought campaign, the exhausted survivors of these two groups evacuated to Australia in early March 1942.[1]

Fortunately, American forces and supplies had been flowing into Australia. Initially these were from convoys destined for the Philippines that were redirected to Australia after the outbreak of war. They were followed by ships sent direct from the US. In the first months of 1942 hundreds of P-39 and P-40 fighters arrived in Australia. Although time was needed to assemble and test fly these aircraft, they were soon equipping newly operational USAAF and RAAF fighter units. Among these was the 49th Fighter Group, USAAF, which began arriving in the Darwin area in March 1942.

For the next several months the 49th FG defended the skies of Darwin from air attack by Japanese units operating from bases in the Netherlands East Indies. The two key units involved were No. 3 *Kokutai* and the Takao *Kokutai* operating Zero fighters and Betty bombers respectively.

Some bombers arrived in Australia in the first months of 1942 after flying the trans-Pacific route from the US, but numbers were very modest. These were B-17E reinforcements for the 19th BG, together with B-25 Mitchell and B-26 medium bombers which equipped the 3rd and 22nd Bombardment Groups based in northern Queensland. Smaller numbers of crated A-20s also arrived, having been originally intended for the Dutch in Java. Subsequently most of these bombers became involved in the fast-escalating war against the Japanese in New Guinea, although as will be seen they also flew missions from the Darwin area.

The only bombers available for permanent service in northern Australia from March 1942 were the RAAF Lockheed Hudsons of Nos. 2 and 13 Squadrons. These aircraft had been acquired for coastal reconnaissance purposes, for which they were well-suited, being modern and reliable. However, they had been used as bombers during the Netherlands East Indies campaign where they had incurred heavy losses. The survivors had withdrawn to Darwin in February, although by March just a handful of Hudsons were still in service. This modest force would shoulder the burden of taking the fight to the Japanese in the North-West Area.

Boeing B-17 Flying Fortress bombers of the 19th BG at Darwin several weeks prior to the start of the Pacific War. The B-17s were making the long ferry flight from the US to the Philippines. In December 1941 some of these bombers returned to Darwin briefly, before moving to Java. (AWM)

---

[1] The 7th BG elements were transferred into the 19th BG, and the 7th BG was subsequently reformed in India.

CHAPTER 2

THE BOMBERS

Nine different types of Allied bombers were used in the NWA to launch attacks against Japanese targets during 1942-1945. The bulk of these missions were flown by three types: Lockheed Hudsons, B-25 Mitchells and B-24 Liberators. American bomber squadrons based in eastern Australia were detached to the NWA and flew a small number of missions using B-17 Flying Fortresses, B-25 Mitchells and B-26 Marauders. An RAAF Vultee Vengeance squadron was based in the NWA but only flew a solitary mission due to the limited range of the type. From 1944 RAAF Bristol Beauforts and Lockheed Venturas saw significant use, while RAAF Catalinas flew occasional bombing missions but were mainly used in the minelaying role.

The table below gives some basic comparative data on these nine bombers, followed by more detailed information for each type. However, some of this data, especially concerning bomb loads and range, should be treated as indicative only. The actual practice in theatre conditions could vary considerably.

Name	Type	Bomb load (pounds)	Range (miles)
B-17 Flying Fortress	Heavy	6,000 to 12,800 lb	1,100
B-26 Marauder	Heavy	5,000	1,150
B-25 Mitchell	Heavy	2,400 to 4,000	1,500
B-24 Liberator	Heavy	2,200	2,200
Catalina	Maritime strike	2,000	3,100
Vultee Vengeance	Dive-bomber	2,000	600
Bristol Beaufort	Medium	2,000	1,600
Lockheed Ventura	Medium	3,000	1,660
Lockheed Hudson	Light	1,600	1,960

CHARACTERISTICS

B-17E Flying Fortress	Wing span	Length	Bomb load (lb)	Crew	Range (miles)	Cruise Speed (mph)	Service ceiling (feet)
Manufacturer Boeing	103'9"	74' 9"	6,000 lb internal but could carry up to 12,800	6-10		250	35,000
Engines	4 x 1,200hp Wright 9-cylinder radial							
Armament (B-17E)	• twin 0.50-inch Brownings in three turrets • 1 x nose gun; 2 x two waist guns; 1 x radio compartment gun							
Notes: • Total made: 12,731 • Described as a "sedate" flyer, B-17s were a reliable performer, although early model Cs deployed to Europe had problems with guns freezing at high altitudes, and a blind spot astern. • *Memphis Belle* pilot Robert Morgan, who flew them as a check pilot and in combat, said they had "a rocky road to the mass-production line". He described the deployment of the C model to Europe for the RAF to fly as "simply disastrous", caused by the British rush to fly them in daylight raids, with "excessive altitude, engine trouble, frozen machine guns and lack of fighter escort cover" which combined to make the raids "worse than ineffective".							

This B-17E (41-2649) served with the 28th Bombardment Squadron, 19th Bombardment Group, which was based in Queensland from March until November 1942. When the 19th BG returned to the US in late 1942 this Fortress was transferred to the 43rd BG.

Vultee Vengeance	Wing span	Length	Bomb load (lb)	Crew	Range (miles)	Cruise Speed (mph)	Service ceiling (feet)
Manufacturer Vultee	48	39' 9"	2,000 lbs	2	600	273	22,000
Engines	1 x Wright 14 cylinder 2-row radial 1,600 hp						
Armament	• 4 x 0.303-inch in wings • 2 x 0.303-inch rear cockpit						

Notes:
- Total made: 1,528
- Although effective, by the time the Vengeance reached optimum production the time of the dive-bomber had been and gone, with ground and ship anti-aircraft defences overcoming their advantages.
- The minimal bombload by comparison with multi-engine aircraft was also a negative factor.
- In flight to the target dive-bombers also usually required fighter cover.

Catalina	Wing span	Length	Bomb load (lb)	Crew	Range (miles)	Cruise Speed (mph)	Service ceiling (feet)
Manufacturer Consolidated	104'	63'11"	2,000	7	3,100	196	18,200
Engines	2 x 1,200hp Pratt and Whitney 14-cylinder 2 row radials						
Armament	• 1 x 0.30-inch or 0.50-inch in nose • 1 x 0.50-inch in each waist blister • 1 x 0.50-inch in tunnel under hull step (Armament is for USN version; RAAF had British armament of 6 x 0.303-inch)						

Notes:
- Total made: 4,000
- Amphibian and boat versions. The former could be moved out of the water on the wheels of the tricycle undercarriage.
- Name of Catalina (from the original designation PB-Y) given by the RAF and adopted by the US.
- Operated by the RAAF in the bombing, mining, reconnaissance and rescue roles.
- Wingtip floats retracted into the wing in cruise, unlike most flying boats in which they are fixed.
- Wing mounted on central pylon raising engines and propellers high above the sea surface. Wing made largely from aluminium, with ailerons and some of the trailing edges covered in fabric. Area of around 1,400 square feet. 1,750 gallons of fuel in centre section.
- Characterised by ability to take punishment and keep flying.

B-25 Mitchell	Wing span	Length	Bomb load (lb)	Crew	Range (miles)	Cruise Speed (mph)	Service ceiling (feet)
Manufacturer North American Aviation	67'7"	54'1" BCJ 54'11" GH 51'	2,400 3,000 A 3,200 H 4,000 J	4-6	1,500 miles	315 A 300 B 284 CG 275 HJ	27,000 A 24,000 later models
Engines	2 x 1,700hp Wright 14-cylinder radials							
Armament	Initial: (see notes below) • 1 x 0.50-inch tail • twin 0.30-inch waist • 1 x 0.30-inch nose							

Notes:
- Total made: 9,816 – constructed in larger quantities that any other US twin-engine bomber.
- The B-25 was progressively improved through the war, with armour; self-sealing fuel tanks following the initial model; and the armament steadily becoming more formidable.
- B: twin 0.5-inch guns in an electric dorsal turret and a retractable ventral turret (tail gun removed)
- G: 75mm gun, and two 0.5-inch guns in the nose, and four 0.5-inch guns on the sides of the nose.
- H: 75mm gun and 14 x 0.5-inch
- J: 13 x 0.5-inch (attack version with another 5)
- The "strafer" version of the B-25 originated under the leadership of Fifth Air Force chief George Kenney in New Guinea, to replace tanks and heavy artillery which, he wrote, "have no place in jungle warfare". They were also known as "commerce destroyers" for their usefulness in sinking ships.

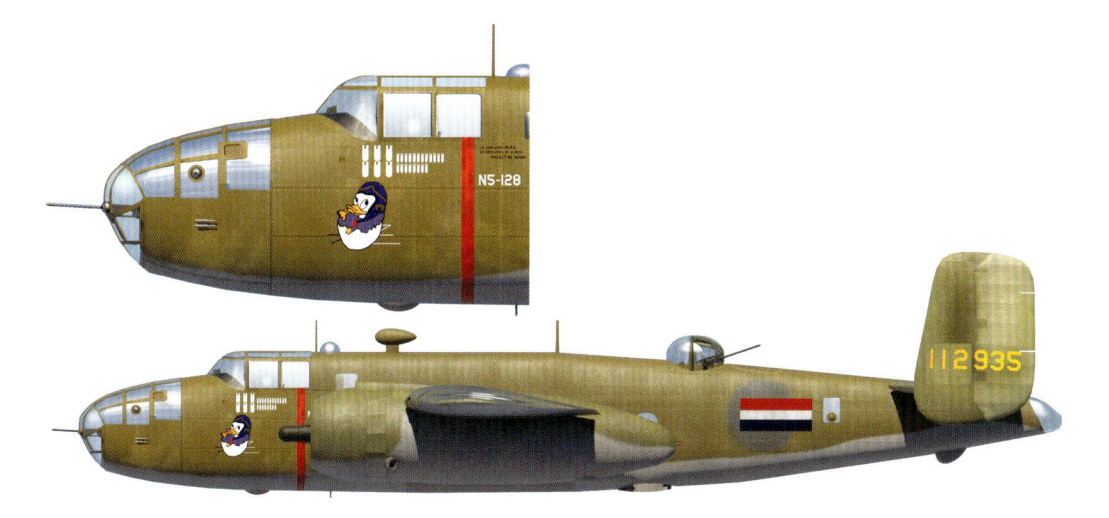

This B-25C Mitchell N5-128 was delivered to No. 18 (NEI) Squadron on 24 August 1942 and ferried to McDonald in the Northern Territory on 27 December 1942. It commenced flying operations there the following month and successfully completed around fifty missions. Profiled as it appeared in late 1944, the Walt Disney hatchling Donald Duck appeared on both sides of the nose. Note the darker area on the fuselage where the original US insignia has been painted out. Following its last mission from Batchelor on 5 January 1945, the airframe was stripped down to natural metal finish and it was used as a transport. Both Donald Duck logos were retained, with a black anti-glare panel painted on the nose. However the aircraft did not last long in this configuration, as it was lost in an accident on 20 January 1945.

B-26 Marauder	Wing span	Length	Bomb load (lb)	Crew	Range (miles)	Cruise Speed (mph)	Service ceiling (feet)
Manufacturer Martin	65' (A) and first 64 of B model, then 71'	56'	5,000	5-7	1,150 miles	310	23,000
Engines	• 2 x 1,850hp Pratt and Whitney 18-cylinder two-row radial							
Armament	• five 0.50-inch Brownings in three positions • two nose guns							

Notes:
- Total made: 5,157
- mainly operated by the US Army, plus approx. 250 for the USN and as trainers.

B-24 Liberator	Wing span	Length	Bomb load (lb)	Crew	Range (miles)	Cruise Speed (mph)	Service ceiling (feet)
Manufacturer Consolidated Vultee	110'	67'2"	5,000	10	2,200	290	28,000
Engines	4 x 1,200hp Pratt and Whitney 14-cylinder 2 row radials							
Armament	• 10 x 0.50-inch guns in four turrets							

Notes:
- Total made: 19,203 in numerous variants.
- Distinguished by being difficult to fly.
- Almost every mechanical component was electrically operated.
- Pilot comments from the time include that the cockpit was "oppressively cramped", and that the bomb bay catwalk was dangerous, having only a nine-inch plank to move across it: "one slip and you'd tumble into the bay, which was fitted with fragile aluminium doors that would tear away with the weight of a falling man."
- Then again, "In time, the men's misgivings about the Liberator fell away. In hundreds of hours of intense training, their plane never failed them. For all its ugliness and quirks, it was a noble thing, rugged and inexhaustible."

This B-24J Liberator (44-40649/A72-40) is profiled as it appeared in service with No. 24 Squadron in the Northern Territory in 1944, before being transferred to No. 7 Operational Training Unit at Tocumwal. These late J model Liberators had a natural metal finish.

Hudson	Wing span	Length	Bomb load (lb)	Crew	Range (miles)	Cruise Speed (mph)	Service ceiling (feet)
Manufacturer Lockheed	65'6"	44'4"	1,600	5	1,960 miles	246	24,500
Engines	2 x 1,100 hp Wright nine-cylinder radials							
Armament	• 7 x 0.303-inch in nose (2 x fixed); dorsal; beam windows and ventral hatch							
Notes: • Total made: 2,584 • A versatile bomber which served in many forces, including the USAAF, USN, RAF and RAAF. • In inexperienced hands the Hudson could be a challenging or even dangerous machine to fly. Robert Morgan called them "prickly" with some "dicey" traits. This included their strange cockpit configuration: twin rudder controls for two pilots, but a control yoke that was designed to "flip over" – "that is, it could be unlocked from the pilot's seat and transferred over to the co-pilot seat." • The Hudson also had "extremely narrow landing gear between two wings". This meant, as Robert Morgan noted "If the landing was not precise, and if you weren't in complete control, the gear could pitch the plane into a ground loop – a radical swerving to the right or left. If the wing touched the tarmac during this out-of-control lurch, the wheel strut could break off and rupture the gas tank, usually igniting a fire."							

This Hudson, A16-117, served with No. 13 Squadron at Batchelor throughout 1942. The yellow surround on the roundel is a legacy from the RAF markings in which it was delivered.

Ventura	Wing span	Length	Bomb load (lb)	Crew	Range (miles)	Cruise Speed (mph)	Service ceiling (feet)
Manufacturer Lockheed	65'6"	51'9"	6 x 500 lb bombs or 6 x 325 lb depth charges	5	1,660 miles	312	27,500
Engines	2 x 2,000 hp Pratt and Whitney R 2800-31							
Armament	• 2 x 0.50-inch fixed guns in nose • 2 x 0.50-inch guns in dorsal turret • 2 x 0.30-inch guns in ventral position							
Notes: • Total made: 2,080 • A torpedo could also be carried in the fuselage bay. • A surviving Ventura – VH-SFF – is owned by the RAAF Museum, awaiting repair to static display condition.							

Beaufort	Wing span	Length	Bomb load (lb)	Crew	Range (miles)	Cruise Speed (mph)	Service ceiling (feet)
Manufacturer Bristol	57'	44'2"	1 x 18" torpedo or 2,000lb	4	1,600	260	16,500
Engines	\multicolumn{7}{l}{2 x 1,130hp 14-cylinder Bristol Taurus or 2 x 1,200hp Pratt and Whitney Twin Wasp}
Armament	<ul><li>2 x 0.303-inch dorsal turret</li><li>1 x fixed forward-firing 0.303-inch</li><li>1 x .303-ichn remote control chin blister</li></ul>OR<ul><li>4 x 0.303-inch in wings</li><li>2 x 0.303-inch manually aimed from windows</li><li>2 x 0.303-inch in dorsal turret</li></ul>

Notes:
- Total made: 2,080
- A distinguishing feature of Australian Beauforts was a larger fin, which was used from the Mk VI on. Australian Beauforts almost all used the Pratt and Whitney Twin Wasp engine due to problems sourcing the Taurus from Britain.
- In total 700 Australian Beauforts were manufactured in six series, including transport and trainer versions.
- Final 140 Australian machines built carried 2 x 0.50-inch machine guns in the dorsal turret.

An RAAF Beaufort light bomber in natural metal finish. Manufactured in Australia, Beauforts served with the RAAF in large numbers during WWII. (RAAF Museum)

CHAPTER 3

THE OPPONENTS: FIGHTERS AND AA GUNS

Death dealt by the enemy to the bomber crew could come from a myriad of sources. In general, it was from two weapons: fighters sent aloft to shoot down the bombers, and anti-aircraft fire from the ground. In general this last was simply called "AA", "ack-ack" or "flak" by the Allies. Ironically the last term came from the German word flak which was an abbreviation of "fliegerabwehrkanone" meaning "air defence gun".

ANTI-AIRCRAFT FIRE

Ground enemy forces would usually be clustered around a target, or in the predicated route to it. Anti-aircraft weapons generally consisted of two types: machine guns and rapid-fire projectile weapons. Machine guns fired from the ground were only effective at very low altitude. Gunners faced obstacles such as the need to allow for deflection, bullet drop, and wind. Solid and explosive shells from bigger AA guns were far more of a threat.

The main Japanese machine gun was the 13.2mm Type 93. Introduced in 1933, its most common variation was a twin-barrel model, placed on four extended stands. The gunner sat astride the breech, reclining, which let him easily look up and around and rotate the weapon. The Type 93 was thought to be most effective by the user and enemy alike and remained in use throughout the war.

The next weapon was the 25mm Type 96 cannon. Developed by the Navy for ship usage, it was quickly adopted for land defence in the many naval airbases across the Pacific. It was a twin-barrel gun capable of firing 220 rounds per minute.

The third main weapon of Japanese anti-aircraft defence was the 75mm Type 88 gun. Nothing to do with the fearsome 88mm German anti-tank gun, this was used by both the Navy and Army. Manually operated and supported by five outriggers which could be folded to a towed trailer for movement, this was capable of 20 rounds per minute. The Type 88 fired 14-pound shells with an effective ceiling of 22,000 feet, although 29,000 feet was the absolute ceiling. The Type 88 was re-worked in 1944 with a longer barrel and a more powerful cartridge capacity, which increased the effective service ceiling to 27,000 feet.

The naval 10cm Model 98 was the most formidable weapon in the Japanese arsenal. It fired a 28-pound shell up to 35,000 feet. It was matched in the Army by the 105mm gun, but this was an antiquated 1928 model only comparable to the early Model 88, and it was used in lesser numbers. The Army also produced early versions of a 120mm gun (35,000 feet) and a 150mm model to fire to 55,000 feet, but they seem to have seen little service.

Anti-aircraft fire could be lessened in effectiveness by constantly changing height and course. Such deviations didn't help navigation though. Flak was often regarded as ineffective, but it got better as the war went on. The shells had to burst at the right height to explode near enough to an aircraft to damage its controls or engines. A direct hit from a big shell – a 3.7-inch, for example – would destroy a bomber completely, or blow a wing off, which usually meant a few survivors trying to parachute out of a spinning flaming wreck.

Armour inside bombers was sometimes derided; sometimes useless, but as the war went on its place became more appreciated. Some forces never fitted it either early on or at all, arguing it was heavy and affected aircraft performance, or lowered aircrew morale. This was often a ground manager perspective – nothing lowered morale as much as seeing a fellow aviator smashed by a cannon shell. RAF fighter pilots in the Battle of Britain, denied backseat armour for their fighters, surreptitiously began fitting it, either made by the squadron mechanics or even salvaged from a wrecked German machine – the Germans had learnt all about it in the Spanish Civil War. Then again, as some gunners found, inadequate armour didn't stop much and often got in the way of seeing an enemy approaching.

Exploding shells threw off flying metal pieces, which could be deadly especially against soft targets such as aircrew. USAAF Lieutenant Norman Freidman was hit "directly on the bridge of the nose between the eyes. The leather on my sunglasses was cut and each glass flew in a different direction without breaking. The flak missed my steel helmet and after hitting my nose, hit my flak suit near my lap and landed on the floor of the plane." Freidman was given novocaine for the pain and the wound was covered in sulphur powder. He spent 12 days in hospital.

FIGHTERS

The Japanese employed a myriad of fighter types against the bombers. In general, their tactics were to get in high and swoop down, but this was if they had the luxury of being pre-warned through radar – developed later than the Allies – or ground spotters.

Generally speaking the Allied bombers flying out of the NWA did not have the luxury of fighter escorts, and hence had to depend on interlocking fire from their own on-board gunners for defence.

So what did the Japanese fighters look like, and how did they fight? From the mid-1930s, armies, air forces, and navies across the world were developing fighter aircraft that looked very much the same.

Instead of the biplane fighters of the Great War, which had ended in 1918, almost of these aircraft had one wing, placed low on the fuselage. Biplanes, it had been found in the previous war, had given tremendous lift, which translated into an ability to climb at a high rate. But speed had been found to be preferable to lift, and two wings created too much turbulence for fast flight.

The new single wing was placed low, for fighter pilots wanted to see above them as much as they could. Sighting the enemy before he pounced on you was a lesson learnt, and a high wing got in the way of seeing the sky. The low wing made for a more difficult landing, but it was still to be preferred than the alternative. Capable fighter pilots learnt quickly that height was an advantage; allowing them both to see prey below and giving them the possibility of converting height to speed. Conversely, pilots knew their attackers liked to wait up high, preferably in the sun.

Upfront you wanted an engine of as much power as you could get, to be on top of the opposition before he saw you coming, and to get away as fast as possible. The power-to-weight ratio of most WWII fighters made the machines overpowered, which was definitely what was needed. Supercharging, turbocharging, fuel injection, and emergency boosting were often added for even more power.

A strong airframe that took punishment was most desirable. Wheels added drag, so a retractable undercarriage was needed. These aircraft took punishment in combat, but also in being rough handled on grass or dirt airstrips, and from pilots without much training in finesse. The ability to take bullet or cannon hits and still get home was much prized. Many WWII aircraft lacked armour, particularly for the pilot, but this was often added as the war progressed, although more weight chopped off speed, and could upset the aircraft's performance. But this was better that than a bullet in the back, for from behind was where a pilot liked to attack from. Conversely the advantage of many fighters was speed, and a lot of that came from lightness – and hence no armour.

Pilots also wanted agility. "Dogfighting" – the art of air-to-air fighting between fighters – was won by a combination of skill, power, durability, and the ability to fling an aircraft around to get on the tail of an opponent in an aerial duel. Tight turns; the ability to roll inverted, and being able to dive or zoom as fast as possible all added into a combination of engineering and construction which made up what was necessary to win in the air. Strength was needed too: there was no point in being able to out-dive a pursuer if the wings came off when pulling out of a dive.

So why were some fighters better than others? Why were some quite appalling? There were around 77 fighters produced in the war from a range of countries, although some machines, it must be admitted, were variants of a single design. There were experiments too, with twin-engines, and with rocket and jet propulsion, but overall, it can be said that WWII was dominated by single-engined monoplane propeller fighters.

FIGHTER TYPES

Throughout the Pacific War the mainstay Japanese fighter was the superb Zero, as operated by the Japanese Navy. But in various theatres where the JAAF operated the Zero was absent. However, to many Allied aviators, all Japanese fighters were reported as "Zeros": it was the most recognised and most famous of Japanese aircraft. Understandably many airmen didn't care too much for what it was that attacked them; they were merely interested in downing it or avoiding it.

Allied bombers from the NWA ranging over the NEI encountered eight known types of Japanese fighter.[1] Five of these were operated by the IJN: the Zero, Irving, Rufe, Pete and Rex. The last three types were floatplane fighters. The other three types were operated by the JAAF: the Oscar, Nick and Tony. Characteristics of these types are listed below.

Zero	Wing span	Length	Weight (lb) empty	Max. climb rate (fps)	Range (miles)	Max speed (mph)	Service ceiling (feet)
Manufacturer Mitsubishi Nakajima	39'4.5"	29'9"	3,704 lb	4,500	1,940 with drop tank	316	33,790
Engine	925 hp NK1C Sakae 12 14-cylinder two-row air-cooled radial piston engine							
Armament	2 x 20mm cannon in wings 2 x 7.7mm machine guns in engine cowling							
Notes: • Total made: 10,937 • Carrier-based fighter successfully used extensively on land. • A6M2 was the most numerous model made and is the specification quoted here. • Often fitted with a drop tank. • Could carry small underwing bombs.							

---

1   A Mabel three-seater light bomber was encountered on 23 June 1943 when it rammed and brought down a B-24. Its characteristics have not been listed here, as it was only in the area in transit and the attack appeared opportunistic.

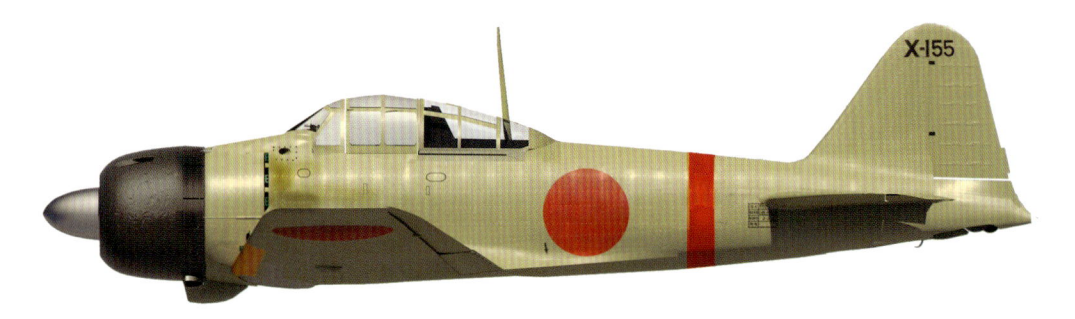

This A6M3 Model 32 Zero served with No. 3 Ku in the NEI during 1942. Both Model 21 and 32s were in the inventory of No. 3 Ku and when it became No. 202 Ku in November 1942.

Irving	Wing span	Length	Weight (lb) empty	Max. climb rate (fps)	Range (miles)	Max speed (mph)	Service ceiling (feet)
Manufacturer Nakajima	55'8"	39'11"	10,697	1,968	1,585	315	30,578
Engine	2 x 1,130 hp Sakae 21 14-cylinder two-row air-cooled radial piston engine							
Armament	1 x 20mm cannon in nose 2 x 7.7mm machine gun 4 x 20mm cannon in rear cockpit – 2 upward firing; 2 down							
Notes: • Twin engine night fighter. • Two-seater in this configuration; a three-man reconnaissance version was also made. • Equipped with nose radar.							

This Nakajima J1N1 Irving served with No. 202 Ku at Manggar in the NEI in 1944. No. 202 Ku was mainly equipped with Zeros, but in response to night raids on Balikpapan by B-24s in August 1943, the unit was assigned a flight of Irvings. By the end of 1943, five had been assigned into No. 202 Ku, and were based at Balikpapan in Borneo and at Makassar in the Celebes. When No. 202 Ku was redeployed to the Central Pacific in February 1944, all of its Irvings were reassigned to No. 381 Ku, a newly arrived fighter unit which continued operating in the NEI. On 1 April 1944, the unit was redesignated as No. 902 Fighter Detachment. This particular Irving was captured at Manggar, revealing a stylised red tail code with white piping.

THE OPPONENTS: FIGHTERS AND AA GUNS

Rufe	Wing span	Length	Weight (lb) empty	Max. climb rate (fps)	Range (miles)	Max speed (mph)	Service ceiling (feet)
Manufacturer Nakajima	39'4.5"	33'2"	4,215		713	270	33,000
Engine	925 hp NK1C Sakae 12 14-cylinder two-row air-cooled radial piston engine							
Armament	2 x 20mm cannon in wings 2 x 7.7mm machine guns in engine cowling							
Notes:							
• Total made: 327 • Floatplane version of the Zero, used primarily in reconnaissance and interceptor roles. • A single main float with two auxiliary wing floats. • Performance degraded by the non-retractable main float beneath the fuselage.							

Pete	Wing span	Length	Weight (lb) empty	Max. climb rate (fps)	Range (miles)	Max speed (mph)	Service ceiling (feet)
Manufacturer Mitsubishi	36'1"	31'2"	4,330	1,969	276 670 with over-load	230	30,970
Engine	1 x 875hp Mitsubishi 14 cylinder two row radial							
Armament	2 7.7mm above engine; one manually aimed from rear cockpit Underwing racks for two 60kg bombs							
Notes:							
• Two-seater. • 524 manufactured. • Good without being exceptional in all roles: area defence fighter, light bomber, anti-submarine, convoy escort, ocean rescue.							

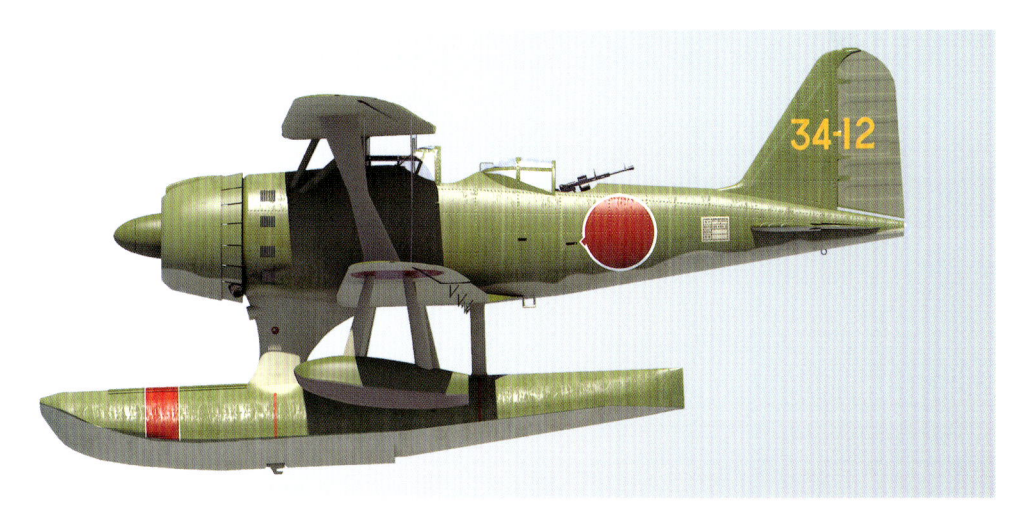

This Mitsubishi F1M2 Pete served with No. 934 Ku at Manokwari in Dutch New Guinea in February 1944. From April to December 1943 the unit was based at Taberfane in the Aru Islands, after which it redeployed to Manokwari. No. 934 Ku had an official allotment of eight Jakes and eight F1M2 Petes, prior to it being disbanded on 1 October 1944.

Oscar	Wing span	Length	Weight (lb) empty	Max. climb rate (fps)	Range (miles)	Max speed (mph)	Service ceiling (feet)
Manufacturer Nakajima	37'10"	37'6"	4,354	3,250	746 (I)	308	38,500
Engine	\multicolumn{7}{l}{1 x 975 hp Sakae 14-cylinder two-row air-cooled radial piston engine}
Armament	\multicolumn{7}{l}{Ia: 2 x 7.7mm machine guns Ib: 1 x 7.7mm machine gun + 1 x 12.7mm Ic: 2 x 12.7mm machine guns II: 2 x 12.7mm machine guns plus wing racks for two 551-pound bombs IIIb: 20mm cannon plus bomb racks}

Notes:
- The most numerous – behind the Zero – of all Japanese warplanes, and the primary fighter of the Army.
- Range for models (II,III) 1,060 miles and 1,864 with drop tanks.
- Only involved in one raid on Australia but present in quantities in Japanese-held territory to the north.

This Nakajima Ki-43-II Oscar was operated by the 59th Sentai which was staffed by experienced combat veterans and was the first JAAF air regiment to operate the Oscar. After receiving the first allocation of Oscars in China in 1941, it proceeded to serve in the NEI. With a unit strength of 27 Ki-43-IIs, the 59th Sentai redeployed to New Guinea on 15 August 1943.

Tony	Wing span	Length	Weight (lb) empty	Max. climb rate (fps)	Range (miles)	Max speed (mph)	Service ceiling (feet)
Manufacturer Kawasaki	39'4"	29'4"	1 5,798 2 6,294 3 5,567	2,200 2,200 3,280	990 1,100 1,243	348 379 367	32,800 36,089 37,729
Engine	\multicolumn{7}{l}{1 1 x 1,175 Kawasaki Ha-40 inverted V 12 cylinder (liquid-cooled – only such fighter for Japan) 2 1 x 1,450 Kawasaki Ha-40 inverted V 12 cylinder (liquid-cooled) 3 1 x 1,500 Mitsubishi Ha-112-II 14-cylinder two row radial – designated Ki-100}
Armament	\multicolumn{7}{l}{1 2 x 20mm cannon in wings 2 x 7.7mm machine guns above engine 2 4 x 20mm in wings 3 2 x 20mm in wings plus 2 x 12.7mm in wings plus two underwing 551-pound bomb racks}

Notes:
- Total made: 2,654 (another account 2,750) + 275 of Mk3
- Single-seat fighter originally fitted with Mauser MG 151 cannon with electrically fused ammunition – 800 supplied by submarine from Germany.
- Version 2 made in 1944 with unreliable engine and bigger wing and new canopy.
- Version 3 was a test-engine fit which was 727 pounds lighter than Version 2 and faster than Version 1.
- Proved surprisingly excellent in all spheres and 275 aircraft were quickly produced.

CHAPTER 4

THE ALLIES STRIKE BACK

Following the devastating attack on Darwin on 19 February, the RAAF moved its North-Western Area headquarters almost 400 miles to the south, setting up at Daly Waters on 28 February. They were joined by Nos. 2 and 13 Squadrons, leaving only No. 13 Squadron's B Flight along with the commanding officer to control operations at Darwin. In a February 1942 letter to his mother, Pilot Officer John Venn wrote:

> Well at last things over here are beginning to move. I am posted to No. 2 Squadron at Daly Waters … another chap, Arthur Sharp, and I are flying up there … whenever the [aircraft] is ready.

No. 2 Squadron moved back to Darwin at the end of February, though Daly Waters remained as the servicing base for the two Hudson squadrons and Darwin effectively became a forward base for operations. At the time work was proceeding on new airfields in the area, reflecting a construction program which had commenced on 29 December 1941.

Flight Lieutenant John Yeaman was instructed to proceed to Darwin to implement the programme, the aim of which was outlined in an instruction requiring that:

> … five major aerodromes were to be located between Darwin and Batchelor, and five major aerodromes between Adelaide River and Birdum, each [major] aerodrome to be associated with a minimum of two satellite grounds and as many road[side] strips as possible …

Enlisting the services of Colonel Sverdrup, an engineer with the US Army, Yeaman led a small team to survey new airfield sites. Based on the advice of the Director of Mines, Mr Hughes, the aerodrome opposite the old Bynoe Road – and named for him – was to be the major new aerodrome with the 27-Mile (Strauss) and 34-Mile (Livingstone) roadside airstrips as its satellites. Over the next few months some 6,000 square miles was surveyed and bomber airfield sites named Fenton, Long, Gill, McDonald and Manbulloo were all selected.

Around Easter time in 1942:

> … A/Cdre Bladin, the new AOC North-Western Area, arranged for Flight Lieutenant CC Fenton be posted to North-Western Area to assist with aerodrome selection works. The strategic situation demanded that a runway be developed somewhere in the vicinity of Brocks Creek, and … Fenton made an aerial reconnaissance of this area.

The major bomber airfield was subsequently named for him. Known as the "Flying Doctor", Fenton was already famous as a medical man who had brought health services to isolated Australians across the Outback.

Two American engineering units, the 808th Engineer (Aviation) Battalion and the 43rd Engineer General Service Regiment had arrived in Australia. In conjunction with Australian civilian workers, they began the herculean job of developing a series of airfields from the scrub.

Working in primitive conditions and without much of their heavy equipment the Americans improved or developed eleven airfields, often using – to flatten the land – earth-filled 44-gallon fuel drums. The 43rd Engineers developed Manbulloo west of Katherine among others, and Tom Skillman recalled camping in:

> … 2 and 8 man tents with dirt floors … with only a hand dug well for water … the flies were terrible – I averaged swallowing at least one live fly a day … we swam in the river until we were getting an ear fungus that was very painful.

The 808th Engineers moved up from the Katherine area in March 1942 and commenced the development of Hughes airfield, along with the 27-Mile and 34-Mile roadside airstrips. By mid-July they had cleared, graded and gravelled Pine Creek, McDonald, Fenton, Hughes, and the roadside 'strips, while the 43rd Engineers had completed Manbulloo and developed Kit Carson (Tindal) and Wilson (Venn). None were bitumised due to a shortage of materials, and this was later completed by RAAF units and the Australian authorities.

With Hughes airfield completed and the arrival of replacement Hudsons and personnel, Nos. 2 and 13 Squadrons moved to the new airfield on 30 April. By 5 May they had settled into their new, albeit extremely primitive surroundings. From there they were to carry the offensive to the Japanese while the American units consolidated and commenced their missions from Queensland and New Guinea.

Earlier, from Daly Waters the bombers continued armed reconnaissance sorties against the Japanese to the north, while steadily losing men and machines in the process. On 13 March No. 13 Squadron's B Flight under Flight Lieutenant Bob Dalkin commenced night operations from Darwin, though only three Hudsons were available between the two squadrons. A16-109 was shot down over Koepang taking the crew of Sergeants JL Wright, DJJ Horsburgh and JR Maddern with it. However, the pilot, Flight Lieutenant JL MacAlister, was able to parachute to safety and became a POW.

On 17 March three Nos. 2 and 13 Squadron aircraft mounted a further night attack on Koepang. Bob Dalkin recalled:

> It was only a three aircraft attack, but it was a start … We were back there at Koepang the next night, and two nights later, and in fact a total of six nights out of eleven – with a long reconnaissance to Ambon and travel flights back to base from the rough Drysdale Mission strip thrown in.

John Venn ran short of fuel following one of these night operations over Koepang on 20 March but was able to land Hudson A16-100 in the shallows off Bathurst Island. The crew was uninjured but, as Bob Dalkin wrote:

> A few broken limbs would have been splendid as we saw their aircraft blown to pieces at Ambon three weeks later.

Dalkin went on to describe the strain of night operations, recalling that sometimes:

> … because, the weather and the concealment it offered, and the heavy towering clouds could be our friend; but the heavy tropical storms and lightning … could also be another … unforgiving enemy … to come in low over a ridge at night, to take in the situation at an airfield quickly, to know that, although the Japanese to our knowledge had no early warning radar … they did have a reasonably effective ground warning system, - to be faced from the start with heavy and direct fire – not knowing whether fighter aircraft were already airborne – posed enough problems and usually caused the adrenalin to flow.

Recalling the 17 March night operation over Koepang, he wrote that even though the:

> … rugged and lofty hills, ridges and valleys … of the Koepang area provided some element

of concealment and surprise, [sometimes] we were the ones surprised … there were many aircraft on the ground and some flying in the circuit area … [so] at high speed I raised the flap, climbed to about fifteen hundred feet, above and behind a couple of [Japanese] aircraft in the circuit, which we kept in sight; - opened the bomb doors, turned downwind and into wind towards the flarepath, selected some parked and taxying aircraft as the aiming point, got the bombs away, realised that I was too low, and with the blinding flashes of the explosions felt that awful thump in the behind and the uplift of the aircraft … not knowing if we were still in one piece, one quick turn to give the crew a chance with their .303s, then it was low level … to the nearby flying boat base at Hansisi. There were some aircraft on the water and these we attacked with gunnery … one solitary 45mm was firing at us … forcing me down towards the water [and] I came close to digging a wing into the sea. It was quite a night.

Meanwhile American and Filipino soldiers on the Bataan peninsula in the Philippines surrendered on 9 April, and plans were laid to break the Japanese blockade for the 10,000 Americans who were holed up on the immense island fortress of Corregidor. Parts of Mindanao were still in American or Filipino hands, including Del Monte airfield, and the plan was to bring bombers in to attack Japanese shipping.

Very few of the 19th BG's B-17s were operational following the Java campaign. Fortunately, the 3rd BG was receiving B-25 Mitchells which, with extra fuel tanks, could make it to the target. Eleven B-25s and three B-17s were assigned to the force led by Brigadier General Ralph Royce.

The men of the 3rd BG volunteered for the mission. Paul Gunn, known by his nickname "Pappy", a former mechanic and naval aviator who had started his own airline in the Philippines, was included. Gunn had flown several relief missions in and out of the Philippines before escaping to Australia. He was commissioned as a captain for the operation. Living up to his name as a scrounger, he was able to acquire bombsights for the B-25s from No. 18 (Netherlands East Indies) Squadron which was a new unit forming within the RAAF.

On 11 April the bombers arrived in Darwin in the early hours and refuelled for the flight to Del Monte. However, one B-25 blew a tyre, leaving ten B-25s and three B-17s. Departing the following morning, they flew a 1,500-mile dogleg route to avoid Japanese fighters on Ambon and arrived at Del Monte that evening. The B-25s were then dispersed at the outlying airfields of Maramag and Valencia. The B-17s, one of which had lost an engine due to mechanical failure, remained at Del Monte.

Following some attacks against the Japanese, Royce realised that Del Monte was not safe from Japanese attacks and ordered the B-17s back to Australia. Loaded with as many passengers as they could, they took off before dawn on 13 April to avoid any Japanese raids.

Meanwhile the remaining nine B-25s had their ferry tanks re-fitted. After loading as many passengers as possible, they departed before dawn the next morning. Pappy Gunn's B-25 had holes in the fuel tanks and could not make the flight, so he remained behind to fit replacement tanks from wrecked aircraft. He subsequently took on as many passengers as possible and landed safely at Darwin on 15 April.

The Royce Mission failed to sink any Japanese vessels or to break the blockade. In effect, it was regarded as a failure, even as a propaganda exercise. It seemed that Australia was going to have to be the base for future offensive operations, for at least the foreseeable future.

While the mission was underway the RAAF Hudsons continued their operations. Most were

Lockheed Hudsons of No. 13 Squadron at RAAF Darwin. The tri-colour roundels suggest this picture likely dates from the first half of 1942, or even slightly earlier. (Bob Alford)

combined Nos. 2 and 13 Squadron operations as both units remained understrength, while a number of routine sea searches were also carried out.

During a 13 April attack over Koepang harbour by No. 13 Squadron, Sergeant D Gitsham was wounded when the aircraft was intercepted by Japanese fighters. The same day saw the loss of A16-159 when it was shot down by three Japanese fighters near Koepang. The pilot, Flight Lieutenant HO Cook, a pre-war Guinea Airways pilot, and his co-pilot Pilot Officer VC Leithhead, managed to free themselves from the wreckage. The other two crewmembers were injured but were also able to be extracted. They were assisted by local natives who gave them ponies to ride, and a chance for rescue. Cook and Leithhead were guided to a pick-up point where they and 31 other Australians were evacuated aboard the US Navy's submarine *Searaven*.[1] However, the two other men from the Cook's crew, Sergeants WD Witham and HF Hearle, were too badly injured to move. They were captured and executed on 8 May.

The following day a further raid saw the loss of A16-137 and its crew of Pilot Officers PG Taylor and A Lockley, along with Sergeants K Orchard and DJ Thompson. They were believed to have been shot down and were posted missing.

Ten days later on 23-24 April, A16-182 failed to return from a combined Nos. 2 and 13 Squadron night operation over Koepang. The crew of Flying Officer R Blanchard, along with Sergeants Jacobs, D Woods and O Guy was posted missing. With the Hudson crews continuing to harass the Japanese over Dili, Koepang and Ambon the losses mounted. Under severe stress those remaining were exhausted. Bob Dalkin recalled his crew's reception following one particularly difficult mission, when he and the crew [were in]:

> … that Operations Room. We were exhausted and we were hungry … we [wore] our Mae Wests with not even a shirt underneath, greasy dirty shorts. There was a bunch of half a dozen visiting staff officers … they were looking at us as if we'd come back from another world … they were probably right. We *had* come back from another world.

Adding weight to Dalkin's recollections, No. 2 Squadron pilot, Flight Lieutenant Dick Overheu, recorded his first mission on 20 March, the day following his arrival at Daly Waters. Flying up to Darwin for refuelling and arming with four 250-pound bombs, he then flew to Drysdale and on to Koepang in a high-level pattern attack. Following his initial success, he then flew five further sorties to the end of March, including two seaward patrols and two further attacks

---

1   Leithhead later joined No. 31 Squadron; his luck lasted until 21 August 1943 when his Beaufighter was shot down in the vicinity of Koepang.

on Koepang. On 27 March Overheu attacked Koepang and the flying boat base at Hansisi, claiming a H6K4 Mavis probably destroyed at its moorings. Two nights later he repeated the effort only to have his undercarriage collapse on landing at Drysdale.

In April Overheu flew fourteen sorties, four of these missions to Koepang and two seaward patrols. In May he flew eleven seaward patrols and an attack on Ambon during which his flights were engaged by five Japanese fighters. Other missions were an armed reconnaissance to Ambon and two raids on Dili on 21 and 29 May.

John Venn's logbook told a similar story. During April he flew 19 sorties, six of these were patrols to Timor and one on 14 April was a search for A16-159 and its crew. Three raids on Koepang and Beco on Timor followed, along with an attack on Ambon and travel flights, completing the month's tally of 91 hours in the air. In May Venn flew five patrols to Timor, and then searches from Milingimbi before flying to Darwin in preparation for an attack on shipping in Ambon harbour. His logbook ends on 13 May with the entry, "A16-183 P/O Angel Batchelor – Darwin .45 [minutes]…" Hours later the 20-year-old was to be killed during the Ambon attack.

How did this mission – a typical story of how an aircraft was lost in wartime – eventuate? Reconnaissance had confirmed a build-up of shipping in Ambon Bay, and on 13 May Squadron Leader AB "Tich" McFarlane led six No. 2 Squadron Hudsons from Darwin. Sweeping in over the hills and surprising the Japanese, each pilot selected a ship and attacked at masthead height. Flying in Hudson A16-196, Venn's four 250-pound bombs scored a direct hit on a 3,000-ton vessel. The vessel exploded and Venn's aircraft was caught in the blast and disintegrated. Venn was killed, however his crew, Sergeants BA Kilpatrick, LA Omsby and JA Graham somehow survived but were badly injured. Both Omsby and Kilpatrick were soon executed while Graham was later executed on 28 June 1943.

McFarlane's formation was closely followed by three No. 13 Squadron Hudsons in what was considered a successful raid, despite the loss of Venn's aircraft.[2] Ambon was at the extreme range of Hudson endurance, but all of the remaining aircraft returned safely to Darwin.

Nine days later Hudsons A16-174 and A16-187 were shot down by heavy anti-aircraft fire during a repeat Ambon attack once again led by Squadron Leader McFarlane. The crewmen Flying Officer PG Brooks, Flying Officer AW Moss, Sergeant EA Vercoe and Sergeant PC Roll were all killed. Flying Officer GWC Allchin and his crew of Pilot Officers KI Kersten and WC McLay, along with Sergeant LJ Montgomerie, were all captured and executed.

In mid-May the Americans provided a brief respite for the Hudson crews, who were shouldering the burden of the Allied bombing offensive in the NEI and were in desperate need of rest. On 17 May eleven USAAF B-17s flew into Daly Waters and while one remained, ten flew on to Batchelor. One later returned to Daly Waters with engine trouble.

The following morning the nine B-17s, each armed with four 500-pound demolition bombs took off to attack Penfui aerodrome and shipping off Koepang. Penfui was obscured by cloud and instead five vessels in Koepang Bay were bombed from 25,000 to 29,000 feet, with only one ship hit. Light and heavy anti-aircraft fire was reported as ineffective, and while several fighters were seen taking off they failed to intercept the bombers. The aircraft returned to Daly Waters. On 19 May only five aircraft were serviceable enough to fly to Batchelor for a repeat mission planned for the following day.

---

2   An airfield south of Katherine was named Venn in his honour, although it was never widely used.

Following a briefing led by the commanding officer of the NWA, Air Commodore Frank Bladin, five B-17s took off from Batchelor early on 20 May to bomb Penfui. They were armed with four 500-pound bombs with instantaneous fuses. Arriving over the target at 23,000 to 28,000 feet in clear skies the aircraft released their bombs. Most fell accurately on or near runways, with the NWA Intelligence Officer later reporting:

> Direct hits were made on one bomber … and two smaller aircraft … [other bombs] fell near two other bombers and aircraft pens. A large fire was started … probably caused by a hit on an ammunition or fuel dump. Six bombers and fifteen fighters were on the aerodrome and a number of fighters were observed taking off … there was no engagement with enemy aircraft.

However, it was impossible to sustain these raids, as the NWA Intelligence Officer remarked:

> The high rate of unserviceability amongst the B-17s … confirms the necessity for providing suitable maintenance facilities and stocks of spares in the area. Unless this is done, the efficient operation of these aircraft … will be impossible … In future attacks on Penfoie Aerodrome it is suggested that 100 lb. bombs, instantaneous fuse [sic] be used [to] cause the maximum damage to dispersed aircraft, fuel and ammunition dumps, and buildings.

It had been a token effort and the B-17s made only one further appearance in mid-June. High command had plans for another heavy bombardment group to operate in the NWA, with personnel of the 43rd Bombardment Group at Daly Waters and Fenton from May to September. However frustratingly the unit had no aircraft for most of this period. It later moved to Queensland and commenced missions in New Guinea under the tutelage of the 19th BG. At Fenton the personnel idled away their time in constructing revetments and roads until they moved out in late September. During this time the unit historian of the 64th Bombardment Squadron noted the tedium: "no change in events on this date", "nothing eventful happened on this date", "No change in events" and the classic "The Squadron Commander's pet parrot died today".

Meanwhile the Hudson squadrons maintained the pressure on the Japanese. Flight Lieutenant Ivor Black in A16-177 bombed Namlea on 13 May in a nine-hour 25-minute flight, with four hours and 25 minutes flown at night. Wireless Air Gunner[3] Harry Riley with No. 13 Squadron wrote of the flying routine:

> 29th April. Out on patrol at 0500 hours – very quiet day. 30 April. Same as above. 1st to 5th May. Routine the same … Ric, Aub and I had our photos taken being the only original flying men of 13 SQN left now. 6th May. Our 9th day of continuous flying and look like going on a raid tonight. If we keep this up we will have flown 130 hours for the month which should be pretty near a record.

Seaward searches were flown and supplies were dropped to Sparrow Force on Timor on 23 May. At the time Sparrow Force was waging a guerrilla campaign against the Japanese. It comprised elements of the 2/40th Infantry Battalion, the 2/2nd Independent Company and local Timorese personnel that had not surrendered after the Japanese invasion of Timor in February. The mountainous nature of Portuguese Timor initially suited the guerrilla tactics.

A night strike on the port at Dili was flown by five Hudsons on 30 May. The Hudsons of No. 2 Squadron flew seaward searches from 23-27 and 30 May along with a reconnaissance of Dili on 29 May.

---

3   The rather strange position of Wireless Air Gunner (WAG) saw those in the role split their duties between operating the aircraft's radio, assisting the navigator and manning a machine gun where necessary.

To end the month, Dick Overheu was part of a six aircraft mission to attack parked aircraft at Penfui, with the powerhouse the secondary alternative. Poor visibility obscured the targets and though some aircraft released their bombs, the results were not observed. Dick Overheu's logbook entry reads succinctly, "Raid on Koepang from Darwin. Target obscured by cloud. No bombs dropped." He had flown 108 hours and 35 minutes for the month.

The Hudsons continued their raids from early June, ranging as far as Timor, Ambon, Timoeka, Merauke (in Dutch New Guinea), the Moluccas and the Tanimbar Islands. Meanwhile routine sea patrols covered the Arafura, Timor and Banda Seas.

The cockpit of an RAAF Hudson. As the Hudson was derived from the Super Electra airliner, the cockpit was relatively spacious compared to most contemporary bomber types. (RAAF Museum)

The month started badly for No. 13 Squadron when A16-108 collided with A16-143 during a night attack on Dili on 2 June. The crew of Pilot Officers RL Gill and DG Campbell along with Sergeants SL Inglis and LR Keally were killed when their aircraft crashed in flames. Flight Lieutenant Lindsay Trewren and his crew nursed a badly damaged A16-143 back to Darwin. "They were a fairly shaken-up crew", Bob Dalkin remarked.

June saw Nos. 2 and 13 Squadrons fly 34 searches and patrol missions, eighteen of those by No. 13 Squadron. Attacks were flown against Koepang and Dili on 15 and 26 June. One aircraft, A16-175 of No. 2 Squadron, was forced to ditch offshore in Hyland Bay southwest of Darwin on 16 June, with the crew rescued by local Aborigines. Photo reconnaissance missions were flown over Atamboea – one of which was intercepted by fighters – Weetah, Ombai Strait, Ambon and Laha. On 9 June a single aircraft attacked enemy shipping in the Maloea Strait. Meteorological data was collected over Koepang on the 15 June while on the same date three aircraft attacked enemy positions between Nikiniki and Keffananoe. Three days later a supply drop was made over Beco.

On 17 June A16-132 went missing on operations in the Timor Sea. The body of the pilot, Pilot Officer GR Crawford, was recovered and later interred at Ambon. However, the remaining crew, Pilot Officers CV Cantor and BE Long along with Sergeants LR Hayward and M McGuire remain missing.

In late June, in an effort to enhance the Allied striking power in the NEI, the B-17s of the 19th BG's 30th and 93rd Squadrons were deployed from Townsville to Batchelor. Initially flying reconnaissance missions, four B-17s attacked Kendari, destroying or damaging a number of aircraft on the ground on 30 June. The same day two B-17s flew single missions, attacking Japanese installations at Koepang and Dili.

Returning from the Kendari strike in the early hours of 30 June, B-17 41-9014 *Red "A" Baby* crashed south of the Noonamah siding near the 49th Fighter Control Squadron's camp. Hit during the raid, the aircraft, flown by Captain Weldon Smith, was damaged. However, Smith managed to fly the aircraft to the Darwin area. Then, on the approach to what he thought was Batchelor, Smith was forced to shut down another engine. The aircraft crashed at Noonamah just short of Hughes airfield.

One of the crew of the ill-fated aircraft, Lieutenant Everett "Stinky" Davis, recalled:

> ... the 93rd Bomb Squadron ... launched a strike against the Japanese Air Depot at Kendari in the Celebes Islands ... [and] our formation was attacked by several Zeros ... [A] running air battle lasted approximately 30 minutes. During this time, our aircraft was damaged ... The number 3 engine was shot out and the right aileron had been severely damaged. On our return to Port Darwin, we were unable to find our landing field ... Another engine on our aircraft failed and was feathered.

Continuing, Davis remembered:

> After several attempts to locate our landing field, another engine began to lose power and we crashed into the jungle. The aircraft hit on the nose and right wing and turned over on its back ... Shortly after the removal of the last crew member, the main wheel tires exploded and the incendiary bombs in the bomb bay were set off by heat.

Killed in the crash were Sergeants Glover Burke, Robert French and Bryson West. They were interred at Adelaide River the next day. Lieutenant Everett Davis, the aircraft bombardier, was recommended for a Distinguished Service Cross following his efforts to rescue fellow crew members.

July commenced with both Hudson squadrons mounting attacks in support of Sparrow Force. Four attacks on Koepang, Penfui, Atamboea and Dili were flown in the first nine days of the month. Buildings, barracks, shipping and enemy installations were bombed and strafed, while reconnaissance of Ambon was maintained. Reports from the returning crew confirmed a lack of anti-aircraft fire and fighter interception. A strike by three 19th BG B-17s on 3 July destroyed several aircraft on the ground at Penfui, further adding to intelligence reports of waning enemy strength.

Raids were made against targets at Dili and Koepang throughout the month and attacks were mounted on shipping in nearby waters. Dick Overheu recorded three raids on Dili and Koepang, a reconnaissance of Ambon, an attack on a Japanese cruiser on 31 July and the usual seaward patrols. On 17 July he was part of a reconnaissance of Koepang by three Hudsons, A16-207, -237

Conditions at the airfields south of Darwin remained relatively primitive throughout the war. This is a view of the No. 2 Squadron instrument workshop at Batchelor in October 1942. (AWM)

and -234. Flying Officer Hay in A16-234 completed his run over Koepang, noting a 3,000-4,000-ton vessel at the pier, and turned for home. They were just short of the coast when three Zeros were spotted, one of which approached from the starboard side. The belly gunner fired two bursts at the enemy aircraft, and it was seen to bank sharply. The pilot abandoned the aircraft, which went down in flames. The remaining Zeros were evaded in cloud and the Hudsons returned to Darwin.

Two weeks later A16-234 was on an armed reconnaissance over Saumlaki in the Tanimbar Islands when it went missing. A Japanese news broadcast picked up by Australian intelligence reported that a Hudson had collided with a Japanese floatplane and crashed into the sea near the Kai Islands.

The No. 36 *Kokutai* E13A1 Jake floatplane, crewed by Ensign Kasuka Sasaki and two others, was patrolling to provide cover as part of Operation *T-Sakusen*, the invasion of the Sunda Islands. Sasaki reporte:

> The enemy made a rapid skilful … attack. But … because of our counterattack the co-pilot was either killed or seriously wounded and because of the low altitude, the pilot didn't have time to recover … he crash landed on the sea.

The Hudson crew comprising Flying Officers Robert C Muecke and Frank S Moss, Pilot Officer Lloyd M Miners and Sergeant James E Laman had no time to send a radio message and were posted missing presumed killed.

On 31 July, Bob Dalkin was on a patrol and was some 30 miles from the Banda Islands to the southeast of Ambon. He decided that never having seen the islands he would take look. Dalkin recalled:

> I came in low and slow … around the steep cliffs, and into the straits and the harbour, past the remains of a very old … castle …it was all rather a beautiful and peaceful sight, [when] I was very suddenly confronted … by a large Japanese cruiser at anchor together with one or two smaller warships … the vital action was to immediately report the … sighting in plain language to Darwin. I had no room to maneuvre [sic] so it was a case of full power, open bomb doors, climb as quickly as possible, get the bombs away by which time I was almost over the vessel … and we were well away down the bay before a single medium rapid-firing anti-aircraft gun started to fire, with no success.

Alerted by Bob Dalkin's report No. 13 Squadron sent Hudsons to attack the vessels. The flotilla comprised a cruiser, a possible cruiser, three destroyers and seven other vessels. Three of the Hudsons broke away to attack a destroyer reported in the area but failed to locate the vessel. The enemy naval force was attacked, with the attention focused on the cruiser, however only near misses were reported near the wharf and installations. Three Hudsons of No. 2 Squadron were also sent out and released twelve 250-pound bombs resulting in near misses. A number of flying boats and floatplanes were reported at anchor nearby.

Nine aircraft were sent out to resume the attack the following day. However, the floatplanes of No. 36 *Kokutai* were flying protective patrols, and this factor combined with the anti-aircraft fire meant that only two of the Hudsons broke through to bomb the ships. After reporting more near misses, all of the Hudsons returned to base safely.

THE OTHER SIDE OF THE PICTURE – JAPANESE ATTACKS

It is important to remember what this book does not cover: while the Allied bombers were beginning their offensive the Japanese bombers were doing the same thing – attacking Australia and its outlying islands wherever they could. Although the carriers never returned after the 19 February 1942 raid, they were replaced by a relentless procession of aircraft which pounded northern targets steadily over the rest of the year and throughout 1943.

The main aircraft utilised were IJN Betty bombers escorted by Zero fighters, although occasionally other types were present. They were guided by photo reconnaissance of possible targets taken by at first single-engine Babs navigation aircraft, which were then replaced by the faster, high flying and more sophisticated twin-engine Dinahs.[4]

The Allied response was three-fold: radar, fighters and a communications network. The radar told the air headquarters a raid was incoming; the fighters were sent aloft, and the communications radio system tied it all together in a network which grew more sophisticated as time went on. Searchlights backed up the radar at night. The defenders flew P-40s in 1942, which were replaced the following year by RAAF and RAF Spitfires.

This response was not without its problems – it failed at times, as most wartime efforts do as they are developing. But it became better and better at meeting the Japanese bombers before they delivered their bombs to their targets. Eventually it turned the situation around from one of the defenders being overwhelmed to one of making it too costly for the enemy to keep up the missions.

Lastly it must be noted that the air war was mainly fought in the northern Australian dry season when flying conditions were best. The dry season runs approximately from May until October, although in 1942 significant Japanese air activity began in March and lasted until the end of August. During the wet season activity was characterised by reconnaissance flights and occasional nuisance raids, often at night.

This picture is outside the scope of this book, but to understand what was happening in northern Australia in WWII the reader is recommended to examine this other side of the war.

No. 3 Kokutai Zeros at Penfui, Timor, ready themselves for a mission to Darwin while a Takao Kokutai Betty bomber passes overhead. Because this airfield was often targeted by Allied aircraft in the first half of 1942, it was subsequently only used as a forward base by the Japanese. (Bob Alford)

---

4   See the same author's *The Empire Strikes South*, and *Eagles over Darwin*, both published by Avonmore Books. The first book uses Japanese records to describe more than 200 air missions flown over northern Australia, and the second covers the 1942 defence against these raids by the 49th FG, USAAF.

CHAPTER 5
THE END OF THE BEGINNING

By August 1942 the Japanese were on the back foot in the face of concerted attacks on their airfields, towns, installations and shipping by the RAAF Hudsons. Meanwhile 49th FG P-40s had been intercepting daylight raids, forcing the Japanese to commence night raids against Darwin and its hinterland. These were countered with searchlights and the beginnings of a "fused defence" of the area.

The Hudsons of Nos. 2 and 13 Squadrons, along with the 49th Fighter Group and No. 12 Squadron's Wirraways were the only operational units in the NWA. Support units included the Operational Base Units at Darwin, Batchelor and Hughes while No. 5 Fighter Sector provided the operational control of the fighters.

Changes and an enhanced operational role for the RAAF were in train. The 49th FG received orders to move from the Darwin area to New Guinea, while a new squadron, No. 31, formed at Wagga Wagga on 14 August. Equipped with the Bristol Beaufighter twin-engine fighter the squadron was destined for the NWA. In the attack role the unit was to ease the pressure on the Hudsons with its long-range missions over the NEI. In addition, No. 77 Squadron's P-40s were to provide for Darwin's aerial defence pending the arrival of the much-vaunted Spitfires of No. 1 Fighter Wing.

The bombing offensive was steadily increasing in power and size. A Dutch-Australian unit, No. 18 (NEI) Squadron, was working up at Canberra prior to its move to the NWA, while negotiations were underway for the RAAF to receive heavy bombers. The USAAF was also to take a more prominent role in providing a heavy bombardment squadron and later an entire bombardment group to carry the offensive beyond the range of the hard worked Hudsons.

The later months of 1942 saw the Hudsons continue to carry the offensive load with operations throughout the southern fringe of the NEI. Missions were flown against various targets including Koepang, Dili, Penfui and Beco. Ambon, the Tanimbar, Aru and Kai islands along with their floatplane bases also received attention, while routine sea searches were maintained.

To counter the guerrilla operations by Sparrow Force and their local Timorese allies, the Japanese were landing troops at Beco, a town on Timor's south coast. To push back against this move from 10 August Hudsons attacked Japanese transports and their escorts. Flight Lieutenant Lindsay Trewren, No. 13 Squadron's A Flight commander, scored direct hits on a 1,200-ton vessel. Squadron Leader Moran hit a 3,000-ton vessel, and Bob Dalkin, after missing with his bombs, strafed the decks instead. Trewren reported:

> The Beco-Mape area had been battered for several days. On the 14th August my target was Mape, and after scoring direct hits on buildings, I was intercepted by four Zekes. One made a pass at my formation but I'd seen them coming, and by that time we were right down on the water. S'Ldr Moran was leading his formation at 500 feet when the Zekes attacked. He lost formation and was last seen turning violently. He got away with just some holes in his Hudson. We'd been expecting interception [as] … we'd been attacking at the same time each day.

While the Hudson squadrons were busy harassing the Japanese in the NEI, on 14 August No. 2 Squadron moved from the RAAF Station to Batchelor. The unit occupied a camp area close to the main road with their aircraft hidden in the camouflaged inserts and taxiways.

The Hudson bombers were over Timor every day for the remainder of August, dropping supplies and attacking Japanese positions. Five Hudsons of No. 2 Squadron flew a support mission for Sparrow Force, attacking Maubisse, Timor. After releasing their bombs on the town, they reconnoitred the roads in the area. However, luck ran out on 21 August for No. 2 Squadron's Flying Officer Sid Wadey and his crew when A16-209 was intercepted and shot down over Maubisse.

Two Zeros of No. 3 *Kokutai* attacked the formation and one set fire to Wadey's Hudson. He was the only one able to bale out before his aircraft crashed into the side of a hill, killing the remaining crew. A Zero then made several attacks on the Hudsons which with one exception remained in protective close formation. Flying Officer NT Badger broke off and flew towards cloud, pursued by a Zero. With the Japanese in pursuit Badger flew low along the valleys until he reached the sea. The Zero attacked again at close range as the Australian bomber was over water, and it was shot down into the sea.

Meanwhile, Wadey, badly burnt, had landed under his parachute. He was taken in by Timorese who handed him over to Sparrow Force. Wadey was later rescued and evacuated to Darwin. The bodies of four members of his crew, Pilot Officer SW Faull and Sergeants WR Edeson, FM O'Reilly and WH Gould were found with the aircraft wreckage and buried on site.

September and October saw more of the same for the Hudson crews, and the losses continued. On 14 September A16-172 of No. 2 Squadron was lost when it was shot down into the sea by Japanese ground fire near Saumlaki in the Tanimbar Islands, taking the crew with it. Killed were Flying Officers KL McDonnell, V Treloar and KJ Ahern; together with Sergeants GS Dobbs and G Wards-Smit.

A highlight during this period was the evasion of four Zeros on 25 September by No. 2 Squadron pilot, Flying Officer RR James and his crew in Hudson A16-160. Part of a three aircraft formation, the target for the mission was Dili and any shipping sighted.

Jame's aircraft was intercepted by four No. 3 *Kokutai* Zeros over Dili, forcing James into evasive action. Flying at low level, into valleys and over hills, James and his crew managed to evade the fighters. In the process they claimed two of them, one brought down by the guns of Sergeant H

A No. 2 Squadron Hudson warms its engines in a dispersal at Batchelor prior to leaving on a mission over Japanese occupied territory in the NEI in October 1942. Trees were purposely left adjoining the dispersals and taxiways, making for very effective concealment in conjunction with camouflage nets. (AWM)

Reilly and another by Sergeant PS Reen. A possible third was claimed when a "Zero pulled away sharply and broke off [the] engagement", James later reported, adding he then "... proceeded at 0 feet towards Darwin", where he managed to land the badly damaged Hudson. As were the vagaries of warfare this did not guarantee immortality – seven months later he and his crew were dead. The claims of Zeros shot down were not to be supported by the Japanese records: the No. 3 *Ku* log shows the four Zeros airborne for an hour, during which they engaged one bomber which they claimed as a "possible". They all landed safely. The overclaiming was not unusual for either side.

October started badly for No. 13 Squadron when A16-243 along with Flying Officer JE Alcock and his crew was shot down by No. 3 *Ku* Zeros near Koepang. Bob Dalkin recalled:

> Alcock and his crew had operated from March ... and had specialised in the dangerous, high level, daylight photographic reconnaissance operations, usually against heavily defended targets. They had completed a magnificent tour of duty and were probably on their last operation when they were killed.

None of Alcock's crew were recovered. Lost were Flying Officers PC Gunson and GV Boynton along with Sergeants FP Kemp and WS Powell. Lindsay Trewren recalled:

> Alcock was regarded as one of the best reconnaissance pilots the squadron had ... he had carried out several successful missions ... The idea was to take photographs of ships in the [Koepang] harbour and then take shots of Penfui drome. When we saw the dust of the fighters taking off from Penfui, we allowed five minutes and then made for home ... I think ... Alcock was shot down by fighters waiting for him or he stayed too long.

On 24 October three No. 2 Squadron Hudsons led by the new commanding officer, Squadron Leader RH Moran, mounted a night raid on Penfui airfield. Bombing from 16,500 feet, they reported a large explosion.

The following day, A16-170 of No. 2 Squadron failed to return from a three aircraft attack on Penfui airfield. The trio made landfall at Cape Mali, before making a run over the target and turning back when A16-170 lost formation and was not seen again. On the return trip one of the pilots, Flying Officer Mills, was forced to make a landing on a beach in Hyland Bay. They were located on 27 October by Flight Lieutenant Clyde Fenton and Dick Overheu in a Tiger Moth biplane. Overheu flew the Hudson out next day with Flying Officer Mills as co-pilot. His logbook entry records succinctly "...Batchelor to beach near Cape Ford...A16-160 Self P/O Mills Beach – Batchelor." Meanwhile Flight Sergeant RKR Dunning and his crew of A16-170, Sergeants DW Francis, LHS Fraser and ML Kenihan, were all killed.

On 27 October the Beaufighters of 31 Squadron arrived at Batchelor before moving to the newly completed Coomalie airfield on 12 November. Five days later they were in action along with the Hudson units.

> The term "Zero" or "Zeke" was used by Allied aircrews to describe any Japanese single engine fighter in the NWA during 1942 and 1943. The main unit equipped with the A6M2 Zero was the IJN's No. 3 *Kokutai*, which was re-numbered as the No. 202 *Kokutai* from 1 November 1942. This unit was widely dispersed over the NEI until September 1943 when it moved to Rabaul. The Japanese Army Air Force arrived in the theatre from September 1942, with the 59th *Hiko Sentai* equipped with the Ki-43 Oscar single engine fighter. This unit was based at Lautem on Timor's north coast, before deploying to New Guinea in late June 1943.

November 1942 saw support for the Hudson squadrons and Sparrow Force increased. Twelve Martin B-26 Marauder aircraft of the 22nd BG, USAAF, arrived at Batchelor from Reid River near Townsville. Missions were flown against Dili on 1 and 2 November and against Aileu, ten miles south of Dili, on 4 November. Two Zeros and a floatplane were reported as being airborne but did not engage the Marauders during the Aileu mission. However, eight No. 3 *Ku* Zeros intercepted the force on 2 November, and only broke off when the Marauders were well out to sea.

The ground fire however was more effective. B-26 40-17593 flown by Lieutenant Charles Hitchcock and his RAAF co-pilot, Sergeant John Simms, was hit by anti-aircraft fire over the target. The starboard engine was damaged, the landing gear was torn off, and a fire was started. Nursing the aircraft towards Darwin, Hitchcock was getting close to Bathurst Island when his remaining port engine failed, and he was forced to ditch into the sea. All the crew managed to scramble free from the aircraft, however the turret gunner, Sergeant GA Campbell, died.

Martin B-26 Marauders of the 22nd BG in July 1942. Based in northern Queensland, the B-26s usually operated in New Guinea but in early November were detached to the NWA for a series of missions over Timor. (AWM)

While Hitchcock was nursing his damaged aircraft towards Darwin, Sparrow Force personnel were monitoring the aircraft frequency. They had watched the Marauders, listening to Hitchcock calling the damage as the aircraft disappeared to the south. Later they radioed Darwin and asked "Did Hitchcock make it?" but received no answer. The next day Marauders appeared in a search for Hitchcock's aircraft and Captain "Bull" Laidlaw of Sparrow Force broke in on the frequency and was advised:

> Thanks Diggers. Stop. Hitchcock made it. Crash landed Bathurst Island.

Two No. 13 Squadron Hudsons were despatched and dropped supplies while HMAS *Forceful* was sent to the scene and rescued the survivors on 3 November.[1] RAAF pilot Sergeant AG Bill Roberts flew as co-pilot in Lieutenant Robert's 40-1430 on 2 November, and then 40-1549 on 4 May, recording the missions simply as "Raid 4 500 lb bombs" and "Raid Rtd [Returned] engine trouble." The Marauders returned to their Queensland base at Reid River on 6 November, bringing their NWA deployment to an end.

During the Marauder deployment the Hudson squadrons continued their attacks on Timor.

---

1   *Forceful*, incidentally, a seagoing tugboat of 37 metres in length, may still be seen on display in the Queensland Maritime Museum today.

A No. 31 Squadron Beaufighter shortly after take-off from its Coomalie Creek base in January 1943. These powerful twin-engine fighters commenced NWA operations from November 1942. (AWM)

A night raid on Bobonaro by six Hudsons on 1 November was followed by a series of attacks, armed reconnaissance missions and seaward searches. On 5 November six No. 13 Squadron Hudsons attacked Bobonaro where the Australians of Sparrow Force were active. A Wireless Air Gunner crew member, John Shaw, recalled that:

> … I don't think the Japs appreciated the Guy Fawkes day display we put on … we formed into three groups of two and bombed buildings and started many fires … an aircraft of one pair dropped its bomb load from above the flight path of another Hudson … [thankfully] missing it. Not so lucky was WAG Bill Andrews, who had his leg broken by shrapnel from a bomb dropped by a preceding Hudson.

On 17 November No. 31 Squadron, operating Bristol Beaufighter fighters, flew its first combat mission in conjunction with a Hudson strike on Maubisse and Bobonaro. It was a bad start for the unit: the commanding officer Squadron Leader Doug Riding and his observer were both lost. While being pursued by a Japanese fighter, Riding dug a wing into the sea and the resultant accident killed both men.

A combined Hudson and Beaufighter operation on 26 November saw ten Hudsons and six Beaufighters attack Timor in the largest RAAF operation to date, leaving Nova Luba and Beco in flames.

The end of the month saw clearing searches mounted by No. 13 Squadron for the corvettes HMAS *Castlemaine* and *Armidale* as part of the withdrawal of Allied forces from Timor. The aircraft sighted two Japanese destroyers near Suai – subsequent attacks on the enemy vessels proved unsuccessful. Following the sinking of the *Armidale* in the Timor Sea by enemy aircraft on 1 December, Nos. 2, 13 and 31 Squadrons along with a Catalina from the North-Eastern Area flew searches and dropped supplies for any survivors.

During December, in an attempt to discourage the enemy from gaining full control of Portuguese Timor, offensive missions were flown against the Japanese in the Kai, Aru and Tanimbar Islands. In these areas the IJN was stepping up development of floatplane bases, from which they were increasing actions against Allied shipping in the Banda and Arafura Seas. A new airfield was also reported at Fuiloro, 60 air miles closer to Darwin than was Dili, while Japanese air strength in the Celebes was reported as 42 aircraft. Meanwhile Timor had been reinforced and had 62 aircraft on hand, an increase of 33.

Fuiloro was designated as a primary target in light of its proximity to Darwin, while Dili, Koepang and Penfui remained under constant attack by both Hudsons and Beaufighters.

On 4 December, three No. 2 Squadron Hudsons were engaged in a running fight with No. 202 *Ku* Zeros near Laga on Timor. One of the three, A16-232, flown by Flying Officer Arthur Cambridge, was experiencing engine trouble and a Zero made several passes at the Hudson, wounding Sergeant Gordon J Thame and badly damaging the aircraft. Cambridge and his co-pilot managed to fly the aircraft back, subsequently crash landing at Batchelor. However, by that time Thame had died of his injuries.

Distraction raids were now carried out by Hudsons and Beaufighters while the mess of Australian Army operations north of Australia was sorted out. From 10-19 December, after nine months of guerrilla warfare against the Japanese, the remnants of Sparrow Force's 2/2nd Independent Company was finally evacuated from Timor. They were accompanied aboard the Dutch destroyer *Tjerk Hiddes* by Dutch and Portuguese civilians and other military personnel. On 23 September reinforcements aboard the destroyer HMAS *Voyager* had been left on Timor after the destroyer ran aground – and was then blown up to prevent her capture by the enemy – during unloading off Betano. The destroyer HMAS *Arunta* took the last of the reinforcements off Timor on the night of 9-10 January 1943.

On 23 December No. 13 Squadron Hudsons were sent to search for floatplane bases around the Aru Islands, and to attack any on the water as far as Usir island with Dobo as the alternative target. The bomber formation was attacked by an enemy aircraft some 80 miles from the Aru Islands but these were driven off. Dobo was then bombed and the Hudsons were attacked by a floatplane, which was set alight by return fire from the Hudsons.

The first of two losses for December saw No. 13 Squadron's Flying Officer PG Thompson lost on Christmas Eve when his Hudson A16-166 was shot down south of Cape Lore by "Zeros". Four Hudsons of Nos. 2 and 13 Squadron had been sent to attack a destroyer and four transports in the Wetar Strait off Lavai. No hits were scored on the vessels; and Thompson and his crew of Sergeants GP Dunbar, KG Chote, RM Clark and RM West were all killed.

Three days later, A16-210 of No. 2 Squadron was lost to enemy fighters during an attack on stores at Laval. Six Hudsons led by Squadron Leader Moran were attacked by three No. 202 *Ku* Zeros during their bombing run. One flight went on to the secondary target but was again attacked by Zeros and was forced to jettison its bombs. The second flight saw the aircraft of Flying Officer MWC Johns shot down, with the loss of all on board: Johns plus Pilot Officer JF Nixon and Sergeants DK Tyler, K Ross and JC Horseman. The Zeros continued their attacks over the next 15 minutes but lost one when the belly gunner in Flight Lieutenant JW Robertson's aircraft hit it at close range. The remaining Hudsons, all damaged, landed safely at Batchelor.

By late December RAAF squadron dispositions in the Darwin area were:

- No. 2 Sqn – 18 Hudsons at Batchelor
- No. 12 Sqn – 6 Wirraways and 18 Vultee Vengeances at Batchelor
- No. 13 Sqn – 18 Hudsons at Hughes
- No. 31 Sqn – 24 Beaufighters at Coomalie Creek
- No. 1 PRU – 1 Wirraway, 4 Brewster Buffalos, 2 Lockheed Lightnings and 6 Republic Lancers at Coomalie Creek
- No. 77 Sqn – 24 P-40 Kittyhawks at Livingstone
- No. 76 Sqn – 24 P-40 Kittyhawks at Strauss.

For the remainder of the year, the Hudson squadrons flew seaward patrols and armed reconnaissance and bombing missions over Timor. They also attacked the Aru, Tanimbar and Kai islands and their floatplane bases and flew security patrols over convoys. This last task included an action over the Australian vessel MV *Alagna* and its escorting RAN corvettes during which a No. 36 *Ku* floatplane was driven off.

On New Year's Eve No. 13 Squadron Hudsons joined a search for a missing Beaufighter, the second loss in one day. On 29 December the crew of Beaufighter A19-71 was forced to parachute from their aircraft off Cape Helvetius on Bathurst Island, to the north of Darwin. Both crew members were rescued by Corporal Bill Woodnutt who was manning a forward observation post on the island. The same day saw A19-20 forced to ditch off the coast of Timor after being hit by anti-aircraft fire. Both crewmen swam ashore and managed to evade the Japanese before being rescued by a Sparrow Force patrol. They were later returned to Darwin on HMAS *Arunta*.

From 23 March 1942 to year's end the Hudson squadrons had lost sixteen aircraft, while 64 aircrew had been lost on operations. An article in Brisbane's *The Courier Mail* highlighted the role of the bombers:

> Heroes of the air in Northern Australian are two Lockheed Hudson squadrons, who have been battling with the Japanese ever since the Pacific War began … first from islands in the Netherlands East Indies and since their fall from the Australian mainland. Their record is one of courage, skill and hard work. In their 130 "strikes" against the enemy they have covered about 104,000 miles across the tricky Timor Sea and many thousands more in seaward patrols and other duties, which are the every-day life of the … Hudsons.
>
> RAAF Hudsons fly only with their own guns to protect them against the hovering Zeros so they often have a deadly task – to bomb their target and beat off Zeros. Several of these have found the Hudsons' sting fatal. In spite of the heavy odds against them in distance, weather and fighter and ground opposition, these squadrons are still smashing Japanese bases and immobilising Japanese aircraft, troops and supplies … Fifteen flying strips in Northern Australia have been named after members of the two squadrons who have lost their lives …

A pair of No. 2 Squadron Hudsons at Batchelor on 28 October 1942, about to embark on a mission over the NEI. (AWM)

CHAPTER 6

A TURNING OF THE TIDE, AND THE DUTCH ARRIVE

On 26 December 1942 a new phase in the air war over the NWA commenced, with the arrival of No. 18 (NEI) Squadron. This was a Dutch unit operating under the administrative umbrella of the RAAF.[1] The squadron and its B-25 Mitchells flew into McDonald airfield near Pine Creek. Although the aircrews were largely made up of Dutch nationals, the RAAF supplied many co-pilots, air gunners, bombardiers, photographers and ground staff.

The Dutch were reasonably appalled by what they had arrived at. They had spent months being frustrated in the southern states and were keen to get at the enemy – many of them traumatised by the situation of their families, many of whom had become prisoners of the Japanese in their old colonial lands. They found in the Northern Territory – instead of an airbase ready to operate from – a field where the runway was too short for their B-25s; little in the way of facilities, and to make matters worse it was the beginning of "The Wet": the months-long period of high humidity and usually daily torrential rain.

The new unit flew a number of familiarisation and training flights before its first mission on 18 January 1943 with a reconnaissance of the Tanimbar Islands. A search for reported enemy shipping was also carried out. The following day a follow-up armed reconnaissance of Toel in the Kai Islands saw a B-25 hit by Japanese ground fire. On 20 January two Zeros were claimed as "probably destroyed" during an engagement over Fuiloro, while a floatplane was claimed as a probable over Dobo.

The location of McDonald airfield so far south of Darwin meant that these missions required the B-25s to fly north to Darwin to refuel and then be ready on standby. On 31 January a six-aircraft mission was launched against Dili, with the priorities being shipping and the aerodrome. Led by Lieutenant Gus Winckel, visibility obscured the targets, and no bombs were released. Both N5-134 and N5-139 ran short of fuel on the return trip and jettisoned their bombs before landing southwest of Darwin: N5-134 at the Port Keats airstrip and N5-139 on the nearby Moyle River floodplains.

On 2 February N5-144 carried out a successful attack on Dobo. Two days later No. 18 Squadron suffered its first loss in the NWA, though it was not combat related. N5-132 was one of three aircraft of No. 2 Flight flying to Darwin to be on standby for a mission. It crashed north of McDonald airfield shortly after take-off and two of its bombs detonated.

Ted Lewis was the duty fire tender driver that morning and recalled:

> Two of the B-25s took off … and the third was just airborne when a flash in the sky was seen followed by … detonations. [I] later had to go and pick up the remains, one of whom was LAC Palamountain … he'd been married [for] a fortnight. Another was Sergeant Walton.

---

1   See Appendix 1 for a detailed summary of No. 18 Squadron by Dutch author Eler Mesman.

Two Dutch No. 18 Squadron personnel load a 500-pound bomb into the bomb bay of a B-25 at Batchelor in February 1943. (AWM)

A Dutch air gunner tests the turret of a No. 18 Squadron B-25 at McDonald in May 1943. (AWM)

Walton lingered for a time but died before he could be hospitalised. Killed in the crash were Lieutenant L Schalk; Sergeants L Heile, Harold O Walton (RAAF), David L McPherson (RAAF), GF Abeleven, A Maarschalkereerd and JJLM Janssen; Sergeant Major NMW Kessels and their passenger LAC Max T Palamountain.

Three days later, nine aircraft of Nos. 3, 4 and 5 Flights successfully attacked Dobo, reporting no interception. Offensive missions were flown almost daily and on 18 February Nos. 2 and 5 Flights each of three aircraft departed to attack shipping and aerodromes in the Dili area. Each aircraft was armed with three 500-pound bombs and 34 smaller incendiaries. Despite releasing their bombs over a heavily camouflaged ship in Dili harbour no hits were observed. Heavy anti-aircraft fire was encountered before five 59th *Sentai* Ki-43 Oscar fighters intercepted the formation.

In a running fight lasting over 45 minutes, two Oscars were claimed as shot down – but in fact the 59th *Sentai* lost no Oscars that day – while N5-144 of No. 5 Flight was hit in the port engine. Both the pilot, Lieutenant BJQ Grummels and the navigator/bomb aimer, Sergeant RG "Tim" Tyler were killed. The co-pilot was then forced to ditch in the sea where the remaining crew got into their dinghy despite the presence of a large shark. Later that day three No. 13 Squadron Hudsons, alerted by signal flares fired from the boat, flew over the survivors and dropped supplies. The destroyer HMAS *Vendetta* subsequently rescued the group.

In the meantime, a new unit had arrived in January to fulfil the requirement for a reconnaissance/strike force to operate in the Ceram, Celebes and Western New Guinea areas. This advance element of the 319th Bombardment Squadron of the 90th Bombardment Group was led by Captain Harry J Bullis and was equipped with Consolidated B-24 Liberators. The long endurance of the Liberator would enable the aircraft to penetrate into distant parts of the NEI, including Dutch New Guinea.

On 2 February the 319th BS settled in at Fenton. Bill Haggerty, a crew chief with the squadron recalled:

> … a desolate place out in the back country there … Outback as they called it … and the only thing around there was critters [American slang for snakes and scorpions and suchlike].

Four reconnaissance missions were flown over the period – one each to Menado, Kendari, Macassar and Ambon. During a three aircraft mission to Ambon on 21 January the formation was attacked by No. 202 *Kokutai* Zeros resulting in the photographer aboard one aircraft being killed.

Eight aircraft, led by Captain Charles Jones, took off for an attack on Ambon on 5 February. However, Jones had engine trouble and Captain Paul Johnson led the remainder through the intercepting fighters to the target. On 9 February Jones led the squadron on a twelve-hour mission to Kendari. "A funny thing", commented Lieutenant Charles Hesse after the mission, "… They put 2,350 gallons of fuel into the tanks whose total capacity is supposed to be 2343 gallons … time for our flight was 12 hours and 30 minutes."

While the wet season kept them grounded for a week, a mission was flown to Ambon on 15 February during which two hits were scored on a large transport in the harbour. With the wet season keeping the bombers grounded once again, it was a further six days before eleven aircraft again hit Ambon, this time through heavy anti-aircraft fire. Paul Johnson wrote:

> Jones and my flight[s] were intercepted by 6-8 Zeros about 15 min before reaching the

The crew of 319th BS B-24D 41-23753 Lady Millie pose with their aircraft. Part of the 90th BG, the 319th BS arrived in Australia in November 1942 and operated from Iron Range in Far North Queensland for several weeks before transfer to the NWA early in 1943. Judging by the mission markers on the aircraft, the photo was likely taken shortly before Lady Millie's loss in a take-off accident at Fenton on 2 March 1943. (Bob Livingstone)

target. They tried to drop phosphorous bombs into our formation, and they came pretty close too! … Ack Ack was terrific, but no one hit except by Zeros. 2 holes in my ship.

To date the unit had suffered only one death, the photographer killed on 21 January. However, the inevitability of losses caught up with the 319th BS on 2 March when B-24D 41-23753 *Lady Millie* crashed shortly after take-off, bound for a reconnaissance of Ambon.

This machine was the usual aircraft of Lieutenant Clarence "Bud" Eckert and named for his wife. On this occasion the aircraft was flown by Lieutenant Anderson. Of the eleven crew members only Anderson and Sergeants Clark and Stewart survived. Killed were Lieutenants William Belcher, William Q Flessert and Thomas J McHarris; Staff Sergeants Jack S Mueller and John H Wallace; Sergeants Robert Cooper and Robert W Slunaker; and Private Raymond A Keiran.

On 8 March Lieutenant Charles Hesse took off for an eight-hour armed reconnaissance flight to the Celebes and Dili. However, on testing the guns he found the top turret guns were inoperative. Rather than risk the fighters he dropped his six 500-pound demolition bombs on an alternative target of Saumlaki in the Tanimbars, as well as conducting a leaflet drop over Babar Island.

Eight days later a further armed reconnaissance was flown by four Liberators in search of shipping along the southern coast of New Guinea. Led by Captain Charles E Jones, the others were flown by Charles Hesse along with Lieutenants Hal Havener and John Wilson. Reaching the New Guinea coast, Jones and Havener headed east while Hesse and Wilson flew west. Sighting three or four ships Hesse and Wilson released their bombs, though no hits were observed. Arriving back at Fenton Havener informed them that Jones and his crew had perished when their aircraft, B-24D 41-23731 *Dirty Gertie*, exploded in mid-air. Paul Johnson wrote:

> Today we suffered a great loss to the squadron … Jonesy, our C.O., was lost with his entire crew when his ship blew up … nothing was left of plane or … 12 good men … We will try to carry on, but it is going to be very hard … with our best pal gone.

Captain Charles E Jones' crew comprised Lieutenants Howard Q Daniel, George O Munker and Roland W Russell; Master Sergeants William Hamby and Thomas N Spink; Staff Sergeant

B-24D 41-11869 One Time from the 319th BS, in flight over the Darwin area in early 1943 in company with a No. 1 Fighter Wing Spitfire. (Bob Livingstone)

James C Roberts; Sergeants Alfonso W Maslaskas, John Salemi and Lowell F Smead; along with Corporals Bruce E Baker and Darcy AJ Sharland, an RAAF photographer.

On 18 March, Lieutenant Aldan Currie flew a single plane mission to Ambon during which he and his crew were intercepted by ten Zeros. In the ensuing combat Currie's gunners claimed two fighters while one of the bomber's gunners was shot in the hand. Currie landed his badly damaged B-24D 41-11869 *One Time* at RAAF Darwin where it was written off.

The first night attack on Ambon was flown by six aircraft the following night, though one aborted with electrical problems. With the times and heights of bomb release prescribed, Charles Hesse was third in and recalled the:

> … ack-ack fire … appeared more intense than … during our daylight raids. As we started our bomb run it appeared that we would have to penetrate a solid wall of tracer fire. We made it through unscathed … [and though] we could not assess how much damage we did … it is safe to say that a lot of Japanese lost a lot of sleep that night.

The wreck of B-24D 41-11869 One Time being salvaged for parts after crash landing at Darwin on 18 March 1943 following combat with Zeros over Ambon. (Bob Livingstone)

A TURNING OF THE TIDE, AND THE DUTCH ARRIVE

For the remainder of March to the end of June the 319th BS flew the longest missions from the NWA to date, flying for up to twelve hours to attack targets as distant as northern New Guinea. They flew 33 missions, either bombing, armed reconnaissance or reconnaissance to Ambon, Kendari, Dobo, Nabirre, Manokwari, Maikoor River, Laha, Babo, Maubisse, Penfoie, Kaimana and Koepang. They flew in the face of anti-aircraft fire and enemy fighters including No. 202 *Ku* Zeros and 59th *Sentai* Ki-43 Oscars. Towns, aerodromes, ships and floatplane bases were all targets. The one fatality was Staff Sergeant Harold H Helzer, who died from injuries received in combat during a mission to Kendari on 4 April in B-24 41-23752.

On 4 May eleven B-24s of the newly arrived 380th Bombardment Group arrived at Fenton following ground personnel who arrived in late April. Bill Haggerty wrote:

> The 380th was sent in … from the States to relieve the 319th Squadron, so we could rejoin our group over at Port Moresby … So we had to indoctrinate them on combat tactics and the … maintenance people had to help them maintain their aircraft.

The pilots of the 380th BG participated in a number of missions, initially as co-pilots, prior to the departure of the 319th BS to Port Moresby in early July 1943.

The same day, 4 May, an attack on Babo was flown. Charles Hesse overflew Dobo on the return trip and further on a gunner noticed what he thought were birds on the water below. He quickly corrected himself to exclaim, "They are float-planes: Look like fighters!" Six Rufes[2] and a floatplane took off but failed to catch the Liberators. Two days later Hesse recalled the intelligence officer telling him the enemy base had been attacked by No. 31 Squadron Beaufighters. "Good work, mates!" he wrote.

Indeed, six Beaufighters had staged through Milingimbi (a forward base to the east of Darwin) on 6 May with orders to attack any floatplanes at the mouth of the Maikoor River or in the Taberfane area. Nine Japanese floatplanes of No. 934 *Kokutai* were destroyed on the beach or on the water. One Beaufighter, A19-60 and its two crew, failed to return.

On 23 June 1943, three 319th BS and fourteen of the newly arrived 380th BG aircraft took off for a bombing mission against Macassar and its installations including the Wilhelmina wharf area. The distance from Darwin to Macassar had seen the Japanese consider it safe from attack. So the surprise was complete when the B-24s attacked with a mix of 500- and 2,000-pound bombs and incendiary clusters. Four destroyers of the Kymina class along with freighters were at anchor, while a small convoy was spotted entering the harbour. With surprise on their side the B-24s bombing results were considered excellent.

Over the target area an unusual enemy aircraft was noticed. Initially identified as a Ki-27 Nate single seat fighter, it was a Mitsubishi B5M1 Mabel three seat attack aircraft (Type 97 Carrier Attack Aircraft Mark 2) of No. 932 *Kokutai* based at Mandai airfield. It had flown in from Soerabaya following repairs and had taken off when the B-24s arrived overhead. On reaching the height of the bombers, the pilot of the Mabel selected the B-24D of Captain Roy W Olsen and rammed it, severing the bomber's right wing. Olsen and his crew had no chance to escape as both aircraft spiralled into the sea.

The Mabel was piloted by Reserve Lieutenant Yuji Kino and his radio operator FPO2c Tsuruo Manabe. As reported in a Combined Fleet All Forces Bulletin, this:

---

2   The Rufe was a floatplane version of the A6M Zero, produced by Nakajima.

B-24D 41-24248 Alley Oop of the 319th BS. Operating as a lone squadron, the 319th BS established a good record during five months of operations in the NWA before returning to its parent group in New Guinea in July 1943. (Bob Livingstone)

… was the first ramming victory in the Japanese Southwestern Area. The crew were awarded a posthumous double promotion of rank.

No such honours awaited Roy Olsen and his crew: Lieutenants Thomas H Durkin, Russell R Setterblade and Kenneth F Strong; Technical Sergeants Robert F Cole and Robert K Enders; Staff Sergeants Frank A Hudspeth, Harold Muscato and William C Simon; and RAAF photographer Sergeant John A Graham.

On 8 July the 319th BS departed Fenton, bound for its new base at Port Moresby. Charles Hesse returned from leave in Sydney and was told the squadron had flown out for Moresby. He and his crew flew out on 9 July, taking seven hours for the flight. The 319th BS's five-month stay had paved the way for the long-range missions over the NEI to be flown by the 380th BG and eventually the RAAF's B-24 Liberators.

Meanwhile, concurrent with the USAAF B-24 operations, the two Hudson squadrons and No. 18 Squadron had maintained their attacks on the Japanese during the first half of 1943, ranging over the NEI and the Arafura and Banda Seas. In January 1943, the Hudsons had maintained support for the Allied forces on Timor with supply drops to Lancer Force.[3] For No. 13 Squadron it was a busy month when they flew 82 sorties during which they were engaged by enemy aircraft. A further 89 sorties were flown including missions to Dobo and the islands in the Banda Sea.

On 27 February Hudson A16-212 of No. 13 Squadron was destroyed while landing during a heavy storm following a test flight. Four of the six persons on board were killed: Sergeant William Robert Robertson and LACs Charles Conroy Jennings, Roy Gordon Bradley and PR Lazarus. The pilot, Sergeant KD Danks-Brown, and crewman LAC KEG Edwards survived the crash.

During March the No. 13 Squadron flew 61 sorties as far afield as Dobo, Saumlaki and Langgoer (in the Kai island group). Seaward patrols, an anti-submarine patrol – ahead of the HMAS *Latrobe* and MV *Tulagi* convoy – and reconnaissance missions continued. By that time however No. 13 Squadron was winding down its operations in the NWA. On 30 March the unit flew its last mission with Hudson aircraft. Six aircraft were sent to bomb Timoeka on the southwestern coast of Dutch New Guinea. Staging through Milingimbi, the aircraft carried

---

3   Lancer Force was the codename for a small number of troops landed in Timor to continue the guerrilla campaign following the evacuation of Sparrow Force. However, the Japanese had by now become much more efficient at hunting such forces, making their position on the island untenable. The force was evacuated by an American submarine in February 1943.

out their mission and returned to Hughes, marking the end of No. 13 Squadron's current operations in the NWA.

Early April 1943 saw No. 13 Squadron engaged in searchlight cooperation flights over Darwin while personnel were busy packing for the trip south to Canberra. On 12 April squadron personnel departed Hughes. While 30 aircrew flew out from Batchelor in the last six Hudsons, 186 airmen proceeded by rail to Adelaide. The squadron would later return to the Northern Territory in 1944 after conversion to the Lockheed PV-1 Ventura patrol aircraft.

An RAAF Hudson seen during a raid on Dobo, an IJN floatplane base in the Aru Islands, in March 1943. (AWM)

For No. 2 Squadron, the missions continued. On 6 April aircraft A16-247, *The Saint*, was detailed to carry out a single aircraft search for shipping around Timoeka. No shipping was sighted, and instead the aircraft attacked installations at Timoeka. Anti-aircraft fire was experienced with several hits received, damaging the aircraft. A crash landing at Milingimbi, following port brake problems in the landing roll, causing a ground loop collapsing the starboard undercarriage. The crew were not injured.

Meanwhile over the period February to April, No. 18 Squadron was also mounting up the missions, flying 60 sorties from over the main targets of Dili and Dobo, but also attacks on shipping and airstrips. In return they experienced the inevitable anti-aircraft fire and intercepts by enemy fighters.

On 30 March N5-133 took off from Darwin for an armed reconnaissance over Kaimana Bay. Completing the mission, the B-25 turned for home but was intercepted by two A6M Zeros. During the engagement the oil line to the starboard engine was damaged, putting the engine out of action. Both enemy fighters were claimed as shot down by gunners. The pilot, Lieutenant Rudy Swane, then attempted to reach Darwin on one engine but instead was forced to make a wheels up landing on Melville Island. One crewman was slightly injured.

On 3 April, eight B-25s were sent on an armed reconnaissance to the Kai Islands to attack shipping and the town of Toeal. Each aircraft was armed with three 500-pound bombs and incendiaries. However they failed to release on both N5-136 and -141, while only one bomb released on N5-129. As the aircraft departed the target internal fires and smoke were reported, but all the aircraft managed a safe return.

Two days later three aircraft, N5-130, '140 and '145 were on night standby at Darwin when they were ordered on a reconnaissance of Dili, Bacau and north Timor. Led by Lieutenant Gus Winckel, N5-130 and -145 took off at 0400 and circled, awaiting aircraft N5-140 to join up.

When contact was not made, they proceeded with the mission. At Darwin N5-140 had taken off but crashed into the sea off Nightcliff shortly after, killing the crew. Those who died were Sergeant Major G Tijmons; Sergeants K Van Bremen, GB Weller (RAAF) and Sergeant Major FJM van Wylick; along with RAAF Flight Sergeant RJ Hill. A sign in the present-day Nightcliff foreshore park commemorates the loss.

During April the range of the B-25s was raised as an issue, as was the political significance of the Dutch squadron being retained in the NWA against some suggestion of it moving to the North Eastern Area. Further, the commanding officer of the NWA pointed out that their range of 1,200 miles allowed for attacks on Dili and Koepang in favourable conditions at night in light of a lack of fighter cover.

On 13 April the squadron began a move to Batchelor. During the move the squadron had continued its attacks on Dili, Bacau and Koepang, and reconnaissance missions against shipping. The last operation from McDonald was flown on 7 May when 20,000 leaflets were scattered over Koepang and Dili. The move was completed two days later. The Dutch B-25s were also undergoing a slow process of having drop tanks fitted to increase their range, and their weapons replaced by those of heavier calibre.

As if to emphasise the need for more forward armament and the release of bombs by the pilot, on 28 April four B-25s were sent to attack shipping to the west of the Aru Islands. Vessels of around 2,000 and 1,000 tons were sighted south of Ceram accompanied with an armed escort and the B-25s went in to attack. N5-135 was hit by anti-aircraft fire which blew off a wing before the aircraft burst into flames and crashed into the sea. Lost were the crew of Lieutenants AF Oudraad and JBF de Knecht; Sergeant AH de Jong; and RAAF Sergeants NGW Morris and GA O'Hea.

At the time, poor visibility and the difficulty of aiming and bringing guns to bear on ship anti-aircraft guns were causing problems in attacks on shipping at masthead height. A solution was the fitment of gun packs on the fuselage sides along with the installation of four 0.50-inch calibre machine guns in the former bomb aimer's compartment. The primary work was carried out by the Americans at the Townsville depot, with a first aircraft modified in this "strafer" configuration at Townsville before the remainder were modified at Batchelor by No. 18 Squadron fitters. The belly turrets were also removed and replaced with extra fuel tanks, increasing the range by a further 300 miles. The first strafer missions from Batchelor were

The sign commemorating the loss of No. 18 Squadron B-25 N5-140 in Nightcliff foreshore park, Darwin. Parts of the wreck can still be seen at very low tide. (Author photo)

Armourers service twin 0.50-inch calibre machine guns on the side of the fuselage of an RAAF B-25 at Hughes in 1945. Dutch B-25s of No. 18 Squadron received this modification in 1943. (AWM)

flown on 11 May with a reconnaissance of the Tanimbar Islands and Ambon, along with operations over Dili and Koepang harbour.

Meanwhile No. 2 Squadron was continuing its offensive operations against Japanese shipping, airfields and installations along with seaward sweeps. During March 1943, Dick Overheu flew four seaward sweeps, during which he bombed Saumlaki on 24 March, and three missions over Koepang and Dili. The squadron was also on the move. On 10 April the unit moved to Hughes airfield while the remainder of No. 13 Squadron was preparing to vacate.

A raid on shipping in Kaimana Bay on 2 April was met by enemy fighters, one of which was claimed to have been shot down into the sea. A raid on Saumlaki in early April was met with heavy anti-aircraft fire. And still, the losses mounted. A raid on Timoeka in Dutch New Guinea on 2 April saw A16-169 shot down by anti-aircraft fire during a low-level attack on the airstrip with five other Hudsons. The doomed aircraft was observed at 200 feet when a red flash was seen. The pilot pulled up and to starboard and travelled a further 500 metres before it dived into the ground killing all of the crew: Squadron Leader MC Burns; Pilot Officer LR Jope; along with Sergeants K Jones, RJ Johnstone and AA Dean.

Two aircraft were lost along with their crews on 19 April when they collided shortly after taking off from Milingimbi on an armed reconnaissance mission to Timoeka in Dutch New Guinea. Four minutes after taking off, A16-183 and -197 collided and crashed some 600 metres apart on Rabuma, one of the nearby Crocodile Islands. Both crews were killed. In A16-183 Flying Officers KR Mills and RE John along with Sergeants HH Hadley, JL Barnes and TW Bassen perished. Also lost was the entire crew of A16-197: Flying Officers KE Daniel and J Laws; and Sergeants TW Wilson, WJ Gove and JG Butler. All were buried at the site.

On 28 April, luck ran out for the Flying Officer James crew – who had successfully evaded fighters over Timor the previous September – when their Hudson was shot down during a patrol over Arafura Sea. The Hudson was one of six aircraft sent on an armed reconnaissance and had departed Milingimbi when 40 minutes later it signalled, "one engine gone." A further signal nine minutes later stated "X200 about 30 minutes Milingimbi." No further news was heard and the crew was reported missing. A Japanese pilot had intercepted what he identified as a B-25, which was James' Hudson. Missing believed killed were Flying Officer RR James; Warrant Officer NE Cutten; along with Sergeants RE Norris, RD Ryan, KD Krech and PS Reen.

It had been a period of intense operational activity for the Hudsons. Some 629 operational strikes had been flown and 224 tons of bombs released in the six months to May. In addition they were carrying out an average of 110 patrols, reconnaissance sorties and convoy escort duties each month.

On 7 May A16-171 was detailed to fly an armed reconnaissance of the Maikoor and Taberfane area as part of a five aircraft operation. After forming up, fighters were seen in the vicinity and the flight leader throttled back to allow a coordinated defence. Two Rufes attacked and with A16-171 lagging behind one of them scored hits on the Hudson. It climbed steeply to starboard before turning on its back and crashing into the sea killing all of the crew: Warrant Officer VL Jackman, Flying Officer DR Hicks, Flight Sergeants E Quinn and IW McKenzie; and Sergeant DA Emery. A further Hudson, A16-211 *The Tojo Busters*, was badly damaged during the engagement and crash-landed at Milingimbi. It was later written off.

Accidents also took their toll. On 12 June Flight Lieutenant John Mason, the B Flight commander, was tasked to test fly A16-186. After being airborne for 30 minutes he was seen making a single engine approach to Hughes, then raising the undercarriage as if to overshoot. The Hudson disappeared below the trees before crashing north of the airfield, killing all aboard including three Hudson captains. Those who died were Flight Lieutenants John Mason and JR Wood; Flying Officers IG Knauer and TW Swann; and Sergeant GR Rowland.

Hudson A16-227 was flying an armed reconnaissance over the Aru Islands on 20 June when surprised by a Rufe flown by Warrant Officer Takeshi Kawaguchi of No. 934 *Kokutai*. Kawaguchi, probably short on fuel, returned to his base and claimed a victory. However, Flying Officer John Cameron and his crew returned safely to base. A16-227 lasted only a further seven days before it landed at Milingimbi with a flat tyre and collapsed the undercarriage. The aircraft was written off.

The wreck of No. 2 Squadron Hudson A16-211 The Tojo Busters at Milingimbi sometime after its crash landing on 7 May 1943 following combat with IJN floatplanes. (AWM)

Sergeant G Wynnands in the cockpit of No. 18 Squadron B-25 N5-128 on 4 May 1943, pointing to the Donald Duck nose art. At this time the squadron's aircraft were being converted to "strafer" configuration with the addition of fuselage gun packs. (AWM)

CHAPTER 7

BIGGER, BETTER AND FASTER

By mid-1943 the overall war outlook from the NWA was looking increasingly positive for the Allies, with a focus on future offensive rather than defensive operations.

The long road back in the Pacific, therefore, consisted of steadily pressing north to the Japanese home islands. At the same time a key factor in respect to the Allied effort was the "Germany First" imperative. In mid-December 1941, British Prime Minister Winston Churchill met with US President Franklin D Roosevelt in Washington DC. The meetings, known as the Arcadia Conference, had significant outcomes. The USA and Great Britain agreed to share military resources. They also agreed to prioritise the war against Germany, rather than try and stretch themselves to fight everywhere at once. So the war in the Pacific was more a holding action at first, before eventually becoming offensive in nature.

On 5 June 1943 a summary of the RAAF's operational aerodrome requirements for the western and north-western areas was issued by the Forward Echelon. In it a number of new and remedial works were proposed, including a new seaplane Operational Base Unit at Groote Eylandt and the requirement for:

> …not less than five new moorings … and the base should be equipped adequately to handle those aircraft staging through.

A new joint land and sea base was also planned for Arnhem Bay in far east Arnhem Land, with an intention to base three squadrons there. These were to be a flying boat squadron, a general reconnaissance/bomber squadron and a fighter squadron.

At Darwin it was proposed to provide maintenance and seaplane refuelling facilities in expectation of increased Catalina operations.[1] Drysdale in the Kimberley region of Western Australia was to be maintained to extend the range of Hudsons and Beaufighters. Further, a runway was to be positioned in accordance with the prevailing wet season wind conditions and was to be surfaced with eighteen dispersal bays "…up to the dimensions of the Ventura type [of aircraft]." For Fenton requirements for the 380th BG were clarified. While no specific works for Fenton were detailed it is known that dispersal bays, reveted bays, sealed roads and camp areas were developed both with the 380th BG and the RAAF's (future) heavy bomber squadrons in mind.

During April 1943, RAAF headquarters had laid out a plan for the reconnaissance of Japanese held areas as a guide for any discovery of an enemy attack. The plan included the following reconnaissance missions:

- A twice weekly reconnaissance of likely assembly points and anchorages [in] Timor
- A daily reconnaissance of similar points in the Tanimbar, Kai and Aru Islands, and
- A reconnaissance of Dutch New Guinea between Babo and Frederik Hendrik Island at least every three days.

By early June, replacement flights of No. 18 Squadron personnel were becoming available from the Dutch training base at Jackson, Mississippi, in the US. Two flights were planned to arrive on 15 and 30 September followed by two flights in October and the remainder during

---

1   The RAAF had operated Catalina flying boats since 1941, but from east coast bases and in New Guinea.

November. The Dutch B-25 crew composition remained at two pilots, a radio operator and a bomb aimer – the latter surplus to requirements on the new "strafer" versions, while the RAAF filled the remaining crew positions.

At the same time the formation of an NEI Reserve Squadron was clarified to:

a. provide means of maintaining flying practice for crews relieved from the … operational squadron;

b. maintain and improve flying standards for replacement crews; and

c. provide a pool in which reserve B.25 [sic] aircraft could be held

The squadron was to form as No. 119 (NEI) Squadron, but it failed to eventuate. However, an NEI personnel and equipment pool was formed in Canberra in September 1943.

Early June 1943 saw the losses continue for No. 18 Squadron. On 2 June, N5-150 and its crew was lost during a masthead attack on a Japanese destroyer off Vila Nova Malacca (Lautem) on Timor's north coast. Killed were Lieutenant H Van Den Berg and Flight Sergeant TEW Williams, along with Sergeants A Bouwman and RAAF members RL Morrison and FC Pritchard. Part of a planned attack on vessels off Lautem, the aircraft was to attack the smallest of four ships. However, the target turned out to be a "5,000-ton destroyer" and the aircraft was shot down by anti-aircraft fire.

Not all losses were due to enemy action. Gus Winckel recalled taking off at 0400 for a raid on Fudors:
> … with 3 Mitchells fully loaded with petrol and 5-300 lb. bombs [when] a huge kangaroo ran into the landing lights and then into the right engine. I was doing nearly 100 miles [sic] … heard a terrific bang … could not stop, just had to continue, the right engine became really rough. I had to carefully drop the bombs into the sea and slowly did a … circuit to land again. The prop was badly bent [and] this was the only ever mission not fulfilled by me.

While suggested requirements for aerodromes was slowly doing the rounds of the defence bureaucracy, Fenton airfield was buzzing with activity. The B-24 Liberators of the USAAF's 380th BG and its four squadrons – the 528th, 529th, 530th and the 531st Bombardment Squadrons – under Lieutenant Colonel Bill Miller were planning to settle into their new home. Fenton was to be their home base with an established strength of 35 aircraft. To enable the crews to gain experience in operational conditions, twelve aircraft were to operate with the 319th BS while the remainder to were operate with the 90th and 43rd Bombardment Groups from Port Moresby.

Eleven aircraft and their crews of the 528th BS flew into Fenton on 3 and 4 May expecting the facilities to be ready for them. They weren't. The 380th BG historian wrote:
> This place called Fenton Field gave new meaning to the adjectives "remote" and "primitive" … their tower lacked radio equipment and only one permanent building stood [there] … tents provided the only other shelter … the field had been carved out of a dense forest that still harboured a variety of creatures … the runway was not level … [and] all maintenance was done outdoors.

In the event the 528th BS commanding officer, Captain Zed Smith, sent seven of the aircraft to Batchelor while improvements were made, all the while with an eye on getting the group operational. The first operational mission flown by the 380th BG was on 6 May when Captain John Henschke flew as co-pilot to Captain Paul Johnson of the 319th BS to Manokwari in a long flight lasting ten hours and 45 minutes.

B-24D 42-40500 Careless trails smoke over enemy territory prior to crashing on 11 June 1943. (Bob Livingstone)

By 14 May facilities at Fenton had improved enough for the aircraft at Batchelor to return to Fenton. They joined the 319th BS in a number of missions, some of them from the remote Corunna Downs in the Pilbara region of Western Australia where temperatures reached 50° C, or 122 Fahrenheit in the scale the Allies were using then. The NWA commander, Air Commodore Frank Bladin, ordered the first mission from Corunna Downs for 29 May, however it was delayed for a day. A reconnaissance mission to Soerabaya, it was flown by Captains Jack Banks and Bill Shek, with the latter experiencing engine trouble on the return flight. Dropping only one 45-pound bomb they brought back photos of the Wonokromo oil refinery and Malang airfield crammed with over 60 aircraft. Corunna Downs vastly increased the range of the B-24s deep into the NEI, enabling missions over Java, Bali, the Celebes and Borneo. It was kept in mind for further missions despite the heat, poor conditions and being described as "…a God-forsaken spot…inhabited chiefly by flies."

That first flight was also significant in that it was the first of a B-24 fitted with radar countermeasures, known as RCM. This equipment was manned by RAAF-trained operators, such as Sergeant Dick Dakeyne of the RAAF's secretive Section 22. The RCM equipment was able to locate Japanese radar emissions, determine the frequencies it was using and plot its effective range. Posted to No. 44 Radar Wing in late April and then to the 319th BS in early May, Dakeyne flew a number of missions as both a gunner and photographer before a posting to the 530th BS of the 380th BG. There he flew two tours, the first from May to December 1943 and the second from March to August 1944 flying as both an RCM operator and gunner. Over the two tours he clocked up 69 missions and 1,239 combat hours.

Membership of Section 22 was hazardous. Dick Dakeyne and Joe Holohan tossed a coin to see who went with Jack Banks on a Java mission. Dakeyne won and Holohan was killed on 11 June 1943 along with the crew of B-24D 42-40500 *Careless* that was shot down by anti-aircraft fire and No. 202 *Ku* Zeros. Killed in *Careless* were Captain James H Dienelt; Lieutenants John B Payne, Joseph A Donovan and John A Palmer; Technical Sergeants Clarence E Neville and Alvin J Schulte; Staff Sergeants Bernard Greenfield, William J Kelly, Carl A Ochala, Donald D Russell and Emil F Vanek; along with Joseph Holohan of the RAAF.

B-24D 42-40486 Dis-Gusted! after its wheels up landing at Fenton on 2 June 1943. At the end of that month it was burnt out as a result of a Japanese bombing raid on Fenton. (Bob Livingstone)

Another RAAF RCM operator, Pilot Officer Keith Bevan, died on 21 November 1943 when B-24 42-40967 *Black Widow* and Lieutenant Maurice Beller's crew perished when the aircraft disintegrated after reportedly being hit by anti-aircraft fire over Manokwari. Two No. 202 *Ku* Zeros carrying phosphorous bombs spotted the seven B-24s approaching the target and attacked.[2] The Zeros were joined by two No. 934 *Ku* Rufes.

While the Zeros and Rufes didn't prevent the B-24s from bombing the target, Beller's *Black Widow* was downed and two other B-24s damaged while a Japanese fighter was downed by the B-24 gunners. The Rufes claimed one kill and two damaged while anti-aircraft gunners claimed Beller's aircraft. Killed in *Black Widow* were Lieutenants Maurice W Beller, Kenneth R Adkins and John W Trexler; Flight Officer Lee A Root; Staff Sergeants Paul Nigrini, Floyd E Rakow and Ernest Rivera; Technical Sergeants Arnold W Churchek and Lincoln Johnson; plus Private William M Thomas and Pilot Officer Keith H Bevan, RAAF.

The Beller crew had previously flown on the first mission by the 380th BG after gaining full operational status. On 2 June Lieutenant Colonel Bill Miller and Captain Zed Smith flew an armed reconnaissance of Lautem, home of the 59th *Sentai* with its Ki-43 Oscars and Ki-46 Dinahs of the 70th *Dokuritsu Chutai* reconnaissance unit.

Miller took Beller in B-24 42-40393 *Black Magic* while Smith took the Captain Charles Sowa crew in B-24D 42-40486 *Dis-Gusted!*. Over the target they met heavy anti-aircraft fire, damaging an engine, puncturing fuel tanks, severing hydraulic lines and hitting bomb racks in Miller's aircraft. Smith was attacked by three Ki-43 Oscars led by Captain Shigeo Nango, commander of the 59th *Sentai* No. 2 *chutai*. Both B-24s made it back to Fenton, however Smith had to land wheels up after discovering two punctured main wheel tyres.

During this period of early operations the 380th BG suffered several further losses. On 11 June 531st BS B-24D 42-40527 *Lelia Belle* and the crew of Captain Paul G Smith failed to return from a night mission over New Britain. Four days later Lieutenant Benjamin G Parker's crew in B-24D 42-40517 *Kathy* was lost when the machine was involved in a mid-air collision south southeast of Port Moresby during a night mission to Rabaul. The other aircraft involved, B-24D 42-40528 *Dauntless Dabbie,* was forced to ditch off the south coast of New Guinea, with the loss of two crewmen. On 10 July B-24D 42-40507 *Esmeralda II* and Captain Howard Merkel

---

2   The Japanese made occasional use of aerial bombs which were released over Allied bomber formations. While a promising idea, such weapons suffered numerous practical limitations and were rarely successful.

and his crew were lost following an attack by a 59th *Sentai* Ki-43 Oscar over Babo. The same day Lieutenant Francis G McDowell, his crew and B-24D 42-40492 *Miss Mary* were lost over Kaimana after being intercepted by fighters.

The RCM unit was a useful addition in a war that was becoming ever-more technical. RCM aviator, Bernard Hosie, recalled:

> In July I was posted to Section 22 which came directly under RAAF Command in Brisbane. Two other Nav (W)[3] made up the group; Sgt Bill Ford and Sgt Don Herbert. Secrecy was at the highest level; we could tell no one what our job was. We lived in the RAAF camp in Brisbane but trained in an old warehouse on the Brisbane River. We were receiving special training as Radar Countermeasures operators; this meant that our job was the identification and location of Japanese radar, determining the frequency they operated on, their range, and methods to trick or blind them.
>
> Not a little of our course consisted of listening to recordings of Japanese radar – mostly a series of squeaks and buzzes; this quickly became very boring. We had one recording with the song "Stormy Weather" on one side and "The Rose in her Hair" on the other side. As soon as the instructors left the room we put on the recording. To this day, fifty years later, those two songs still remind me of the days in the old warehouse on the Brisbane River. I had my 21st birthday, 20 August 1944, in the old warehouse.
>
> In September 1944 the three of us flew to Darwin on a DC3 (Douglas Dakota) RAAF transport plane – landing at Charleville to refuel on the way. In Darwin we joined the US 380th Heavy Bomb Group. The 380th was made up of four squadrons, each with about fifteen B-24 four engine bombers – Liberators as the RAAF called them. I was attached to the 530th squadron.
>
> There were about ten RCM operators with the 380th; all of us Nav (W)s from the RAAF. The Americans had plenty of Navigators and of Radio Operators but did not have men trained in both navigation and radio; for this reason they had borrowed some Australians. There were also about twelve Australian Liberator crews flying with the 380th (three per squadron) prior to setting up an operational Australian Liberator squadron after the 380th moved north from Darwin.[4]
>
> My first bombing mission (or strike as the RAAF called them) was on 28 September, a few days after arriving in Darwin. It was against an airstrip on Ceram, some four hours north of Darwin. Four days later came a night strike against Makassar in the Celebes (Sulawesi as it is to-day). Makassar was one of the main ports in the Celebes and the target for many of our raids; it was a round trip of 11 or 12 hours. We hit Makassar again on another night raid on 5 October.
>
> On 9 October we bombed Koepang Harbour in Timor; as usual on a major strike we had four squadrons each of six planes. The squadron ahead of us ran into very heavy flak (anti-aircraft fire); we saw one plane take a direct hit and go down in flames. Three parachutes opened, but as the Japanese usually beheaded any prisoners we knew their chances were not great. Our squadron leader changed the approach path as it was clear the Japanese guns were trained on the path of the first squadron and we escaped with almost no flak.

---

3   Navigator (Wireless)
4   In 1944 the RAAF was training its own B-24 crews and a number saw service with the 380th BG as the RAAF B-24 squadrons were not yet operational. This is discussed in Chapter 9.

On my return I found that Don Herbert was in the plane that was shot down. Don lived near my Uncle George Hosie in Sydney and his parents thought the three of us were flying in the same plane; when they heard their son was missing they told George; he wrote to my parents to console them on the fact that I was missing and expressing his hopes that I would survive. There were no survivors from the crew.

Only two or three planes in the squadron had the RCM gear so I flew with different crews depending on which crew was allocated to that plane. Sometimes these would be Australian crews, sometimes US.

Meanwhile the 380th BG was now becoming fully operational. Both the 529th and 531st BS moved into Manbulloo, west of Katherine some 200 miles south of Darwin during the first week of June 1943, while the 530th BS moved into Fenton. Manbulloo had been developed enough to support the two squadrons. Despite its poor conditions, the nearby Katherine River provided a respite from the heat and dust, as did the army's ice works. Nearby there was also an Australian General Hospital "…with female nurses…[who] would provide the men with hours of fanciful diversions."

On 1 November the 529th and 531st BS moved forward to Long airfield east of Fenton, and in proximity to a hospital, fuel supplies from the Brocks Creek siding and a combined group headquarters.

The first of the long-range missions was flown in two strikes by 22 aircraft on 13 August 1943, this time to hit the oil refinery at Balikpapan in Borneo, a sixteen hour round trip. To date B-24s had flown to Java, Ambon, the Celebes, Dutch New Guinea and Macassar. Two further aircraft on the Balikpapan strike were to overfly the area to take post-strike photos two days afterwards.

Eleven aircraft flew up to Darwin to upload bombs and take on fuel. Each aircraft carried six 500-pound bombs and 3,500 gallons of fuel for the trip. Led by Captain Forrest Brissey in B-24D 42-40515 *Sooper Drooper*, the initial strike was assigned a variety of targets including the refinery, lubricating oil plant and shipping. Two aircraft failed to bomb due to poor weather. Meanwhile, following a running battle with Japanese fighters, B-24D 42-40387 *Shady Lady* force landed on salt flats near the old Pago Mission in the remote Kimberley area of WA. The crew was rescued and the aircraft was subsequently repaired and flown out.

The crew of B-24D 42-40387 Shady Lady with local Aborigines after force landing on a salt flat in the remote Kimberly region of Western Australia. (Bob Livingstone)

A follow up strike was ordered for the night of 16-17 August. Major Richard Craig in *Gus's Bus* aborted with a fuel leak. Lieutenant Dexter Baker in *The Golden Goose* was "weathered out". However, Lieutenant Bob Fleming in *Prince Valiant* won a Distinguished Flying Cross for bringing his aircraft back on two engines with a burnt-out forward nose area. The bombs dropped over Balikpapan by the 380th BG had not inflicted any great damage, but the success of the two missions confirmed the long-range capabilities of the B-24. They also forced the Japanese to deploy resources to defend the area.

The B-24s had been lucky. Following the raid on 13 August the Japanese quickly deployed elements of No. 202 *Ku* to Manggar airfield near Balikpapan, with veteran Lieutenant Commander Minoru Suzuki as the detachment commander. The move saw the loss of Flying Chief Petty Officer Takeshi Takahashi while intercepting *Miss Giving* on 15 August, while the bomber was taking post-strike photos.

Accidents also accounted for good men and aircraft. A night landing at Fenton on 25 August saw B-24D 41-24248 *Alley Oop* hit a tree, killing Colonel Edward Shepherd, Captain Samuel S Poor, Flight Officer Raymond E Siple and Technical Sergeant Clifford D Cater. On 11 November B-24D 41-41242 of the 528th BS crashed short of Fenton's runway after its bombs were jettisoned and a propellor feathered. Killed were Lieutenants Wilfred L Grenfell, Kenneth M Cochrane, James R Hagerty and Daniel C Hammang; Technical Sergeant Harry T Francis; and Staff Sergeants Charles R Calhoun, William F Gallagher, Raymond Katz, Harold B Markowitz, James F Roubal and RF Shepardson.

Over the months to December 1943, the 380th BG lost a further six aircraft and 60 men on operations. A further 24 men initially survived the actions, of which 20 were taken POW by the Japanese with four known to have been executed.

Photographer Frank McGarry managed to jump clear of B-24D 42-40509 *Nothing Sacred* when it crashed short of Fenton's runway following a mission to attack Langgoer on 21 September. Badly damaged after a fight with six Zeros over the Kai Islands, Lieutenant Hugh B Parris nursed the bomber home. However instead of following orders to land at Darwin he continued on to Fenton. His action cost the lives of himself and his crew comprising Lieutenants Andrew B Edwards, Archibald S Mills and Laverne F Parsons; Staff Sergeants William O Miller, Albert Mirachi, Ralph T Newbold, and Dossie J Odom; and Technical Sergeants Urban V Darlington and Leonard R Greene.

Captain John Farrington's crew all perished off the Celebes on 26 October when their aircraft B-24D 42-40485 *Fyrtle Myrtle* was shot down by fighters after bombing Pomelaa. Lieutenant Frederick Hinze and his crew aboard B-24D 42-40518 *The Golden Gator* were shot up over Pomelaa the same day. Hinze managed to nurse the badly damaged aircraft as far as Timor before he was forced to ditch it, dying of his wounds. Those killed were Flight Officer Francis E Herres; Staff Sergeants Howard G Collett, Mark A Mitchell and Robert R Wolf; and Corporal Aldo A Bottiglio. Four survivors were rescued by Catalina A24-63 near Moa Island the following day.

The Beller and Grenfell incidents of 11 and 21 November 1943 (described above) added to these losses.

On the afternoon of 21 November seven 531st BS B-24s raided Taberfane. They were met by four Rufes flying a combat air patrol. The Japanese aircraft intercepted the B-24s as they left the target area, but one Rufe was shot down and its pilot killed. The B-24s all returned safely to base. While the 380th BG was busy with its long-range missions and bombing of strategic targets throughout the NEI, the B-25 Mitchells of No. 18 Squadron and the Hudsons of No. 2 Squadron were continuing their harassing raids closer to home. Adding weight to the RAAF's operational effectiveness was the commencement of operations from Darwin by the RAAF's PBY Catalinas during August 1943.

The Catalina was slow and unwieldy but it was the one aircraft in the RAAF inventory that could fly further then the B-24 Liberator and more than proved its worth in bombing, mine laying and air sea rescue missions over the two years to August 1945 – as we shall see.

Japanese barracks on fire at Pomelaa in the Celebes after being bombed by 380th BG Liberators on 21 August 1943. On 26 October two B-24s were lost to Japanese fighters during a raid on the same location. (AWM)

CHAPTER 8

THE CATALINAS ARRIVE; THE ALLIES APPLY PRESSURE

Darwin was already acquainted – although by now most of its civilians had left – with the pre-war Empire flying boats which flew on a route from Australia to Britain. These used the harbour as a runway, and their passengers were ferried out to them via launch. Later, in the first weeks of the Pacific War, the Consolidated PBY Catalinas of the US Navy's Patrol Wing 10 used Darwin as a base until the 19 February 1942 attack. However, it was not until the latter half of 1942 that RAAF Catalinas began using Darwin harbour.

On 18 August 1942 a Catalina flew from Cairns to deliver supplies to the commandos on Timor. It returned with wounded men whose conditions prevented them waiting for sea transport. In December a No. 11 Squadron Catalina searched for survivors of the ill-fated HMAS *Armidale* after it was sunk off Timor by Japanese aircraft. Another flew out a covert party, "Walnut 2", from the Aru Islands on 15 February 1943. The first offensive Catalina mission occurred on that same day when two of the flying boats staged through Groote Eylandt to bomb Babo.

Patrols were also flown and on 8 April A24-42 of No. 20 Squadron was lost over the Gulf of Carpentaria when Flight Lieutenant CW Haydon reported his machine on fire. Nothing further was heard from the aircraft and despite searches the aircraft and its crew were posted missing, presumed killed. The crew comprised Haydon, along with Flying Officers LA Elkington, JD Fisk and JG Lancaster; Flight Sergeant LG Adamson and Sergeant LN Oppy.

The first RAAF minelaying missions of the war were flown by Nos. 11 and 20 Squadrons against Kavieng on the nights of 22 and 24 April 1943, with follow up raids on 3 and 13 May. While they originated in north Queensland, these operations set the tone for future Catalina operations in the north. The first operation was carried out in full moonlight and because collisions were a risk, take-off times were widely spaced.

Eight aircraft took off on the evening of 22 April and laid their mines in Kavieng's Silver Sound, with the mission code named "Popsy I". The aircraft all returned safely despite the presence of light and medium anti-aircraft guns. The minefield was replenished by two Catalinas on 27 April, while "Popsy II" was flown two nights later when the passage west of Silver Sound was laid with eight Mark 12 Model 1 and eight Mark 15 mines. These were later replenished with two further mines each in Silver Sound, Staffren Strait and in Byron Strait on 3 May, while four mines were laid in Ysabel Passage on 13 May.

In a report on the "Popsy I" and "Popsy II" operations by the No. 11 Squadron commanding officer, the following conclusions were reached:

> Mine laying can be done without the aid of the moon and is better performed under that condition. Fighter interception is less likely and with no moon a cable seen as low as 500 feet. The risk of collision is greater as aircraft cannot see each other. This can be obviated by sending fewer aircraft per night … replenishments to SILVER SOUND or any defended areas will be done by one or at the most two aircraft … using a glide approach. This is also the only method by which secrecy might be achieved.

Even with the apparent success of the "Popsy" operations, the Catalinas were only used on a part time basis for minelaying over the twelve-month period to April 1944 with Nos. 11 and 20 Squadrons flying an average of only fifteen operations a month. This was because the flying boats were still busy with supply dropping, reconnaissance, bombing, rescue and convoy patrol tasks during this period.

Minelaying continued to June 1943 while the Allies applied pressure on the Japanese and their hold on the Bismarck Archipelago. Lorengau on Manus Island was mined from 27 to 30 May. Babo was struck on 9 June in the longest bombing mission by the Catalinas to date when two aircraft staged through Groote Eylandt. Laha, near Ambon, was also bombed at this time, causing large fires, although only one aircraft found the target in poor weather. A 20 May directive by Lieutenant General George C Kenney called for a show of force in the NWA during June and July. As a result Babo was attacked on four occasions during June, with a crew reporting that thirteen fires, one of them very large, were started during the 10 June mission.

Minelaying was changed from Kavieng to Babo during July 1943 in a new phase of operations in which mines were to be laid in all "mineable" harbours and along shipping routes in the NEI.

On 26 August four Catalinas arrived in Darwin where they were refuelled and armed with mines before setting out for Soerabaya, a major port and naval base in Java. The four flying boats successfully released eight mines over the target and returned to Exmouth Gulf, Western Australia, where the seaplane tender USS *William B Preston* refuelled them after the 20-hour mission.

Catalina A24-50 was lost on 2 September during a minelaying mission to Sorong. After refuelling at Groote Eylandt, the aircraft departed and was not heard from again. The aircraft was posted "missing, believed crashed into mountain", and while no trace of it was found, the aircraft was believed to have crashed at Nuhi Tjut Island near Fak. A24-50 was the first of nine Catalinas lost on minelaying operations emanating from bases in the NWA. The crew of A24-50 comprised Flying Officers JWB Amess, AJP Oliver, EC Smith, EM Howe and AS Boyd; Sergeants RJ Hobbs and MB Tyrell; Corporals A Burns and IL Penrose; along with LAC AH Crough.

On 25 November, A24-45 of No. 11 Squadron under Flying Officer Bob Honan flew into Darwin from its base at Cairns to join a combined mine laying operation code named "Virago" in Soerabaya harbour. Crews from Nos. 11, 20 and 43 Squadrons were briefed the following afternoon. Honan recalled:

We took off at 1800 hours, and headed for a point south of Timor. We were concerned

A Catalina of either No. 11 or No. 20 Squadron at Bowen in north Queensland in 1943. (AWM)

Vultee Vengeance Dianne of No. 12 Squadron, which carried out the only Vengeance bombing mission from Australia in mid-June 1943. (RAAF Museum)

that we would be passing close to Koepang ... so we flew low over the water to avoid radar detection ... [In the face of rapidly deteriorating weather] which removed the threat of fighters [but] the rain poured down so heavily ... [that] the aircraft was hard to control and the slow airspeed caused by the two mines, made the flight dangerous ...

On his first run over Soerabaya harbour Honan missed the datum point and was forced to make a second run:

... at extremely low altitude ... while expecting any minute to be shot out of the sky. There was relief with the mines gone ... and I applied maximum climbing power.

With daylight approaching and the threat of encountering enemy aircraft increasing if they headed for Darwin, they instead flew to Exmouth Gulf to end the nineteen hour 25 minute flight. Three weeks later A24-45 was again caught in severe weather as it flew to Kavieng airfield. Flown by Flight Lieutenant Brooks the aircraft dropped four 250-pound bombs and twenty 30-pound incendiaries across the runway, dispersal areas and a fuel dump before returning to Darwin.

Two further missions were flown from Darwin on 26 and 29 December when the harbour approaches to Batu Kelat and Pomelaa were mined.

In the middle of 1943, what was the only operational mission by Vultee Vengeance dive-bombers from Australia took place. Construction work had been seen on Ceram Island to the north of Australia on 10 June. Work on dispersal loops and blast pens had also been sighted at Penfui. The air route between New Britain and Ambon appeared to be complete, allowing air reinforcement either way. The Japanese had also begun to build an airfield on Selaru Island (in the Tanimbars), only 300 miles from Darwin, and three new airstrips at Fuiloro in Timor. Air Vice Marshal Bladin decided to neutralise them.

In mid-June, twelve No. 12 Squadron Vultee Vengeance dive bombers were assigned to attack the nearest of these sites, Selaru, in company with six No. 31 Squadron Beaufighters. The aircraft flew from Batchelor to Bathurst Island for a final fuelling. One plane could not take off again due of electrical trouble, but the remainder carried out the first bombing attack by Vengeances in the South-West Pacific. The raid was carried out successfully without opposition and all the aircraft returned to base safely.

The Vengeance was not used again in anger from Australia, although the type was used in anti-submarine patrols off both the east and west coasts. The dive-bomber saw limited service in New Guinea before replacement by multi-engine machines that could carry a much greater bombload. In fact, when General Kenney found out that its escorting Kittyhawks could tote a 1,000-pound bomb – the bomb limit of the Vengeance – he asked all RAAF Vengeances to vacate Nadzab airbase as they were taking up too much room.[1]

In the meantime, both Nos. 2 and 18 Squadrons had continued their operations. Throughout July and August 1943 Mitchells of No. 18 Squadron had bombed and strafed Dili, Lautem, Fuiloro, and Chater airfield while under fire from anti-aircraft defences and enemy fighters. On 6 August two aircraft attacked Lautem West airfield when one of the pair was intercepted by seven fighters, forcing the pilot to jettison his bombs. Cloud cover provided the opportunity to escape, and both returned to Batchelor. Similar experiences were encountered on 14 August in an attack on Ambon town and again four days later over Koepang when enemy fighters intercepted, fortunately with no casualties.

Over the period of 22-27 August shipping at Larat, Koepang and Dili was attacked. A suspected Japanese headquarters was bombed on 27 August causing large fires visible for some 45 miles. No. 18 Squadron B-25 N5-136 was attacked by fighters and forced to ditch during a search of the "Giraffe" area near Soembawa on 7 October, with only the wireless operator, Sergeant J Van Burg surviving the ditching. Those who died were Lieutenant PL Zeydel together with Sergeants C Visser, HJ de Hoog, LJ Gerards and R Hootjij.

During November the squadron commenced a period of intense activity, attacking Japanese air bases and shipping in combined operations with No. 31 Squadron Beaufighters. In the period 17 November to 4 January 1944, six Japanese ships and numerous vessels were attacked and sunk. A typical operation was flown against Trangan Island on 2 November. Six Beaufighters joined with six B-25s and on the return trip N5-159 was attacked by three No. 934 *Ku* Rufes led by FPO2c Toshio Imada. After firing a short burst, the Mitchell turret gunner left the Rufe to the Beaufighters.

Three Beaufighters accompanied three No. 18 Squadron Mitchells on the 13 November when a 200-500-ton vessel was attacked and sunk. This was followed by a further sinking on 17 November after the Beaufighters had neutralised the anti-aircraft guns. The combined operation was successful again on 21 November when an attack on enemy shipping saw one vessel sunk by six Mitchells off Maikoor.

B-25 N5-159 was lost when it was shot down during a masthead attack on shipping in the Aru Islands. Two Rufes of No. 934 *Ku* were flying a combat air patrol and intercepted the No. 18 Squadron formation, however one of the fighters was shot down. While the other claimed the victory, the remaining Allied aircraft returned safely to base. None of the crew of N5-159 survived. Those who died were Lieutenant GH Paalman along with Sergeants W de Putter, MP van Kan, WF van der Coevering and RH van Yperen.

Five B-25s attacked shipping near Lautem on 15 December, during which two vessels were hit and reported as burning fiercely and sinking. A further successful attack was flown on Christmas Eve when the barracks area at Atamboea was hit.

Meanwhile the Hudsons of No. 2 Squadron soldiered on, continuing their attacks on Japanese shipping, bases and airfields while maintaining seaward patrols and reconnaissance missions

---

1   A single Vengeance is preserved in Australia in the Camden Museum of Aviation.

from July 1943 to the year's end. Regular targets for the Hudson crews were Dobo in the Aru Islands (a 980 mile return flight from Hughes), Toel and Taberfane in the Kai group (950 miles), Koepang and Penfui (1,000 miles), Saumlaki in the Tanimbars (610 miles) and Langgoer in the Kai group (900 miles), among others.

The major role for No. 2 Squadron had now become searches for enemy shipping, seaward patrols and anti-submarine escort patrols for Allied shipping. Searches were staged through Milingimbi and were conducted over coded areas, including "Zebra", which was flown north over the Banda Sea to the Aru Islands. These flights all came with the continued risk of meeting up with No. 934 *Ku* floatplanes or No. 202 *Ku* Zeros.

Hudson A16-230 flown by Flying Officer Don Thomas was flying an anti-submarine patrol for a small convoy escorted by HMAS *Latrobe* on 2 July. As it approached the convoy two Japanese aircraft, a E13A1 Jake and a Rufe, were spotted attacking the vessels. Thomas intercepted the Japanese aircraft and recalled:

> … came up underneath the first Jap and gave him a long burst from the two fixed nose guns. The [Jake] broke off his run, did a sudden steep turn and dived … for the deck. We … followed him … [and] closed to within 50 yards … I knew we had hit him when he started to trail smoke.

The Rufe, flown by FPO1c Mitsugu Ichikawa, then attacked the Hudson but was driven off by the turret gunner and withdrew. The Hudson gunners then concentrated on the Jake during a 30-mile chase, and despite:

> … accurate return fire Thomas pressed his attack to close range to shoot the bomber [sic] down in flames using fixed forward firing machine guns.

Ensign Seiichi Nakano's crew were killed, and when Ichikawa reached base and landed, his damaged Rufe sank. Thomas and his crew continued the patrol despite damage to the nose, fuselage and wings of the Hudson.

During May General Kenney, the SWPA Allied Air Forces commander, directed RAAF command to direct its attention against Koepang. This was in realising the importance of Penfui as a base not only for the attacks on Darwin but in its role as a forward base for the Zeros of No. 202 *Ku*. Seemingly forgotten were the Ki-43 Oscars of the 59th *Sentai* and the reconnaissance value to the Japanese of the Dinahs of the 70th DC, with both JAAF units also

A quartet of No. 2 Squadron Hudsons over northern Australia in 1943, likely on their way to attack Japanese targets on Timor. (AWM)

based on Timor. The RAAF command, repeated the directive, ordering a "…maximum effort during the first part of July."

While No. 2 Squadron was mainly engaged in the seaward patrols, it increased its attention towards Koepang and Penfui in line with the directive above. The first in a series of attacks came on 6 July when Flight Lieutenant SJ "Bunny" Austin in A16-207 led five Hudsons in an attack on Koepang. The following night he led seven aircraft against the Penfui airfield in a pre-dawn attack prior to a raid by 380th BG B-24 Liberators. During the attack Austin's aircraft was caught in the enemy searchlights and it was only by his violent evasive action and switching on and off his IFF (Identification Friend or Foe transmitter) set that the lights went out. Austin had flown with RAF Coastal Command and had been with the Hudsons since the dark days of the Japanese advances through the NEI from late 1941. Speaking of such men, a *Wings* correspondent wrote:

> Those … terrible days in the North when the threat of invasion was present … But the Hudsons, and their Australian air crews, did fight back magnificently.

During a pre-dawn raid on 8 July, Flying Officer Mick Helsham in A16-160 took on the role of pathfinder to the Hudsons and incoming B-24s, which were:

> … preceded over the target by a Hudson, which dropped high explosive and incendiary bombs on the runways and dispersal pens during the night. Flying Officer M Helsham … made sure of hitting the target by diving to 2,000 feet before releasing his bombs.

Squadron Leader Jock Whyte handed over to the new No. 2 Squadron commanding officer, Squadron Leader Cyril Williams, on 7 July and paid tribute to his aircrew:

> These boys are good. They are full of fighting spirit and fly with enthusiasm against the best that the Japanese can send against their long operational tour.

Williams flew his first operation in A16-195 two nights later in a four aircraft raid to Penfui. Again "Bunny" Austin led the attackers, however they struck poor weather as they approached Timor. Three aircraft – A16-244 (Austin), A16-189 and A-16235 – turned back, but nothing further was heard from Williams or his crew. Flying Officer Ted Stacy was in A16-189 and recalled hitting a:

> … very heavy front about 100 miles from the target. I went through a towering cumulus at 10,000 feet but failed to see the target owing to cloud layers … and experienced the roughest possible conditions on turning for home.

The wreckage of Williams' aircraft was later found by natives near the summit of Mount Kekneno 60 miles northeast of Koepang. Those who died with their commanding officer were Flight Lieutenant AM Fowler; Flying Officers RC Lindsay and WA Hepworth; along with Flight Sergeant DC Farmer.

Air Vice Marshal Adrian "King" Cole took over from Air Vice Marshal Frank Bladin as the NWA commander during July 1943. He also acquired an awareness of the need for new equipment if he was to abide by Kenney's directive along with General MacArthur's plan to bypass Rabaul by island hopping. Hence the area of attention for No. 2 Squadron remained in the Arafura Sea north to the Dutch New Guinea coast. While raids were maintained against Koepang and Dili, the floatplane bases of No. 934 *Ku* in the Kai and Aru Islands also received attention.

A No. 2 Squadron Hudson crew walking past one of the squadron's aircraft at Hughes in 1943. (AWM)

In early August, Portuguese Timor and the Tanimbar Islands were identified as points where the Japanese appeared to be most active. These areas were systematically attacked by the Hudsons, along with targets in Dutch New Guinea. On 6 August Hudsons A16-213 and A16-219 departed Milingimbi on a search for enemy shipping with Kokenau, southwest of Timoeka, the alternative target. A16-219 bombed Aroeke due to cloud cover while A16-213 dived to 1,500 feet and bombed Kokenau and then strafed a merchant vessel and barges off the coast.

On 15 August Sergeant John Lamb in A16-181 and Flying Officer McKenzie in A16-233 were tasked with a seaward reconnaissance followed by an attack on Keaukwa village near Timoeka. Both aircraft departed Milingimbi. However no further news was heard from A16-181. McKenzie released his bombs at 6,500 feet as two fighters, possibly No. 202 *Ku* Zeros, intercepted his aircraft. During the engagement he evaded the fighters and returned to base at low level. A16-181 was posted missing on operations, suspected of having been shot down by the fighters. Lamb and his crew, comprising Sergeants Ikin, N McLean and M Jackson were posted missing presumed killed in action.

Shipping reconnaissance missions were also flown over new areas, including "Giraffe" (around Timor), "Horse" (around the Tanimbars), "Jackass" (between Timor and the Tanimbars) and "Koala" (around the Arus). It was during a reconnaissance of "Horse" on 8 September that Flying Officer Lynn Martin and his crew in A16-233 disappeared. No news was heard following take-off, however a Japanese broadcast a week later revealed that a twin engine bomber had attacked a small vessel, the *Sugi Maru*, north of Tanimbar Island and had been shot down. Sergeants Maurice Graham and Jack Boanas had baled out of the stricken aircraft. They were captured and executed at Ambon a month later. Martin and his remaining crew comprising Pilot Officers MC Wettenhall and RH Williams were killed.

Thirteen days after the loss of A16-233, two Hudsons flew an armed reconnaissance over the Aru and Kai Islands and were intercepted by four No. 934 *Ku* Rufes. Led by Lieutenant Ikeda the Rufes only managed to damage Hudson A16-204, and both No. 2 Squadron aircraft made it safely back to base.

October saw the loss of two Hudsons, one posted missing and the other written off following a mission over Langgoer. On 10 October A16-213 was one of five aircraft attacking Japanese installations at Langgoer. During the attack the bomber, flown by Flying Officer Mick Helsham, was hit by anti-aircraft fire. A correspondent for *Wings* magazine reported:

> The aircraft went into a right-hand spiral dive … dropping towards the sea with the controls shot away. The radio had also been shot out. And Australia was 430 miles away. By increasing the power to the starboard engine Helsham and his co-pilot, Flying Officer Hollingsworth, were able to control the aircraft. They managed to climb to 5,000 feet and head for home despite the aircraft controls being limited to the port aileron, port elevator and a lack of rudder control. Without any flaps, a wheels-up landing was made at Darwin. However, the aircraft swung to starboard prior to touch down, causing the aircraft to veer into the adjacent scrub. The aircraft was severely damaged, but the crew escaped unharmed.

In contrast Hudson A16-178 seemingly vanished. On 16 October the bomber and its crew departed Milingimbi at 1230 for a shipping reconnaissance patrol over "Koala". No further news was heard from the aircraft, and it was posted missing. The crew, comprising Pilot Officer JP Oldridge; Sergeants RFN Drake-Brockman and Sergeant DJ Petch; along with Flight Sergeants DN Rumble and JF Cullen, were posted missing, presumed killed. Two Hudsons were assigned to search for the aircraft. The conclusions were that the missing aircraft's track would have taken it to within 28 miles of the Aru Islands and 24 miles from Dutch New Guinea. Deaths of the crew were officially presumed as of 16 October 1943.

Accidents had also taken their toll during 1943. Hudson A16-237 exploded and was destroyed during refuelling on 15 March while A16-242 crash landed at Point Annisley on the Coburg Peninsula on 14 May when the pilot Flying Officer TS Graham made an emergency belly landing. After jettisoning his bombs Graham landed the aircraft, which skidded to a stop after swinging 180 degrees. A16-186 crashed on landing at Hughes on 12 June. The aircraft was at 500 feet with the undercarriage extended and with the port airscrew feathered due to engine problems. The pilot, Flight Lieutenant JF Mason, then raised the undercarriage and applied power to the starboard engine, however the aircraft pulled to port and begun to lose height. The aircraft crashed one mile northeast of Hughes and was destroyed in the impact and ensuing fire. All of the crew died: Mason, Flight Lieutenant JR Wood, Flying Officers TW Swann and GL Knauer; Flight Sergeants RJ Flaherty and RD Woods; along with Sergeant GR Rowland.

A16-202 crashed during take-off from Hughes for a night training flight on 6 October, when the aircraft swung on take-off, ground looped and collapsed the undercarriage. The aircraft then caught fire and burned, however the crew escaped unharmed.

Over the period October to 31 December 1943, No. 2 Squadron flew 259 sorties without loss through enemy action: 97 in October; 76 during November (one a search for a missing Catalina A24-67) and 81 in December. During the period they flew armed reconnaissance missions, seaward patrols, anti-submarine patrols, convoy escort, and searchlight cooperation exercises. Attacks were flown against Koepang, Dili, Penfui, Soerabaya, Langgoer, Fuiloro and Dutch New Guinea plus the Tanimbar, Aru and Kai island groups.

One mission on 14 November saw four Hudsons sent to attack Koepang. Flight Sergeant Bruce Wallace, the Wireless Air Gunner in A16-177 recorded:

> We saw the target, the dispersal area at the eastern end of the strip at about 11.15PM … A kite or two had been in before us and left a couple of small fires. We came in at 9,000 feet from the NW over Koepang towards the strip. Over the town I was very busy throwing pamphlets out [of] the belly gun [position]. The navigator thought he saw another kite so we dived down to 2,000 feet to port … As we made our run over the target the Nips came to life. On "Bombs gone" I began pushing out bottles, pamphlets and the incendiaries [we] … carried … A searchlight came sweeping towards us and a red line of Bofors shells laced upwards … One shell left the line and passed right under us … Then we were out of the target area and making for the sea. Our bombs and incendiaries landed on the target and left four fires in their wake.[2]

Wallace was out again four days later on a search over the Koala route and again on 4 and 13 January. On 19 March 1944 his luck ran out when A16-230 was lost with the Scott crew. Captured, they were taken to Ambon where Wallace was executed on 16 August.

A TRAGIC ACCIDENT

Although non-combat related accidents are not covered in this work, one is presented here as it illustrates an explanation for the many dozens of aircraft wrecks which still are often found in the bush and sea of northern Australia.

On 21 October 1943, No. 18 Squadron B-25 N5-156 took off from Hughes airstrip, some 30 miles to the south of Darwin. The aircraft was piloted by Sergeant Cornelis Keesmaat on a night training mission. A flare aboard exploded shortly after take-off, and the aircraft caught fire. The crew with the exception of the pilot baled out successfully. The plane crashed east of the field.

Today the crash site is still littered with wreckage. A plaque commemorating the death of Keesmaat has been placed there. There are many similar sites around northern Australia. A common complaint from visitors to these places is that "the government" should do something about them, but in truth to gather up the remnants and even store them – let alone display them – would cost tens of millions of dollars. And the local museums are not funded to the extent they can display their collections in climate-controlled environments, which would slow the deterioration of the items from decades to centuries.

The wreck of B-25 N5-156 in bushland near the wartime Hughes airfield, in April 2022. (Courtesy Children of 18 Squadron NEI-RAAF)

---

2 The propaganda leaflets referenced by Wallace typically encouraged resistance against the Japanese. Empty beer bottles were often dropped from aircraft by RAAF crews during night raids due to the nuisance value of their loud whistling sound.

CHAPTER 9

A NEW WING AND NEW AIRCRAFT

On 1 December 1943 No. 79 Wing RAAF was formed under Group Captain Charles "Moth" Eaton. The Wing comprised Nos. 2, 18 and 31 Squadrons and No. 53 Operational Base Unit at Batchelor. No. 1 Squadron and its Beaufort light bombers were also expected in the NWA to join the wing in the new year. However, the squadron was not expected to be operational before 15 March 1944.

On 4 January 1944 No. 18 Squadron continued its offensive operations over the NEI with an attack by six B-25s against shipping near Hansisi. With top cover provided by No. 31 Squadron Beaufighters led by Squadron Leader "Butch" Gordon, the Mitchells destroyed one vessel while Gordon shot down an intruding Ki-21 Sally bomber.

The same day saw a strike on shipping by the Mitchells in Tenau harbour, again under cover of the Beaufighters. During the attack a 4,000-ton vessel was hit, however B-25 N5-157 was hit in the starboard wing by anti-aircraft fire causing it to veer towards N5-137. The pilot of N5-137 took evasive action but the aircraft struck the mast of the vessel and spun into the sea. All of the crew died: Captain AJ Rees, Lieutenant WAC Coedam, plus Sergeants Arsil Sahoer, CB Gontha and Kwee Wan Tjoe. Captain CM Holswilder in N5-129 continued the attack and scored a direct hit on the vessel.

During January and February, the unit flew seaward searches of the Jackass, Heron and Gull areas along with reconnaissance and searchlight cooperation flights. Attacks on Laha, the Tanimbars, Toel, Ambon and barges off Naira Island were flown on 4, 6, 8, 15, 18 and 27 February. Six Beaufighters escorted six Mitchells in an attack on a bridge over the Mina River in Timor on 19 February. Strikes by three, six, eight and eleven aircraft successfully carried out the attacks. It was during a night attack on Toel by nine aircraft that N5-179 and the crew of Sergeant Soeterik failed to return. Posted missing presumed killed were Sergeants E Soeterik, W de Eerens, S Bilgrai and Edward R Howley (RAAF); along with Lieutenant B Vromen and Corporal L Rogier.

Strikes were also mounted with masthead attacks against shipping in the Selaru to Babar Islands area while nine aircraft struck Toel on 27 February.

During March 1944 the tempo increased for No. 18 Squadron when intelligence reports indicated a possible Japanese attack on the west coast Australia. The squadron moved to the Potshot airfield in Exmouth Gulf on the 10 March. Sixteen B-25s were supported by eight C-47s in preparation for a two-week period of operations. Beaufighters of No. 31 Squadron also made the move while the Spitfires of Nos. 452 and 457 Squadrons deployed to cover the Perth area. While armed patrols were flown the threat failed to eventuate and the aircraft and personnel had returned to Batchelor just before the end of the month. Regular operations quickly resumed with a night strike on Penfui by eight Mitchells on 30 March.

The first weeks of April saw intensified operations from Darwin as a prelude to the invasions of Hollandia and Aitape under Operations *Reckless* and *Persecution*. No. 1 Squadron became semi-operational under Squadron Leader DIW Campbell on 20 March and mainly flew seaward patrols over the Jackass, Heron and Gull areas.

A No. 18 Squadron B-25 over northern Australia in mid-February 1944. (AWM)

At the same time No. 18 Squadron had acquired a number of the newer B-25D Mitchells. In the first three weeks of April 78 sorties against Koepang, Dili and Penfui were flown. On 16 April ten Mitchells, along with No. 1 Squadron Beauforts, flew a night raid against Koepang, starting new fires and reigniting previous ones. Twelve aircraft attacked Soe two nights later. It was followed up on 19 April with an attack on the Soe village and camp area by twelve Mitchells, fifteen Beauforts and eight Beaufighters.

Three nights later eleven Mitchells attacked Dili, while six Beaufighters provided top cover. This was followed up with a daylight attack by twelve Mitchells and six Beaufighters on 29 April. It was now obvious that No. 79 Wing was fully operational and working cohesively.

May 1944 saw the operational strength of No. 18 Squadron established at eighteen B-25 Mitchells. The actual strength was twenty aircraft, which now had the nose guns and fuselage side packs fitted along with extra bomb stations. On 2 May eleven B-25s attacked Koepang, while Langgoer was struck with seventeen aircraft on 6 and 9 May.

A sweep of the Tanimbars was made on 18 May with four Mitchells attacking Saumlaki, Larat and shipping at these locations. Atamboea was attacked by a dozen aircraft on 19 May when N5-177 was shot down during a masthead attack against shipping. Killed were Lieutenants JH Geerke and Soute; Sergeant Major F Belling; Sergeants P Wallaart and LH Heys; and James Cowey, RAAF.

On 12 May six aircraft were deployed to Merauke in Dutch New Guinea from where they attacked the Wissel Lakes area. Ground patrols reported Japanese at Waniboega and up to six H6K4 Mavis flying boats on Lake Paniai, providing operations planners with further targets. The aircrews were kept busy. Sergeant John Marks, for example, was an air gunner with No. 18 Squadron. He flew nine sorties during May. A strafing attack on Doku Barat on 22 May was followed by an attack on Soe two days later. Seaward searches of Jackass and Heron on 24 and 31 May along with gunnery and gunnery practice flights rounded off his month, flying 33 hours and ten minutes in total.

During May Soemba and Penfui were also targeted. An attack on Soe village by twelve B-25s on 26 May ended the combat missions for the month, which were augmented by the usual seaward patrols, searchlight cooperation flying and transport sorties.

On 30 May N5-176 and its crew were lost. The Mitchell had been engaged in practice bombing on Range L over Grose Island to the west of Darwin with three other aircraft when it crashed. Captain Paul Van Buuren, the pilot of N5-188 recalled:

> We took off for an operational training flight over Range "L"… together with three other aircraft, N5-171, N5-176 and N5-188. When over Range "L" the aircraft formed pairs to make bombing runs, N5-176 [was] paired with N5-188 and carried out three bombing runs at mast height. On the fourth run, N5-176 came in to bomb at a slightly different course causing the port wing of the aircraft to be hit by a column of water caused by the explosion of the bomb released by N5-188. I saw the port wing blown from N5-176, which turned on its back immediately and crashed into the water. I circled the scene … [but] the plane did not appear … A Tiger Moth immediately searched the scene of the crash, but no survivors were found.

Killed in the crash were Lieutenants R Bouche, A Visser, R Fruin and Liem Yoe Hien along with Sergeant David J Crosbie. Crosbie had joined No. 18 Squadron as an air gunner on 5 February 1944, and had flown 164.05 hours including attacks on Koepang, Penfui barracks, Langgoer, Ambon, Dili and Soe along with the seaward patrols. He'd filled out his last logbook entry as "30 May 0930 Lieutenant Visser Skip bombing prac Grose Is. 1.00 [hour]" An annotation to his logbook reads "A plane crashed & airman failed to return to Squadron."

A diary kept by an RAAF transport driver, LAC Lindsay Knight, kept tabs on the movements of the B-25s. An extract of his diary throughout the second half of May reads:

16.5.1944	Quite a few test flights, and we had an exciting day. N5-180. Five ground staff had to bail out when raft came adrift and hung on tail plane. It took nearly all day to find the five survivors. (I can still see them drifting down like posts swinging in the air). N5-164 shot through wing.
18.5.44	4 planes out on operations. N5-177 did not return. Lost 6 men.
19.5.44	12 planes out. All back safely.
22.5.44	Four planes out. All back.
23.5.44	Four planes out. Two were shot up but back OK.
26.5.44	14 planes out. All back.
30.5.44	N5-176 went into the drink with [the] loss of 6 men.
4.6.44	12 planes out. All returned.

June 1944 commenced with No. 18 Squadron concentrating on Japanese shipping along the north coast of Timor and adjoining areas. On 10 June fourteen aircraft attacked Atamboea. Four days later fourteen Mitchells attacked Lautem west, while fifteen attacked Cape Chater on 19 June. The attack on the airstrip at Cape Chater was followed up with three further attacks during the month, with Beaufighters providing top cover for the Mitchells during an attack on 25 June.

On 23 June an attack on shipping around Timor saw the No. 18 Squadron commanding officer, Lieutenant Colonel EJT de Roller, killed during a masthead attack when N5-162 was shot down by anti-aircraft fire from shore batteries and the targeted ships. Also killed in the crash were Lieutenants HJ Jansen, W Reedijk and Th W van Lier along with Sergeants G Th Willems and

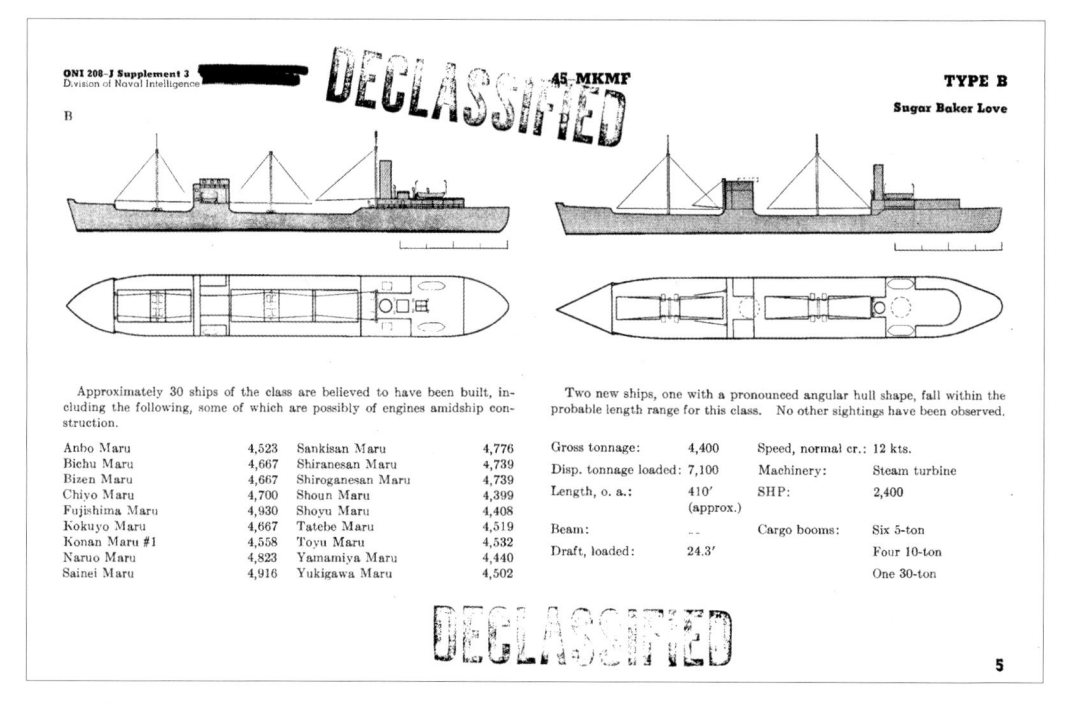

A page from a USN Japanese merchant ship recognition book illustrating a Sugar-Baker-Love type vessel.

BR Clark, RAAF. During the attack by four Mitchells a convoy of two *Sugar-Charlie* vessels towing barges, all guided by a *Fox-Tare-Dog* vessel was bombed and strafed.[1] Three vessels were destroyed or badly damaged.

A planned night attack on Penfui on 26 June by eight No. 18 Squadron Mitchells saw three aircraft return with hung bombs after they failed to release. During June the usual seaward searches along the Jackass, Heron and Gull areas were maintained along with reconnaissance flights.

Meanwhile the B-24 Liberators of the 380th Bomb Group had begun 1944 with:

> … an uneventful strike on the nickel mines at Pomelaa [on 2 January] followed by missions to Waingapoe and Tenau over the following two days.

These routine missions gave no hint of what was to come, for January 1944 would prove the worst month of the war for the group.

On 5 January 1944 the Fifth Air Force released the elements of the group which had been deployed to Dobodura, New Guinea, to work with the 43rd and 90th Bombardment Groups. That same day a request from Air Vice Marshal "King" Cole saw Colonel Bill Miller lead six B-24s to the Straits of Samaroe to attack a 4,000-ton merchant vessel. It had previously been attacked by No. 31 Squadron Beaufighters which had expended all their ammunition without sinking the ship.

Miller led his aircraft to the area and found the vessel awash. Instead, the formation flew to a secondary target area of Koepang harbour where they attempted to bomb another ship without luck. Two days later Miller asked Lieutenant Max Hastings if he would fly one last mission

---

1 The code names refer to the silhouette shape of the vessel in a USN recognition book *Merchant Ship Shapes*, with identification to be made in such terms according to the number and placement of funnels; superstructure of the vessel above the weather deck; presence of cranes and so on.

in his tour, a planned attack on an oil storage area at Boela, Ceram. Hastings and his crew accepted – except for the radio operator who did not want to tempt fate on a final mission.

Flying the relatively new B-24J 42-73449, Hastings led seven B-24s in the early afternoon of 7 January and after bombing the target they flew on to Manokwari where they hit the docks and shipping. Flying into poor weather east of Babo, the formation split up and each aircraft flew on alone. Hastings was not heard from again and he and his crew were posted missing. It was not until 1949 that a Graves Registration party learned of an aircraft crashing into Wademen Bay, Orraegi Island. One of the local natives produced Hastings' wallet with his ID card and photos. The deaths of Hastings and his crew were then confirmed: Lieutenants Raymond E Gilmore, Fredrick J Estes, and Marvin H Robinson; Staff Sergeants Joseph T Allen, Peter H Finck, Charles W Garrison and Arthur N Willer; Technical Sergeants William A Marshall and Francis L Moshier; and Sergeant Thomas E Guilfoyle.

The Battle Action report – the *Kodochosho* – of No. 934 *Ku* provides a further clue to the disappearance of the Hastings crew. A raid on Manokwari was recorded by seven B-24s during which four Rufes led by Flying Chief Petty Officer Sadayoshi Yokota were flying a combat air patrol. The Japanese pursued the bombers for some distance before the Liberators escaped. Hence, it was likely the weather that claimed Hastings and his crew.

On 8 January a strike on Kendari was mounted by thirteen of a planned eighteen aircraft attack. Two aircraft had aborted before take-off while three others returned with mechanical problems leaving Lieutenant Harold S Mulhollen to lead the attack. Like Frank Hastings before him this was intended as his final 30th mission in the theatre. As the formation approached Kendari some thirteen No. 202 *Ku* Zeros attacked them. The B-24s managed to bomb the barracks area although the results were believed poor. Mulhollen's aircraft, B-24J 42-73115, had both starboard engines shot out and his aircraft was badly damaged. It went into a flat spin and crashed into the sea off Wowoni Island, killing all on board. The crew were Lieutenants Russell P Fleming, Clarence F Jerge and Keith K Ramsdell; Staff Sergeants William E Miller, Leonard G Patterson, Eugene O Schell and John C Stevenson; Technical Sergeant William G Whitacre and Sergeant Rex Stewart.

A third loss occurred on 12 January when the crew of Lieutenant Curtiss Hagler was downed over Balikpapan. Hagler's B-24D 42-41214 *B.T.O.* was one of eighteen aircraft flying in a night attack on the Balikpapan oil fields when searchlights and anti-aircraft fire met them, only to suddenly stop.[2] The B-24 crew failed to realise that joining them in the night sky were two of No. 202 *Ku*'s new J1N1 Irving twin-engine night fighters equipped with upward firing 20mm cannon. A6M5 Model 52 Zeros of the newly arrived No. 381 *Ku* were also in the air and attacking the bombers. Hagler's aircraft failed to return and when Lieutenant Joe Vicks' aircraft, *Quack Wac*, was examined the next morning 20mm shell holes were found to have come from below. Japanese records show the Irvings claimed three definite kills though only Hagler's aircraft was lost.

The Hagler crew was posted missing and presumed to have been shot down by night fighters. Later confirmed as dead were Lieutenants Curtiss Hagler, Howard K Marshall, Howard E Gad and James Gardner; Staff Sergeants Vernon E Dewey, Harold C Pafahl, Richard R Rhoads and George L Wertzler; together with Technical Sergeants Jack C Monisko and Gaylord N Stauffer.

---

2   The initials B.T.O. stood for Big Time Operator.

On 16 January fourteen Liberators of the 530th and 531st BS attacked Amahai while six aircraft of the 528th BS attacked Ambon. Japanese radar had tracked the formations as the B-24s bombed their targets. Then they were attacked by JAAF Ki-45 Nick twin engine fighters of the 5th *Sentai* from Liang and the floatplanes of No. 934 *Ku* from Halong. The floatplanes were seven of the new Kawanishi N1K Rex fighters, with one of the Japanese pilots claiming a victory as darkness set in. Captain Jack Banks' B-24J was badly damaged with one engine shot out and hydraulic lines to the nose turret severed. By lowering the undercarriage manually, Banks later landed without flaps or brakes and sheared off the nose wheel before coming to a stop.

Captain Virgil H Stevens joined the 380th BG on 14 January when he arrived at the 529th BS base at Long airfield. He flew his first mission three days later in a four aircraft armed reconnaissance of the Aru Islands. Flying a newer B-24J model in a mission of fourteen hours and 15 minutes, Stevens said they:

> Went from Long Strip to Aru Islands (Babo) – New Guinea (Mabaroe) – Moa Noem Isle – to Noemfoor Isla – 25 miles So of Manokwari, New Guinea (jumped by 4 float type fighters 2 head on attacks & 2 from starboard side) no damage – from S.W. of Manokwari went N.W. to Waiges Isle to Kofian Isle to Misool Isle to Ceram Isle to Banda Isle (dropped bombs on town of Bandanaira) to Jambena Isle to Darwin & back to Fenton Strip.

The floatplanes encountered by the B-24s were six No. 934 *Ku* Rufes led by Lieutenant Ikeda, and while they had superior numbers, they were only able to claim three of the B-24s as damaged.

Front view of a Kawanishi N1K Rex floatplane fighter preserved at a Smithsonian Institute in the USA. No. 934 Ku Rex floatplane fighters were encountered by 380th BG B-24s near Ambon on 16 January 1944. (Author photo)

Stevens flew a further three missions for the month. The first was a mission to Soemba on 21 January during which Waingapoe was bombed. Then came Sorong on 27 January during which the Allied aircraft were attacked by four fighters which attempted to drop two phosphorous aerial bombs on the B-24s. Then came Ceram on 31 January during which they were attacked by No. 202 *Ku* Zeros and by two No. 934 *Ku* Rex floatplanes.

On 17 January Lieutenant Tom Jones experienced engine problems shortly after take-off and was forced to land B-24D 42-41236 at Long airstrip. Landing without flaps he struck B-24D *Sack Time* and then spun into B-24D *Bebe* before 42-41236 disintegrated, killing all eleven of the crew. Those who died were Lieutenants Thomas M Jones, Earl Bennett, Dan A Dunning and Hugh S Kelly; Staff Sergeants Marvin L Drean, Lee E Ferguson, John J Krist, Robert F Peterson and Robert W Welch; along with Technical Sergeants Monte L Fike and Bennett H Longfield. *Bebe* was also written off in this accident.

On 19 January B-24J 42-73187 *Paper Doll* flown by Lieutenant Harold Van Wormer was attacked by fighters following a 22 aircraft raid on Ambon. Seven No. 934 *Ku* Rex floatplanes from Halong intercepted the B-24s, claiming three kills and one probable. However, the bombers fought back: Flying Chief Petty Officer Sadayoshi Yokota was shot down and killed during the prolonged engagement. Then five Ki-45-*Kai* Nicks of the 5th *Sentai*'s No. 1 *chutai* joined the combat and Van Wormer's *Paper Doll* – flying on only its second mission – was badly damaged and was forced to ditch. While four of Van Wormer's crew were killed – two of them by strafing in the water – the remaining seven were captured but survived their experience as POWs. Those killed were Lieutenant Herman J Dias along with Staff Sergeants Louis J Aiani, William F Barbee and Thomas J O'Donnell.

Also badly damaged was *Doodlebug*, which was ditched by Lieutenant Gorman Smith off Seroea Island although six of the crew were killed: Staff Sergeants William G Benshoff, Boyd H Lewallen and Samuel Zelby; along with Sergeants Charles R Owen, JT Parks and Billie R Templeton. Five survivors were picked up by an RAAF Catalina the following day.

Doodlebug was the seventh and last 380th BG loss during January 1944. It had been a catastrophic month for the group with 52 crewmen killed and others taken POW. However, the group was looking forward to a number of newly trained Australian crews coming through No. 7 OTU at Tocumwal and the Combat Replacement Training Center (CRTC) at Nadzab in New Guinea.

As early as December 1941, when the RAAF was using Ambon as a forward base, Wing Commander ED Scott had signalled RAAF headquarters:

> … it would be preferable if large aircraft of the B-17 type or preferably the B-24 could be borrowed or acquired by the RAAF for offensive action against the Japanese … at the moment absolutely nothing can be done to interfere with the Japanese plans … it is urgently recommended that the B-17 aircraft be placed under the control of ACH [Area Combined Headquarters] Ambon forthwith [and that] steps should be taken to acquire long range (not less than 2,000 nautical miles) heavy bombers for employment by the RAAF.

Unfortunately, Scott was forced to rely on the Lockheed Hudsons. It was a further fifteen months before Australian Government minister Dr HV Evatt travelled to America to further proposals for the allocation of heavy bombers to the RAAF. In early 1944 President Roosevelt gave an undertaking to Air Marshal Sir Richard Williams that he would give the matter his personal attention. Following political games including General George Kenney "…showing

A formation of 380th BG Liberators departing northern Australia for another raid over the NEI. The group lost seven B-24s during January 1944, its worst single month of operations. (Bob Livingstone)

little inclination to assist…" and the refusal of Britain to release RAAF aircraft from the RAF, the RAAF received an initial lot of six war weary B-24Ds from Kenney's stock. With the subsequent intervention of Roosevelt, Williams, Evatt and others the RAAF would eventually acquire a total of 286 Liberators.

Flight Lieutenant Ed Crabtree had been among the first four RAAF pilots to fly with the 380th BG beginning as co-pilot to a number of USAAF aircraft captains from August 1943. Over the following months the Australians flew on operations to Ceram, the Celebes, Balikpapan and the Aru Islands among other targets before being posted to No. 7 OTU as instructors. During the period March to September 1944 American pilot Virgil Stevens flew with Flight Lieutenants McCombe, John Napier, Flying Officer ER Jacobs and an RAN pilot, Lieutenant Bob Young, as co-pilots.

The 26 February 1944 edition of *Wings* reported:

> Australians have been selected to fly Liberator bombers … the men are on tip-toe with keen-ness to show what they can do … and are confident they will add to the outstanding record the RAAF has gained … overseas and in Australia

Flight Lieutenant Mick Jacques, a highly experienced Hudson pilot, recalled one flight in which his instructor was:

> …a brand-new shave tail straight from the states, with about 300 hours in his log book. I forget who was … more surprised when we discovered he was to teach me to fly heavies.

Lieutenant Tommy Thompson was another USAAF pilot who recalled instructing the Australians at Fenton. He was impressed:

> We did a couple of circuits and landings before I handed over … he greased that B-24 onto

Flight Lieutenant Dick Overheu, DFC, far right, with former members of his No. 2 Squadron Hudson crew while undergoing conversion training on B-24s at Nadzab, New Guinea, in February 1944. (AWM)

The nose art on B-24J 42-100214 Six Bitts which RAAF pilot Dick Overheu flew from New Guinea on 31 March 1944 to join the 380th BG in the NWA. As attested by the many mission markers, this aircraft eventually logged 118 combat missions. (Bob Livingstone)

the runway and kept the nose up instead of lowering it on [to] the nose wheel ... I couldn't understand it until the aircraft just slowed down by itself ... he just used the wing and flaps instead ... and I was supposed to be checking this guy out!

Dick Overheu, a former No. 2 Squadron Hudson pilot, converted to the B-24 Liberator at the Nadzab CRTC. He flew into the 380th BG on 31 March 1944 in B-24J 42-100214, later named *Six Bitts*, as co-pilot to Captain Doug Craig, the commanding officer of the 529th BS. During April he flew eleven missions, three of those with Captain Clifton Topperwein while the remainder were flown as captain in attacks on Babo, Namber 'strip, Noemfoor and Kamiri, along with practice bombing and check flights before flying with a full RAAF crew.

Overheu's flight engineer Sergeant Lindsay McDonald had flown with No. 11 Squadron Catalinas before converting to the B-24 and in April flew seven missions. In one 24 April twelve-hour mission, partly flown at night, he wrote of an attack on Kamiri airstrip :

> Kamiri Strip. Dropped 120 frags from 4,500 ft. Then went down to ground level straffing [sic] destroyed 21 aircraft ... one fuel dump on fire barracks area also hit. Fired 100 rounds myself.

The RAAF pilots were taking on full RAAF crews even while flying with the Americans. During the period May to 30 June, Overheu and McDonald flew strike missions to Geelvink Bay in Dutch New Guinea, Manokwari, Noemfoor Island, Utarom and Namlea, before joining No. 24 Squadron, RAAF, on 8 June.[3] The posting commenced with an acceptance flight of RAAF Liberator A72-32 from Amberley to Manbulloo.

The *Argus* newspaper at the time reported enthusiastically:

> Australian airmen flying Liberator heavy bombers ... are highly commended by high-ranking American officers. In a recent action by an American unit ... two complete Australian crews took part to deny the enemy use of an airstrip ... on Noemfoor Island ... Flt-Lt Dick Overheu, DFC, of WA and Flt-Lt Napier [took part in] the engagement officially described as "action which would have done credit to a fighter squadron" [where they] destroyed 17 enemy planes and damaged many others.

At the time, the Liberators were becoming available in numbers enough to bolster NWA heavy bomber operations, and No. 24 Squadron moved to Manbulloo over the period 8 June to 6 July 1944. While the Australians were being posted into newly formed RAAF Liberator squadrons, the 380th BG continued their strikes from Fenton and Long airfields. Over the period February to 30 June, missions were flown to Geelvink Bay, Halong, Namlea, Waingapoe and Manokwari. Covert operatives were dropped into Dutch New Guinea; a 24 aircraft detachment was sent to Jackson Strip, Port Moresby to bomb Hollandia; and missions were flown to Wewak and to support the Allied landings at Los Negros in the Admiralty Islands.

B-24J 42-73126 *Foil Proof Mary* of the 531st BS was hit by anti-aircraft fire over Koepang on 5 February 1944, putting two engines out of action. Over Croker Island, in the Northern Territory, six crew members baled out safely. Lieutenant Arthur A Bates, the pilot in command, force-landed the B-24 on the northern side of the island, near Croker Point. It hit a small depression and the aircraft caught fire. Three crew members were killed in the forced landing. Bates survived

---

3   No. 24 Squadron operated Vengeance dive-bombers in New Guinea for several months until March 1944 when it was withdrawn to Australia for conversion to B-24s. Other former Vengeance units converting to B-24s in 1944-45 included Nos. 21 and 23 Squadrons.

The wreckage of B-24J 42-73126 Foil Proof Mary after force-landing on Croker Island on 5 February 1944. (Bob Livingstone)

only until the next day when eight survivors were rescued by the corvette HMAS *Inverell*.

In early March, three aircraft of the 380th BG Port Moresby detachment were lost. B-24D 42-41133 *Gypsy* went down into Huon Gulf on 5 March and on the same day B-24D 42-41124 crashed during take-off from Nadzab. The third loss was B-24D 42-41225 *Sunshine*, shot down by JAAF Ki-43-IIs east of Wewak on 8 March. Several of its crew were seen to parachute, however the bomber was not located until post-war.

On the night of 18/19 March the crew in Lieutenant Martens' B-24D 42-72801 *Big Ass Bird III* was lost when it slammed into a mountain during a mission to drop special operatives from Z Force into Dutch New Guinea. Reports were later received that several crew were captured and executed by the Japanese on Kairiru Island off Wewak around May/June 1944.

Killed were Lieutenants Otto Martens, Ernest R Hedges, Brian J Kennedy and Clifford M Odegaard; Staff Sergeants Charles F Burtis, Henry P Flanagan, Howard W Musson, and Walter H Dellinger; Technical Sergeants William T Rabbitt and Arthur J Schechtel; and an RAAF observer, Sergeant HW Clapinson. Also killed were five Australian Z Force soldiers.

A turret gunner aboard *Puss & Boots*, Staff Sergeant WR "Dub" Miller, was killed during an intense combat over Noemfoor Island on 23 April. Part of an eighteen aircraft attack force, the B-24s were intercepted by Ki-43 Oscars of the 13th *Sentai*, which had recently moved to Noemfoor from the Halmeheras. The Oscars and Ki-45 Nicks of the 5th *Sentai* then attacked a second formation during which they attempted to release phosphorous bombs over the B-24s. During the attack *Puss & Boots* was hit in the cockpit area by an attacking Nick, wounding the pilot and co-pilot. Miller claimed an attacking Oscar and was firing at a Nick from his turret when he was hit and killed.

On 8 May, the Lieutenant Roy Parker crew was lost in unnamed B-24D 42-41117 when it was shot up by fighters 150 miles south of Jefman Island. Part of a seven aircraft attack on the Vogelkop Peninsula in Dutch New Guinea, the formation was intercepted by A6M5 Zeroes of No. 153 *Ku* from Babo and two 5th *Sentai* Ki-45 Nicks out of Sorong. After Parker had two engines shot out, he became an easy target for the fighters which pressed their attacks. Parker and his co-pilot, Flight Lieutenant Neil T Badger, DFC, (an experienced RAAF Hudson pilot), attempted to fly on before they were forced to ditch the crippled aircraft.

The machine disintegrated on impact and while three survivors were spotted, they failed to survive the night. Killed in the ditching were Flight Lieutenant Neil T Badger; Lieutenants Roy M Parker, Fredrick R Baumann and John G Eggleston; Staff Sergeants James C Holt, David L Haga, Glenn A Miller, Donald A Lewis (photographer) and Russell E Kerns; along with Technical Sergeant Bradley F Farr and Private First Class Clinton Hollingsworth.

The remainder of May to 30 June 1944 saw the 380th BG fly missions throughout the central and eastern NEI as well as Dutch New Guinea, at times with escorts provided by P-38 Lightnings of the 475th Fighter Group. In addition, a search mission was flown to the Bali/Lombok area for missing RAAF Catalina A24-73 and its No. 20 Squadron crew.

Flight Lieutenant Lex Halliday (standing, centre) with his RAAF crew in front of their 380th BG B-24J Toddy. Halliday's was one of a number of wholly Australian crews to fly 380th BG Liberators in 1944. (AWM)

CHAPTER 10

TRADING HUDSONS FOR BEAUFORTS – AND THE BLACK CATS FLY

By the end of January 1944, the number of Hudsons on the strength of No. 2 Squadron had dwindled to just eight. However, these had been supplemented by eleven of the new Bristol Beauforts, which had begun arriving in December 1943.

Hence for No. 2 Squadron the first six months of 1944 was a period of transition, with its future laid out in RAAF Memorandum No. 404 of 17 December 1943, directing that:

1. No. 2 Squadron will be re-armed with Beaufort aircraft to replace the Hudsons presently held on strength. The re-arming will be effected as follows.

2. The Beaufort aircraft of No. 13 Squadron … will move as early as possible into North-Western Area and will arm a flight of 2 Squadron. Beaufort crews of 13 Squadron will be transferred with their aircraft. As the Hudsons of 2 Squadron become due for repair or overhaul they will be withdrawn and replaced by further Beauforts, until the squadron is re-armed to a strength of 18 Beauforts plus one dual Beaufort.

3. Following the transfer of the Beaufort aircraft, 13 Squadron will be re-armed by the allotment of 9 Venturas (Type B-34) as they become available from 1 AD [Air Depot].

4. 13 Squadron will then consist of 9 type PV-1 Venturas and one flight of 9 type B-34 Venturas.

Despite the Directive only eight Beauforts made it to No. 2 Squadron by year's end following the crash of one at Fairbairn.

While the squadron's Hudson numbers were diminishing, the tasks allocated by No. 79 Wing headquarters remained at a punishing pace. They were mostly seaward searches covering the Kiwi (formerly Koala), Heron, Jackass and Gull sectors. The increasingly worn Hudsons flew 55 sorties during January and in February the Beauforts contributed 42 of the 86 sorties flown by the unit. The first operational mission by the Beauforts was on 12 January, when a pair flew a convoy patrol.

The Beauforts were initially confined to flying convoy patrols and seaward searches. On 18 February a trio of Hudsons attacked Manatuto on Timor's north coast and dropped supplies to Allied units in the Laclo River area. By the end of February six Hudsons remained while the Beauforts were up to the full established strength of eighteen aircraft.

During March the Beauforts took on more roles usually flown by the Hudsons. On 7 March six aircraft flew a search for missing No. 18 Squadron B-25 Mitchell N5-179, which had been shot down during a night strike on Toel, while a search for missing Hudson A16-230 was flown by three Beauforts on 28 March.

Hudson A16-230 had taken off for a reconnaissance mission over islands in the Banda Sea on 19 March. However, nothing further was heard from the aircraft or its crew comprising Squadron Leader John L Scott, Flight Sergeant Robert King, Pilot Officer Don C Beddoe and Flight Sergeants Bruce Wallace and Keith Wright. Post-war it was revealed that the crew had

An RAAF Beaufort of No. 100 Squadron over New Guinea, where the type saw extensive use. Beauforts entered service with No. 2 Squadron in early 1944, but after a short period they were replaced with B-25s. (AWM)

survived a ditching near Kai Island and had reached Laneong Island by dinghy. Betrayed, they were captured some two months later and transferred to Saumlaki.

On 24 May a No. 18 Squadron B-25 attacked the vessel transporting the crew and Beddoe was shot and killed when he started waving to the aircraft. The remaining crew reached Ambon and on 16 August were taken to Galala, where they were beheaded under the order of Sub-Lieutenant Katayama, of Headquarters 4 South Dispatched Fleet, who personally executed Scott. After the war, the Australian Army located the four responsible Japanese officers, who were put on trial, convicted and executed for their role in the war crime.

On 30 and 31 March the Beauforts carried out attacks on Penfui, the first by four aircraft which started large fires which could be seen for 80 miles according to the crew reports. Six aircraft followed up the following evening, however the results were not observed. The anti-aircraft fire encountered was described as slight to inaccurate.

By the end of March, only two Hudsons remained. That month the Beauforts had flown 62 sorties and the Hudsons 34. On 3 April there was only one Hudson left after A16-203 departed for Milingimbi and a convoy patrol. Nothing further was heard and when the aircraft failed to arrive at Milingimbi a search was flown. However, no sightings were made and the crew comprising Pilot Officers CD Brockhurst, RJ Philpot, RL Black and HJ Gillies along with Flight Sergeant RG Frew were posted missing.

Searches were carried out by No. 2 Squadron and No. 6 Communications Unit over the following four days without success. It was not until June 1946, that a local crocodile hunter reported finding an aircraft near the Adelaide River, 50 miles to the south of Darwin. Following RAAF investigations, the identity of the aircraft was confirmed as A16-203 and the crew remains were recovered. They were buried at the Adelaide River War Cemetery on 8 October 1946.

During early April 1944 the Beauforts carried out attacks over Timor over six days. On 2 April Dili was struck while five aircraft attacked Koepang two days later. Three Beauforts attacked Dili on 5 April and Lautem was hit over three nights from 6 April. Generally, the results were not observed, however the crews on the 6 and 7 April missions reported seeing fires as the result of their bombing. All the while, the convoy patrols and seaward searches were carried out. By April's end the Beauforts had flown 100 sorties and the remaining Hudsons just four. The last mission flown by the Hudsons was on 8 April when A16-199 flew a convoy patrol.

By the end of April, No. 2 Squadron's strength stood at eleven Beauforts – three of which were unserviceable – and three newly delivered B-25 Mitchells, two of which had arrived on 23 April.[1] The Hudsons, which had carried the RAAF's offensive missions from the NWA from February 1942, were now gone. A 1944 edition of *Army News* featured an article, *Hudson Squadron's Unmatched Record*:

> Of the recently announced decorations awarded bomber and fighter pilots for conspicuous service in the north-west, three DFCs have gone to members of the famous Hudson squadron, which has been operating continuously against the Japanese since the outbreak of the war in the Pacific. This squadron's record is unmatched in the RAAF …

> Until the beginning of this year, when they were reinforced by Mitchells … they carried on alone, bombing Japanese bases and ships to the limit of their range. Though no longer alone, they are still in the thick of it, patrolling, convoying and bombing both day and night …The original crews have been relieved, but the reputation for daring and determination which they left behind them are being more than maintained by those who have replaced them.

During May, No. 2 Squadron received more Mitchells while the Beauforts were gradually withdrawn, in part due to their unsuitably in the tropics. Warrant Officer Jim Henderson, a pilot with No. 2 Squadron, recalled:

> The Beaufort aircraft gave a good deal of trouble … mostly small things … the Beaufort did not perform well in the tropical air of Darwin … [and] having no co-pilot and no auto pilot, a long trip was an exhausting business.

RAAF flier Dudley Davies recalls of his time in Mitchells:

> We were called *Ditchmans Deadbeats*. Once we got the B-25 we had firepower. That's when we used to go on shipping strikes or raids on Penfui and Dili Lauman, that would be at 10,000 feet. And the ship strafing would be down on the deck. We got one we left in a sinking condition, two of our formations did it over. The only hair raising one there was when we came in range of a 4.5 naval gun. It exploded and shot the aircraft up a little.

> Normally with the raid on the airfield we would take off a couple hours before dusk and get there just on dusk and come back in the night. And land back about 9 o'clock and be greeted with a bottle of beer and a buffalo steak.

The remaining aircraft flew seaward searches over the Gull, Heron, Jackass and Kiwi areas along with convoy patrols and cover for ground operations. On 17 May Mitchell A47-20 was damaged when the undercarriage collapsed on landing. At the end of the month the unit's strength was seven Mitchells. June saw a continuance of the patrols, with strikes on Doka airstrip, Lautem and Selaru Island over the latter days of the month.

Four Mitchells attacked Doka on 24 June. Three days later nine aircraft attacked Lautem with 63 x 500-pound bombs reported on target. The following day a Mitchell flew a photo reconnaissance sortie over Selaru Island, and the same day saw three Mitchells make a repeat attack on Doka airstrip. At the end of June No. 2 Squadron's strength had grown to sixteen B-25 Mitchells.

---

1   No.2 Squadron became the only regular RAAF unit to operate the B-25, with the first aircraft being transferred from Dutch stocks in April 1944.

A No. 2 Squadron crew unload their gear from B-25 A47-31 at Hughes in June 1944 following a mission. (AWM)

While No. 2 Squadron worked up with its new Mitchell bombers, the Catalina squadrons were also keeping busy. They used Darwin and the former civil aviation base on Groote Eylandt as staging points before heading north on their long-range missions to disrupt Japanese shipping and land targets. In the meantime, No. 1 Squadron and its Beauforts were flying the missions allocated by No. 79 Wing. During May 1944 they flew seaward searches along the Gull, Heron, Jackass and Kiwi areas together with reconnaissance missions, convoy cover, anti-submarine patrols and supply drops to Allied forces in the NEI.

Six offensive operations were carried out in May. Six aircraft attacked the barracks area at Penfui with 250-pound bombs and incendiaries on the night of 2 May, with the flames from the attack visible for 30 miles. Only light anti-aircraft fire was experienced. Two nights later six aircraft made a return visit via Drysdale. Then on 6 May six aircraft made a night attack on Koepang.

On 8 May Penfui was attacked, however two aircraft failed to return and were posted missing. The crew of Beaufort A9-509, Flight Sergeants William D Sandwell and William J Hamilton along with Warrant Officer Felix E Keon were killed. Post war investigations confirmed the pilot, Flight Sergeant Terrence Wallace, survived the crash but he was captured and died the following day. Meanwhile A9-541 and its crew were never recovered. Those killed were Squadron Leader Roxburgh, Flying Officer Kerr, Warrant Officer Lomas and Flight Sergeant Jamieson.

Penfui was attacked again on 11 May, this time by nine aircraft, following an attack by nine No. 18 Squadron Mitchells which had departed the area a few minutes earlier. Both formations reported the flames from the attacks were visible for 50 miles. The same day saw three Catalinas of No. 43 Squadron search for shipping north of Buru Island before bombing Namlea. Nine days later No. 1 Squadron Beauforts attacked the radio station, anti-aircraft positions and barracks areas on Babar Island, while two aircraft bombed and strafed nearby Tepa village. After releasing 250- and 500-pound bombs and incendiaries, all aircraft reported their bombs fell on the targets.

No. 1 Squadron spent June flying seaward searches and convoy cover along with searchlight cooperation missions. Beaufort A9-392 was lost on 19 June when it was attempting a night landing and overshot the runway at Milingimbi. The pilot attempted to take off again however one engine lost power and the aircraft crashed into mangroves. While Pilot Officer Falconer's crew were uninjured, the aircraft was written off the following month.

July was much of the same with 104 sorties flown for the month. On 19 July a shipping strike on vessels in Dili harbour was flown by fifteen aircraft (one aborted prior to take-off) in two flights. Nine days later nine aircraft in three flights of three flew a night attack on an enemy encampment near Penfui airfield.

The No. 1 Squadron Beauforts concentrated on maritime reconnaissance from August onwards, using Air-to-Surface Vessel radar (ASV) in anti-submarine and shipping operations while taking advantage of the full moon period early in the month. Only one offensive mission was undertaken: a night attack by eight aircraft on Soe on 19 June, while 69 sorties in total were flown. A return visit to Soe was made by nine aircraft on 8 September, while the usual tasks were flown including a detachment of four aircraft and their crews to the newly developed airfield at Gove in far east Arnhem Land. There they were to assist No. 13 Squadron in convoy patrols until the end of the month.

One aircraft was lost when A9-593 crashed on take-off from Gould strip on 16 September. Assigned to convoy patrol, the aircraft left the ground but experienced engine trouble shortly after, forcing the pilot to attempt a landing. The aircraft crashed and burst into flames, killing the pilot Flight Lieutenant TWJ Speet and badly injuring the remaining crew of Flying Officer KWH Wood along with Warrant Officers R Brough and KF Klemm.

Lahane on Timor was attacked by eight aircraft on 6 October, and a further attack was mounted by nine aircraft on 21 October. Beaufort A9-610 flew a photo reconnaissance of the Vila and Salizar area the same day. A total of 116 sorties including the usual taskings by No. 79 Wing were flown for the month including seaward searches along the Gull, Heron, Jackass and Kiwi areas which culminated in attacks on alternate targets.

Dudley Davies recalls a shipping strike and a particularly brave Japanese anti-aircraft gunner:

> The other formation went in first and we went in second. When you are sitting there in the tail and it's all happening up front you miss a lot of the action. Then the pilot says gunner get ready then it's your turn. I saw a lot of the other aircraft strafing. There was a fair bit of flack coming up, 40-50 feet above the ship. One of the bravest things I've ever seen was this Japanese, he was on the forward deck he maintained his gunfire back at us after six aircraft had had a go at him. He just kept firing back at us all the time. I think it was our navigator who knocked him out on the second time around. He didn't give a …. just kept firing back.
>
> Sitting down the tail you hear, right we're going over, you hear the bombs go then you are over it. First time the bloody guns jammed, I was cranky. Second trip I got a burst in. In the Arafura Sea out about three or four hours out. We got four 500-pound bombs on it.

These sorties continued throughout November with single aircraft attacks on Viqueque, Cape Deheri, Larat, Longat, Betano, Bandalontan Island, Babar Island and Atamboea. One aircraft, A9-497, was lost during the month when it was ditched near the tip of North West Island in Clarence Strait on 26 November. Uninjured, the crew took to their dinghy and were rescued by a RAAF marine launch from Darwin the following day.

A No. 1 Squadron Beaufort over Timor in 1944, following a successful strike on the village of Su. (AWM)

December 1944 saw the commanding officer of No. 1 Squadron, Wing Commander CA Lonergan, acknowledge the air and ground crews for their accomplishment over the eight-month period of operations. To date 7,473 flying hours had been flown averaging 906 hours each month, while flying an average of 124 sorties per month. By the end of December, and despite Christmas, 115 sorties were flown, including a supply drop near Fatu Chile at last light on 27 December and shipping search attacks on Viqueque, Larat, Taberfane and Bandanaira. Radar test flights were also flown for the Lee Point radar site near Darwin.

The New Year was heralded in with the last mission for No. 1 Squadron flown by Beauforts A9-570 and -491 on 7 January 1945. Each aircraft carried two 250-pound bombs in an armed reconnaissance of the Tanimbars and Saumlaki. Two days later Wing Commander Lonergan announced that:

> The Squadron is to move to Kingaroy, [in Queensland], to be re-equipped with Mosquito Aircraft. All Beaufort Aircraft on strength are to be ferried to various places of allotment by Squadron Crews, the balance of Personnel to travel by Air and Road.

On 11 January the Beauforts began flying out of Gould followed two days later by the main party. No. 1 Squadron headquarters was officially established at Kingaroy on 15 January 1945.

The land-based squadrons had continued their harassing operations against a fading enemy presence in the NEI. Meanwhile the Catalina units, Nos. 11, 20 and 43 Squadrons, had been kept busy in their mine laying, shipping patrols, supply dropping, bombing and air sea rescue roles. Nos. 11 and 20 Squadrons operated from their Queensland bases before No. 20 Squadron joined Nos. 42 and 43 Squadrons as part of No. 76 Wing in Darwin during September 1944, flying from Groote Eylandt and Darwin's Doctors Gully on long-range missions.

No. 43 Squadron had formed in Queensland in May 1943 before moving to Karumba, a former civilian flying boat base in the Gulf of Carpentaria, in August. By 24 August 1943 the unit was equipped with four Catalinas. It flew its first operational patrols on 8 September, with four aircraft conducting strikes against targets in Ambon. The unit moved to Darwin's Doctors Gully in April 1944, while No. 42 Squadron formed at Doctors Gully on 1 June the same year.

Squadron Leader GW Coventry and his crew in A24-49 was detached to Port Moresby to reconnoitre the Sepik and Yellow Rivers during July. On 9 August, he flew an advance party of

"Mosstroops" covert operatives and their supplies to Lake Kuvanmas. Cut off by the Japanese the party was later evacuated by Coventry and his crew.

Back at Darwin, a mixed force of four aircraft from Nos. 11, 20 and 43 Squadrons was refuelled and armed for a minelaying mission to Soerabaya on the night of 26 August. All eight mines were dropped at very low altitude and while the aircraft were fired on by anti-aircraft defences only A24-50 was hit, wounding a gunner.

Forced to refuel at Exmouth Gulf in Western Australia because of the distance and duration of the flight, the aircraft returned to Darwin where they were refuelled and rearmed before setting off for a return visit to Soerabaya on 29 August. Two further missions were flown from Darwin on 26 and 29 September when mines were laid in the harbour approaches to Batu Kelat and Pomelaa.

At the time, operations by the Catalinas were referred to by code names – Babo was code named "Filly" and Kavieng "Popsy" – and as Lieutenant Commander PE Carr, RAN, the originator of the code names, recalled:

> From the first minelaying operation in April 1943 to September … the orders and plans for each operation were taken … by me from RAAF Command Brisbane by air to Cairns. No orders or instructions were written or signalled. Each operation was referred to by a secret code name and all notes were destroyed immediately after use and [the] charts erased.

On 30 September 1943 A24-67 under Wing Commander SG Stilling took off from Darwin for a night torpedo attack on Pomelaa harbour. The aircraft was shot down over the harbour, with Carr the only survivor of the ten-man crew after Pilot Officer DG Diamed died of his wounds. Captured, Carr spent the rest of the war in captivity without the Japanese knowing the value of their prisoner. None of the crew were recovered. Those lost were Wing Commander SG Stilling (RAF), Flight Lieutenant JR Hyde, Flying Officer RF Dickinson and Pilot Officers NF Dwyre and DG Diamed; Sergeants T McMahon and FH Thomson; along with Corporal SJ Carnell and JH Barnes (RCAF). The loss of A24-67 was confirmed on 8 October when a Japanese radio broadcast stated that the aircraft had been shot down by anti-aircraft fire.

Rescues of downed airmen were also carried out by the Catalinas, such as the rescue of the four survivors from 380th BG B-24D 42-40518 *The Golden Gator* which was shot down in the evening of 26 October 1943 on return from bombing Pomelaa Harbour.

Manokwari was mined in early October while Waingapoe was mined by A24-35 and A24-62 on the night of the 12 October, with each aircraft armed with one mine and a torpedo. After

A No. 43 Squadron Catalina in flight. By the time the squadron moved to Darwin in April 1944 most of the frontline Catalinas were painted black to reflect their largely nocturnal role, earning the nickname "Black Cats". (AWM)

releasing their mines the pair flew on to Koepang, where the pilot of A24-35 released his torpedo at a small vessel. While this aspect of the mission was judged as unsuccessful, the crews did subsequently learn that the harbour had been closed in the belief that mines had been laid by the pair.

During November No. 43 Squadron returned to attack Ambon and Babo, where they started large fires. By 12 November the area around Babo was described as "…a mass of flames, [with] two aircraft also being set alight and four others probably destroyed." Babo was attacked again two nights later starting twelve fires, during which Flying Officer RL "Chick" Chinnick spotted a Japanese night fighter during the attack. However, the fighter failed to intercept the flying boat.

Other targets attacked by No. 43 Squadron in November were Sorong and Langgoer while No. 11 Squadron hit Sorong, Boela and Kaimana. Nos. 11 and 20 Squadrons also laid mines at Kendari, Ceram, Waingapoe, Kavieng and Soerabaya. In one mission on 27 November an enemy fighter intercepted A24-35, however no damage was reported.

The threat of enemy fighters was always present for the Catalina crews, particularly during the early daylight hours following their night attacks. The threat increased when the Japanese introduced night fighters in late 1943 and it was highlighted during a raid on Babo on 12 December 1944. A24-38, flown by Flight Sergeant Don Abbey, was attacked by what was initially and wrongly identified as a twin-engine Ki-46 Dinah but was either a JAAF Ki-45 Nick of the 5th *Sentai* or a newly arrived J1N1 Irving of No. 202 *Ku*. Four attacks on Abbey's aircraft were made while five "Zeros" also joined in, however the pilots were likely new as damage to the Catalina amounted to only a solitary bullet hole.

On 17 December 1943 Catalina A24-45 under Flight Lieutenant Brooks was caught in severe weather. Despite the conditions the aircraft released its load of four 250-pound bombs and 20 incendiaries on the runway, dispersal areas and a fuel dump at Kavieng and made it safely back to Darwin.

From 20 until 29 December Nos. 11, 20 and 43 Squadrons flew nightly against Kavieng, during which:

> Bombs [dropped] south across southeast end of runway and through revetment area and dump area and along Panapai Road toward town starting fires … this caused explosion and [an] ack ack gun in [the] vicinity ceased fire. Many explosions from these fires.

Despite the one gun reported, the anti-aircraft fire was intense. Both A24-57 and A24-40 were hit, the latter flown by Flight Lieutenant Damien Miller. The starboard engine of the aircraft was damaged, and it was feathered while fuel was dumped and all miscellaneous equipment including the guns were thrown overboard. At dawn, limping home, A24-40 was targeted again by more anti-aircraft fire. Finally, after ten hours and 50 minutes on the one engine and with only 16 gallons of fuel left in the tanks they landed at Langermak Bay near Finschhafen.

With the New Year came further raids against Kavieng. On 14 January 1944 six aircraft set off from Darwin for a minelaying mission in Kanoe Bay. Flying Officer Chinnick in A24-65 was forced to return while the remaining five Catalinas successfully released their mines. Despite flying over enemy territory for five hours little opposition was encountered, amounting to some light anti-aircraft fire over the target and an unsuccessful interception attempt by a Japanese fighter near Ambon on the return trip. Further missions were carried out over the nights of 16, 18 and 20 January.

On 7 February Catalina A24-34 under Squadron Leader John Todd took off from Darwin bound for Kavieng on a "nuisance raid". After bombing both Kavieng and Panapai airstrips the aircraft continued on before making landfall over the north coast of New Britain. The armourer, Sergeant Harry Jones, was instructed to take three reconnaissance flares to the bunk compartment and to set them to varying heights. He was setting one flare when it exploded, setting the remaining two flares off. Rated at 750,000 candlepower they burned through a bulkhead. With the aircraft on fire, Todd crash-landed.

Once down the crew decided to split up and head in two opposite directions. However, one group was captured comprising Todd, Flying Officer FR Pocknee, Flight Lieutenant Brian Stacy, Flight Sergeant HL Murphy, Sergeant Fred Woolley and Sergeant EH Kreahe. Out of all of them only Stacy survived. The other party met friendly natives and after two months were evacuated to Australia.

In April 1944 five Catalinas landed in Yampi Sound, Western Australia, an advance base codenamed Shecat, before setting out on a Balikpapan minelaying mission, the first for No. 43 Squadron. Taking off on 21 April the five flew to Balikpapan however A24-53 under Flight Sergeant Don Abbey was shot down and crashed into the entrance of the harbour. Flight Lieutenant Robin Grey in A24-35 was caught in searchlights and the flying boat was badly damaged by heavy anti-aircraft fire, although all of the remaining four returned safely to Shecat. None of the crew of A24-53 were recovered: Abbey; Flying Officer FK Robinson; Warrant Officer RA Swan; Flight Sergeants AM Belshaw, DG Hoffman and BK Winterbon; together with Sergeants WD Reece, KE Thompson and ND Woodhouse.

A post-war report on minelaying operations includes a section on Japanese anti-aircraft fire, probably contributed by Robin Grey and his crew in A24-35 with reference to their experience of the 21 April Balikpapan mission:

> Shore based fire never proved such a serious threat as that encountered from shipping, which was always withheld until the critical moment and was invariably accurate and well directed … shore based … fire was, as a rule, wild, uncontrolled and belated.

Two further minelaying missions on Balikpapan were flown from Yampi Sound by No. 43 Squadron on 24 and 27 April, following which, Japanese shipping notices:

> … showed that the harbor was closed between 20 and 29 April and for an undetermined period thereafter. A delayed action mine evidently sank the old Japanese destroyer *Amagiri* while it was sweeping the harbor on 23 April.

Following single aircraft minelaying operations against Sorong, Kaimana and Manokwari on the nights of 25 and 27 April, a solo aircraft mission was planned to be flown by A24-49 of No. 11 Squadron on the night of the 28 April. After being refuelled at Groote Eylandt the aircraft, under Warrant Officer Warwick Rose, departed at 1445 and set course for Manokwari. The presence of No. 934 *Ku* floatplane fighters in the islands *en route* and the Ki-45 Nicks of the 5th *Sentai* were anticipated. Nothing further was heard from the aircraft and the crew were posted missing comprising: Rose; Flying Officer AR Meakin, Flight Sergeants AJ Hine, JB Miller, LW Stringer and JW Willesden; along with Sergeants PC Carter, HJA Coates, AHB Wadham and GW Whitley. It was not until 28 November 1946 following exhaustive searches for the aircraft that the deaths of the crew were declared.

During May 1944 the three squadrons were engaged in minelaying. Kaimana, Balikpapan and Soerabaya were the main objectives while shipping searches and strikes against targets in the NEI were also carried out. No. 20 Squadron attacked Kaimana on four occasions while No. 43 Squadron also hit Balikpapan. Both Nos. 11 and 20 Squadrons attacked Soerabaya towards the end of the month.

A busy scene at the Darwin flying boat base in June 1944 with Catalina crews being taken to their aircraft on a variety of small motor launches. (AWM)

RAAF ground personnel attach a mine to the underwing pylon of a No. 43 Squadron Catalina at the Darwin flying boat base. (AWM)

CHAPTER 11

THE AMERICANS AND THE DUTCH DEPART; LUCKY 13 RETURNS

With the RAAF's Catalinas busy flying by night and bottling up Japanese-occupied harbours the B-24 Liberators of the 380th BG and B-25 Mitchells of No. 18 Squadron continued their long and medium range missions against the islands of the NEI. However, there were major moves afoot for the NWA.

While RAAF crews were also flying with the 380th BG, others were training at the CRTC at Nadzab, flying with the 380th BG detachment at Port Moresby and at 7 OTU at Tocumwal. At Manbulloo No. 24 Squadron was declared operational on 17 June 1944, though most flights at this time were ferry flights from Amberley to Gorrie and Manbulloo. Dick Overheu had been posted into No. 24 Squadron and flew nineteen such flights during June and July along with his crew including flight engineer Lindsay McDonald. Nos. 21 and 23 Squadrons were also to re-equip with Liberators and were to join No. 24 Squadron as part of No. 82 Wing.

On 28 June 1944 the Fifth Air Force issued a directive that would see the 380th BG operate from the one location and gradually make way for the RAAF's Liberator units:

> [The] … 380th Bombardment Group to move from Fenton to RAAF aerodrome Darwin earliest … As and when operational commitments permit. Attached RAAF personnel to move with squadrons concerned. Advise date move will commence. Request this Headquarters be advised date on which movement of each squadron is completed.

The movement began in July and was completed the following month. While the squadrons operated from four large igloo hangars on the south-eastern area of the RAAF station, headquarters, administration and accommodation was located at the McMillans camp area to the east of the airfield.

Despite the move missions continued. On 29 June 24 Liberators attacked Babo, cratering the runway and causing extensive damage to the revetments and other areas. However, the town was bombed when a newly appointed squadron commander led his aircraft over the wrong target. Two days later 31 aircraft followed after Lieutenant Lawrence Stevens' weather reconnaissance in an attack on Namlea airfield. The results were reported as good, even though twelve of the B-24s attacked shipping instead of the designated target. Captain Virgil "Big Steve" Stevens was one, with his logbook reading:

A line up of 531st BS Liberators at Darwin after their move into the base in mid-1944. By that time most of the 380th BG's bombers had been stripped of their olive drab camouflage in favour of natural metal finish. The aircraft closest to the camera is B-24J 42-73134 Milady which crashed near Darwin in January 1945. (Bob Alford)

The control tower at Fenton, circa 1944. By the time that No. 24 Squadron moved into the base in September 1944, it had been much improved by the Americans since the 319th BS first occupied the site in early 1943. (Bob Livingstone)

… weather shipping recco. Sighted 7 ship convoy on W. Tip of Beroe Isle. 3 destroyer – 2 large merchant ships & 2 unidentified ships. We straffed [sic] numerous small ships & boats & took pictures.

On 4 July Stevens flew a night strike on Amahai strip on Ceram, recording one large fire as a result of the nine-hour 35-minute trip. The same trip saw the B-24 of Flying Officer Harold A Thornton fail to return to Long airfield after his aircraft, B-24D 42-40351 *Big Chief Cockeye*, slammed into a cloud-shrouded mountain on Ceram. Of the eleven-man crew ten were killed: Thornton; Lieutenants William C Karbach, Douglas G McMillin and Max Rubin; Staff Sergeants Steve J Buccia, JD Hawthorne, Peter P Kosciuszek, Harry H Reed and Kenneth R Thoen; and Technical Sergeant Richard W Corbin. Only Sergeant Edward J Gill survived the crash and was captured. He later died of malnutrition.

During July Stevens completed a further two missions: a reconnaissance of Soemba Island on 17 July and a weather and shipping reconnaissance which proved to be "all weather & no shipping." Other flights included one to Port Moresby, travel flights, night transition training for RAAF crews and an instrument check flight. In total he recorded 60 hours and 50 minutes of flying for the month.

Also during July Group Captain Derek Kingwell, who would become the commanding officer of No. 82 Wing, flew his first mission with the 380th BG during a strike on Laha on 27 July, further signalling the RAAF's progress in taking over the heavy bombing role in the NWA. Subsequently No. 82 (Heavy Bomber) Wing formed on 25 August, although it did not become fully operational at Fenton until 11 January 1945.

During August Virgil Stevens flew three armed reconnaissance missions. On 10 August he was part of an eighteen aircraft day strike on Laha with his co-pilot, Pilot Officer WA Cowan, RAAF, during which they struck poor weather. On 22 August he flew in a twelve aircraft attack on Amahai again with Cowan and reported poor bombing. His last mission for the month was as part of an eighteen aircraft return visit to Laha, again with Cowan as his co-pilot.

Even though he was getting close to returning to the USA at the end of his tour, Stevens flew three missions during September 1944. On 1 September he flew a single aircraft reconnaissance with Bob Young, RAN, as his co-pilot during which they bombed Namlea. Three days later he was part of a group strike on Kendari, reporting large fires as a result of the attack. On 8 September he flew in an exercise with the submarine USS *Nautilus*. After flying 263.35 combat hours with the 529th BS, on 16 October Stevens' logbook reads:

S. A. Levandowski – XC-Townsville to Nadzab. Returned to USA 17 Oct 44 –

The artwork on B-24J 44-40398 Patty's Pig which was shot down near Koepang on 9 October 1944. (Bob Livingstone)

While August and September 1944 had seen the 380th BG attack Amahai, Namlea, Ambon, Laha, Liang, Langgoer and Ambesia – a previously unknown airfield complex – without loss, three aircraft were lost during October. On 9 October Lieutenant Bob Prest and his crew perished during a strike on Koepang, when their B-24J 44-40398 *Patty's Pig* was hit by a large calibre anti-aircraft round and crashed into the sea. While five parachutes were seen no Japanese records indicate anyone was captured. The crew was Lieutenants Robert F Prest, John T O'Neill, Harry R Gould and John T O'Loughlin; Staff Sergeants Alanson S Ackerman, Alvin W Beenken, Morris Massin and Lloyd E Williams; Technical Sergeants Charles W Cross and Joseph A Fritschy; and Private First Class Fred C Cave. Flight Sergeant Donald N Herbert, RAAF, the RCM operator with 22 Section, also died.

Two days following the loss of the Bob Prest crew, Technical Sergeant Wallace M Olsen, the radio operator in B-24D 42-41125 *Gus's Bus II* was killed. The aircraft had stalled on take-off from Darwin and a propellor which had pierced the fuselage pinned Olsen to his seat as the aircraft burst into flames. The remaining crew suffered varying injuries.

On the night of 28 October 24 aircraft took off on a mission to Macassar. Early on in the flight Flying Officer Alan Harrison in B-24J 42-110120 *Sleepy Time Gal* radioed Darwin to report fuel transfer problems south of Timor. Nothing further was heard from the aircraft and its RAAF crew. Those lost were Flying Officers Alan L Harrison, Donald J O'Dea and Alan A Cropley; Warrant Officers Stuart H Davidson and Leonard Killen; Flight Sergeants Charles L Wilken and William R Barber; Sergeants Stuart H Jamieson, Frederick W Anstey, Walter J Bird and James E Cook; and an Australian Army observer Major Roger Latrelle. It was the only Australian crew lost on operations with the 380th BG.

Sleepy Time Gal may have been downed by a night fighter which itself was brought down. Lieutenant Forrest "Tommy" Thompson of the 530th BS reported encountering night fighters during the mission, although the engagement was fleeting. The first indication for Thompson was the sound of machine gun fire from the gunners in his aircraft and following that a fireball as a blazing J1N1 Irving night fighter or a Ki-45 Nick went past.

A variation on the normal missions took place on 24 October when Major Howard C Williams, the commanding officer of the 531st BS, flew from Darwin to search for No. 42 Squadron

An IJN twin engine Irving fighter, as preserved in the Smithsonian Institution in the USA. An Irving may have been responsible for shooting down B-24J 42-110120 Sleepy Time Gal near Timor on 28 October 1944. (Author photo)

Catalina A24-100. The flying boat had been forced to land on the water after being hit in one engine by anti-aircraft fire during a minelaying mission at Macassar. After finding it Williams flew top cover with another B-24 and a Northrop P-61 night fighter, while a No. 43 Squadron Catalina landed and picked up the crew of A24-100. Following the rescue, the crippled Catalina was strafed and sunk by the two B-24s.

November 1944 commenced with a further raid on Macassar on the night of 2/3 November, which saw large fires started near the Wilhelmina Wharf, sending smoke 10,000 feet into the air. The fires were reported visible for 100 miles as the B-24s returned to Darwin. Anti-aircraft fire was reported as minimal though Lieutenant Bob Wilkinson had his aircraft, *Morbid Mo*, hit by ground fire as his crew also reported seeing night fighters. Other aircraft were attacked by these night fighters on the outbound leg, however all returned safely to Darwin.

Soembawa was attacked two days later, followed on 7 November by a dozen bombers of the 529th and 531st BS in a follow-up attack. Six aircraft of the 528th BS flew in a search for targets of opportunity in the Macassar area on 9 November, attacking a lone *Fox-Tare-Charlie* vessel with poor results. A later report was critical:

> … all crews were not alert as to the target and the bombing run, and only three crews got their bombs away. The other three crews jettisoned their bombs on the way home.

On the night of 27/28 November Lieutenant Colonel John Henschke flew a night harassment raid over Kendari. The final mission for the month was a 30 November attack on Malingpoen airstrip by eighteen Liberators, ten of them with Australian crews.

By November 1944 one third to a half of the crews flying 380th BG B-24 missions were Australian. With No. 24 Squadron now operational following its arrival at Fenton on 1 September 1944 the unit was jokingly referred to as:

> … the fifth squadron within the Flying Circus.

The 380th BG had earned its "Flying Circus" nickname during an efficiency inspection in the USA when Brigadier General Eugene L Eubank had declared:

> My God, these men are a flying circus!

The men of the 380th BG subsequently wore Eubanks' comment with pride.

A typical RAAF crew was that of Squadron Leader "Mickey" Finlayson with Sergeant Dave Sieber as his nose gunner. Sieber had been with the Finlayson crew through the training at Port Moresby from July 1944 and then with the 531st BS at Darwin. He flew three missions to Amahai, Laha and Liang on 21, 25 and 31 August. During September and October, the Finlayson crew flew ten missions to Kendari, Heroekoe, Liang, Lautem, Laha, Babar Island, the Celebes and Koepang. On 5 October they were forced to turn back from a mission to Macassar with engine trouble. On their final mission before a posting to No. 23 Squadron at Leyburn in Queensland they witnessed the loss of *Patty's Pig* when it was hit by anti-aircraft fire on 9 October.

On 2 December 1944 eighteen B-24s raided Boro Boro and Kendari followed by a "milk run" to Ambesia five days later. Attacks on Kendari, Cape Chater and Flores were flown in the first half of the month. On 20 December, No. 24 Squadron joined the 380th BG in a 30 aircraft attack on Java via Corunna Downs in Western Australia. Eighteen aircraft were to hit Malang while the remainder were to attack the power station at Mendalan. Despite poor weather, Malang was hit with a number of aircraft destroyed on the ground while the Mendalan target was obscured by cloud and poor weather, forcing the aircraft to jettison their bombs at sea.

On 30 December eighteen aircraft attacked an empty airfield outside Macassar, followed by an eighteen aircraft attack on Ambesia in poor weather on New Year's Eve. On 3 January 1945 orders were issued to the 380th BG to move to Mindoro in the Philippines and all but priority missions were suspended in preparation for the move. On New Year's Day an abortive shipping search was flown around Macassar by both the 380th BG and No. 24 Squadron, followed four days later by a mission to destroy three gun emplacements covering Lombok Strait at the request of the US Navy. Missions were flown on 5, 7 and 9 January before the guns were destroyed, much to the pleasure of the USN who sent a congratulatory message:

… Please express the gratitude of all submariners to all concerned for their part.

Even with missions suspended, training continued. On one practice bombing sortie over Quail Island Lieutenant Bobby Neal and a five-man crew aboard B-24J 42-73174 *Milady* crashed on the Cox Peninsula west of Darwin, possibly due to low flying and disorientation. All aboard died: Neal; Lieutenants Walter E Scanlan, William G Ward, and Ricard W Walsh; together with Sergeants Francisco Caballero and Gerald D Sacre. The bodies were recovered the following day by a search party, who were landed on the coast and followed the smoke from the burning aircraft to the crash site.

On 2 February 1945 a dozen aircraft of the 528th and 531st Bombardment Squadrons flew the last mission for the 380th BG from Australia with an attack on Malingpoen airfield and the ship building facilities at Pare Pare. Poor weather prevented them from bombing either target. While the 528th BS bombed the nickel mines at Maniang, the 531st BS split up with three aircraft bombing Pare Pare through cloud. The others went to Dili as a target of last resort.

By late February 1945, only a few 380th BG personnel remained at Darwin. Flying a war-weary B-24D, *Beautiful Betsy,* Lieutenant Bill McDaniel took off on 26 February. Along with his flight crew, two RAF personnel were also on board; Flying Officer Roy Cannon was to get married in Brisbane, while Flight Lieutenant John Cook was to be his best man.

The aircraft simply disappeared. Despite searches over many years, it was not until July 1994 that the wreckage and the remains of the crew were located on Kroombit Tops in Queensland

Fresh supplies being loaded on 380th BG B-24D Beautiful Betsy at Gawler airfield in South Australia, circa 1944. The aircraft was a so-called "Fatcat" Liberator, stripped of combat equipment and used as a transport to take crews south for rest and recreation leave. The Fatcats returned to the NWA loaded with fresh food and other supplies. Beautiful Betsy disappeared on a flight to Queensland in February 1945 with the wreckage not found until 1994. (Bob Livingstone)

some 310 miles north-northwest from Brisbane. The crew comprised Lieutenants Eugene A Kilcheski, Hilary E Route, and Jack W Owen; along with Technical Sergeants Harold J Lemons and Raymond L Tucker.

With the departure of the 380th BG the offensive missions from the NWA fell on No. 18 Squadron, the newly arrived Mitchells of No. 2 Squadron and the Liberators of No. 24 Squadron, while patrols were being flown by the Venturas of No. 13 Squadron from Gove. Even then, Nos. 2, 13 and 18 Squadrons were into their last few months of operations before they too were on the move.

Six months earlier, during July 1944, the Allies had stepped up their reconnaissance effort against enemy coastal luggers and barge concentrations. No. 18 Squadron detached sixteen aircraft to the newly developed airfield at Truscott, on the Anjo Peninsula in the Kimberley region of Western Australia for three days. From Truscott they carried out a reconnaissance of Selaru along with attacks on shipping at Maumere and coordinated attacks with No. 2 Squadron Mitchells. An attack on Penfui was carried out on 29 July by a dozen aircraft of Nos. 2 and 18 Squadrons in an effort to neutralise the airfield. Two nights later another combined attack to destroy shipping, stores and installations at Maumere was carried out by thirteen Mitchells.

Further attacks by the two squadrons were carried out against an enemy camp at Mina Bridge on 2 August by fifteen aircraft. A daylight attack on Langgoer by eleven B-25s on 9 August was followed up by a night attack on Langgoer by twelve aircraft two days later. Twelve Mitchells struck shipping and enemy activity at Tioor Island on 17 August, followed up the same day by eight Mitchells which rendered the airstrip unserviceable. During the attack on Langgoer N5-210 was hit by anti-aircraft fire in the wing and crashed in shallow water off the airfield. Killed were pilot Lieutenant HJ Spoel along with Lieutenants P Van Straalen and Ch Riemens; Sergeants BJ van der Linden and JC Van Polanen Petel; and Flight Sergeant Douglas V Webley, RAAF.

A further aircraft was lost on 24 August when N5-169 failed to return from an armed reconnaissance of Larat in the Tanimbars. It was thought that the aircraft was shot down by anti-aircraft fire. Searches were mounted for the aircraft, during which attacks were made on two vessels in Hom Bay. The crew was not recovered. Lost were: Captain PC Andre de la Porte; Lieutenants JJ Th Draaier, FH Meijer and Lie Kok Hian; along with Sergeants M Samalo and Maurice E Trimnell, RAAF.

Six days later ten Mitchells individually attacked Larat with bombs and incendiaries. September saw more coordinated attacks by Nos. 2 and 18 Squadrons, commencing with a night attack on Langgoer by eight aircraft on 1 September. However, one aircraft, N5-214 and the crew of Lieutenant AA Dreher failed to return to Batchelor and was thought to have been shot down by anti-aircraft fire. Lost were Dreher along with Lieutenants GJ Lught, AE Donk and WG Franken; Sergeant RW Marsman and Flight Sergeant Thomas H Barclay, RAAF.

Langgoer received further attention on 12 and 15 September during which N5-222 was hit by anti-aircraft fire which set the starboard engine on fire. With the flames spreading to the whole aircraft, it went into a steep dive. At 7,500 feet one wing separated and the aircraft exploded as it crashed. None of the crew survived: Lieutenants KG Vogler, HJ Van Renesse and WJM Scholte; Sergeants F Engelsman and R de Rozario; together with Flight Sergeant David BE Bacon, RAAF.

September and October saw No. 18 Squadron attack Saumlaki over a number of days while shipping and coastal vessels and barges were continually harassed. Throughout October armed anti-shipping searches and armed reconnaissance missions were carried out against enemy installations and camps. During late October the squadron was again detached to Truscott from where they attacked Maumere, the Kabiniroe River Bridge and Matawai village in harassing operations. An anti-shipping sweep along the north cast of Soemba was flown on 30 October.

November saw the Mitchells attack enemy troop positions, anti-aircraft sites and shipping in the Alor and Wetar Islands and Hom and Goerita Bays. Photo reconnaissance of Timor was made along with attacks on Dili and Bacau in cooperation with No. 31 Squadron Beaufighters. On 6 November twelve Mitchells of No. 18 Squadron along with No. 2 Squadron flew from Truscott to attack shipping at Waingapoe. While No. 18 Squadron attacked anti-aircraft positions to draw the enemy fire, No. 2 Squadron Mitchells attacked the shipping at low level, damaging the jetty and barges.

On 22 November, again operating from Truscott, a coordinated attack by a dozen aircraft of the two Mitchell squadrons saw enemy supply dumps at Lautem targeted, leaving a number of barges and a *Sugar Dog* vessel burning in the Flores Strait and at Laratoeka.[1] Three days later four Mitchells flew a daylight anti-shipping sweep of the Lewotobi Strait/Flores Island/Maumere/Goemoek area, during which a 150-ton *Sugar Dog* was attacked at low level and left burning. Further anti-shipping sweeps were carried out over the Wetar and Alor Islands and Timor on 28 and 30 November, leaving vessels burning and sinking and inflicting heavy casualties on enemy personnel.

The anti-shipping strikes from Truscott continued into December 1944. Four aircraft sank luggers and schooners off Timor, while Bacau was bombed on 1 December and follow up operations were carried out on both 3 and 5 December. Eight Mitchells attacked the barracks area at Ende on 8 December while leaflets were also dropped. For the remainder of the month the anti-shipping sweeps continued along with armed reconnaissance and concentrated attacks on convoys. Despite some aircraft being hit by anti-aircraft fire none were lost and the attacks saw many sinkings of enemy coastal shipping.

Early December saw the "bush telegraph" working overtime with rumours that No. 18 Squadron

---

1   *Sugar-Dog* vessels were small Japanese supply vessels with a single hatch up to 300 tons, while *Sugar-Charlies* were larger, up to 1,000 tons and with two hatches.

was to move to a new destination. However, it was not until 11 December that Circular No. 232 announced that No. 79 Wing headquarters along with its squadrons were to move to Jacquinot Bay on the south coast of New Britain. Despite the impending move operations continued with a daylight attack on Suai, Atamboea, Lahane and Maubisse by six aircraft. In an anti-shipping sweep on 15 January 1945 one large, four medium and two midget submarines were sighted however they crash-dived before the Mitchells could attack.[2]

Anti-shipping strikes were carried out from Truscott over the month with attacks on barges, luggers and smaller vessels mainly around Timor where leaflets were also released. Over two days from 28 January a visual and photo reconnaissance mission of eastern and central Java was carried out by Major Van Bremen in N5-185.

Over February and March 1945 No. 18 Squadron continued its harassing anti-shipping sweeps. Armed reconnaissance missions over the Alor and Solor Islands and Timor were flown, including the bridges at Ende and strafing attacks on enemy shipping. Despite taking a number of hits by a rapidly fading anti-aircraft presence, the Mitchells suffered no further losses. On 3 April two aircraft carried out an attack on radar stations at Cape Eliase, Selaru Island, followed by a daylight attack the next day by eight Mitchells on stores dumps and dispersal areas at Adoert Bay. A number of small vessels were also strafed and sunk off Kisar Island.

On 6 April ten B-25s, five each from Nos. 2 and 18 Squadrons, along with nine B-24 Liberators of No. 82 Wing were involved in attacking a large enemy naval force. This included the cruiser *Isuzu* escorted by a destroyer and minesweepers, which were in the Flores Sea reportedly evacuating troops from Timor. Departing Truscott, the Mitchells set course:

> … for Cape Dendoe to search for the forces but after proceeding for approximately 45 miles, the formation leader, acting on his opinion that the vessels would be North of or under the direct cloud cover changed course and brought his formation directly over the target. Although the attack was opposed by five (5) enemy single seater fighters (an Oscar, a Tojo and Irvings) [sic] which shot down two Liberators and a Catalina no casualties were suffered by the B-25's which by tight formation flying and concentration of their attack on the *Isuzu* achieved two direct hits.

According to one reliable source 60 bombs were dropped, and the cruiser was slightly damaged near her bows by near misses. The next day the *Isuzu* was targeted by one British and three American submarines. She was torpedoed three times and sank with the loss of 190 of the ship's company.

With the move to Jacquinot Bay looming closer, operations decreased, though armed reconnaissance missions were flown over the Sermata Islands and Timor. The last mission for No. 18 Squadron in the NWA was to bomb and strafe a ditched RAAF Liberator to prevent it falling into enemy hands.

On 21 April 1945 an advance party left Batchelor for the new location, leaving 386 personnel to move from Batchelor by service aircraft. The commanding officer of the RAAF component, Squadron Leader Gray, along with five airmen departed by air for Jacquinot Bay on 26 April. Operations from Batchelor ceased on 1 May and by mid-month the No. 18 Squadron had completed its move.

---

2   A doubtful and likely over-eager reporting. According to their records, almost all Japanese submarines had withdrawn north by this time, and there were no midgets deployed this far south this late in the war.

A *Wings* magazine article described No. 18 Squadron as:

> Unique among the squadrons in the Pacific air war is the Mitchell Bomber Squadron which flies from Darwin deep into Netherlands East Indies. These are the Netherlander and Indonesian Revenge Bombers. They fly to avenge Rotterdam, Pontianar, Terimpah and many other small towns in the Netherlands Indies … Many of the … pilots and navigators are fliers who count who count their flying hours by the thousand. Some of them flew with the airlines and many were fighting the Japs before the fall of Java … The squadron ops log shows raids on targets all over the NW Area, from West Timor to the western tip of Netherlands New Guinea … Each week the squadron adds new achievements. Dutchmen, Indonesians and Australians are fighting side by side, doing a magnificent job. These men are fighting for more than victory.

With the movement of several units from the NWA, one squadron had returned, this time to far east Arnhem Land at Gove. Number 13 Squadron now re-equipped with Venturas was engaged in coastal patrols and convoy escort duties from the airfield.

Based initially at Fairbairn in Canberra following its move from the NWA, the squadron had ten Beauforts and three Lockheed Venturas allotted in July 1943. The first of the Beauforts arrived on 3 August followed in batches by nine more, while the Venturas followed soon after. With the arrival of larger numbers of Venturas, the Beauforts were subsequently allocated to Nos. 2 and 32 Squadrons.

In early September 1943 the squadron was advised of a move and flying training on the new aircraft including night flying, cross country navigational flights and convoy patrols began in earnest. In December the unit moved to Cooktown in north Queensland and on 25 August 1944 moved to Gove and commenced sea and convoy patrols, 76 of which were flown during September. The unit often used Merauke in Dutch New Guinea, Higgins Field on Cape York or Darwin for refuelling.

The sorties increased to 87 in October 1944, one of which ended with A59-83 ditching in Torres Strait after the failure of both engines on 19 October. The uninjured crew of Flying Officer Richard "George" Rudge was able to reach Banks Island in the aircraft's dinghy. They were taken in by local natives before being picked up by the MV *Mangola* and taken to Darwin.

During November 86 sorties were flown, including a number of armed reconnaissances over the Kai, Tanimbar and Aru Islands. While little shipping was sighted, shore installations were destroyed and the buildings and a jetty at Elat Bay were severely damaged. Propaganda leaflets were also released over these islands while light anti-aircraft fire was encountered over Dobo.

In December a total of 84 mainly convoy escort and anti-shipping sweeps over enemy territory were flown. On New Year's Eve the unit commanding officer, Wing Commander William J Keenan, flew A59-71 in the first armed reconnaissance over No. 13 Squadron's old base at Ambon. January 1945 saw No. 13 Squadron carry out 57 sea patrols, while armed reconnaissance sorties were flown over Timoeka and the Aru and Kai Islands.

On 15 January Flying Officer AG Goudie and his crew in A59-70 carried out a low-level attack on shipping in Bima harbour, during which the starboard engine was struck by light anti-aircraft fire. Some 30 minutes later the aircraft filled with smoke and the starboard propellor was feathered. All loose equipment was jettisoned to lighten the load on the port engine. With

A Lockheed Ventura of No. 13 Squadron at Gove in late 1944. (AWM)

single engine procedures carried out the aircraft landed safely at Gove after four hours. The sorties flown by the unit's Venturas lasted anywhere from three to over nine hours.

Two weeks later on 27 January A59-56 crashed into the sea off Bremer Island during a gunnery exercise killing three of the crew: Flight Lieutenant E Calder, Warrant Officer Eric C Peacock and Flight Sergeant Lloyd Ames. The surviving crew members including the pilot, Flying Officer P Clarkson, were rescued by a No. 42 Squadron Catalina, however Clarkson died of his injuries the following day.

The same day saw Ventura A59-84 lost when it crashed into a hill in poor weather while on final approach to Batchelor. The crew was killed: Flight Lieutenant G Anderson; Flying Officers B Poole and C Watts; Pilot Officer Nerdan Chowns; Warrant Officer J Kay and Leading Aircraftman J Pugh. Nerdan "Don" Chowns' logbook entry for the flight was completed by the Adjusting Officer and reads:

26.1.45 A59-84 F/O Anderson. Ops travel GOVE/BATCHELOR 2.30 [flight time].

The No. 13 Squadron commanding officer wrote to Chowns' brother:

> You realise that Don is with us no longer because the job must be done ... and we must go on doing it until it is over ... Don ... has helped up hasten this conclusion of a weary time for all of us.

In late January three aircraft were detached to Merauke. In February the squadron flew 27 shipping patrols along with 23 armed reconnaissance sorties, usually by four or five aircraft, over the islands to the north and east of Timor. One aircraft under Squadron Leader RS Dennis flew from Batchelor and ranged out over the Solor and Aru Islands and released leaflets over villages. Venturas carried out strikes from Truscott in Western Australia on Soemba and Soembawa, hitting a number of barges and *Sugar-Dogs*.

On 22 February Flight Lieutenant Jack Batho and his crew flew an armed reconnaissance over Batahai Strait and were intercepted by a Ki-43 Oscar, possibly of the 21st *Sentai*. No damage was recorded though the bombs were jettisoned over the strait, before the Ventura returned safely to Gove. Flying hours for the month totalled 515 hours while 780 tons of enemy shipping was destroyed and another 740 tons damaged.

Operations decreased significantly during March 1945 with only six convoy patrols flown, while strikes were carried out against targets in the Soembawa and Raki Island area. On 4 March Ray Kennedy-Dwyer and his crew in A59-65 were intercepted by two Ki-43 Oscars, again possibly of the 21st *Sentai*, during an armed reconnaissance of the Bakit Island-Soembawa area. Four barges, one a *Sugar-Dog* and three other vessels, were strafed with one destroyed. No damage resulted from the intercept and the aircraft returned to base safely. During March the squadron flew 476 hours, destroying 315 tons of enemy shipping and damaging a further 1,945 tons.

During March a signal was received from RAAF headquarters indicating that a squadron move was imminent and the commanding officer, Wing Commander Bill Keenan, was summoned to a conference at No. 79 Wing headquarters at Batchelor. As a result, virtually all operational activity ceased from 1 April as the unit prepared for the move to Labuan off the northwest coast of Borneo opposite Brunei Bay. The last No. 13 Squadron personnel left Gove on 6 June when the vessel *William H Seward* departed for Darwin to pick up the personnel and equipment of No. 79 Wing.

In the 7 August 1945 edition of *Wings* magazine a correspondent wrote of the role of No. 13 Squadron and its Venturas from the time of their arrival at Gove:

> … operating from Batchelor, Truscott and Merauke … patrolling long stretches of the Arafura Sea, from Cape York to … WA, [and] from Cape York to the New Guinea coast. Generally its work has been unspectacular … but the Ventura boys have [carried out] highly successful strikes on enemy ships, barges and Japanese positions on … Aru … Kai, Tanimbar and the Flores in the first few months of 1945 … Some of their round-up missions have ranged over 1,000 miles carrying 1,500 lbs of bombs on long trips and up to 5,000 lbs … on shorter strikes … now that the war has moved on, there are few targets left for the Venturas around [the] NWA. But more will certainly be heard of them further north – and soon.

One member of No. 13 Squadron who was to become famous following the war was future Prime Minister of Australia Gough Whitlam. Having joined the RAAF in 1940, he trained as a navigator and was posted to No. 13 Squadron. He flew many operations on Venturas. Whitlam served as a member of Parliament for several decades and became Prime Minister from 1972 to 1975.

A No. 13 Squadron crew prepares for an armed reconnaissance mission from Gove in mid-1945, shortly before the unit departed for Labuan. (AWM)

CHAPTER 12

NO. 2 SQUADRON OPERATIONS AND THE RAAF'S HEAVIES TAKE OVER

Two of the No. 79 Wing units, Nos. 13 and 18 Squadrons, had departed the NWA by mid-1945. They would be joined by No. 2 Squadron which in the meantime had continued operations from Hughes. It will be recalled from Chapter 10 that by mid-1944 the unit had almost completely replaced its Beauforts with B-25 Mitchells, nicknamed "Roger" by squadron operations staff.

Even while flying combined operations with No. 18 Squadron, the Mitchells of No. 2 Squadron also carried out independent anti-shipping sweeps and strikes on enemy targets as part of a wider campaign to assault of northern Dutch New Guinea, including Noemfoor Island. Squadrons from the NWA were to support the campaign with harassing strikes on Ceram and Timor. On 27 June 1944 nine Mitchells of No. 2 Squadron carried out a strike on Lautem West airfield. Each aircraft dropped seven 500-pound bombs from 10,000 feet and two days later a pair of Mitchells bombed Doka Barat.

In a commentary of a typical operation, the navigator of Flying Officer Bob Avery's Mitchell, A47-9, Flight Sergeant Brian Hawthorne recalled his aircraft being:

> … Number Three, and took off last. The Mitchell had 4 five-hundred-pound bombs … The crossing over water was quite uneventful … [and] the other two planes were in loose formation beside us. I could see the navigators sitting in the nose, the pilots at their controls, the turret gunners swinging their guns … and I could make faces at the tail gunner of the next plane. So far, so good.

With a brief crackling of the VHF intercom Hawthorne recalled the tension and excitement and exhilaration of an attack:

> … we were diving gently, testing our guns. I estimated another ten minutes before our arrival over Enoe Island [and] I checked the bombing gear and made what settings I could … then [we were] over the mainland … watching for the target ahead. Yes! The leader saw the clearing over to port and wheeled round towards it. Almost before I knew it we were over the strip … we wheeled around in a broad circuit to the left. I opened the bomb doors as I saw the leader's opening [and] straightened up on the run in … this was the vital 20 seconds in the whole 6-hour job [but] I wasn't thinking of this, nor did I notice the trace[r] from the machine guns leaping up at us from the opposite side of the strip … We were concentrating on formating on the leader … I saw the first bomb fall … and I toggled my switch, remembering … to space the four releases over about 3 seconds. "Bombs gone!" I called … I closed the bomb doors … [and] Les [Pilot Officer Les Smith], from … the tail turret, yelled "*Bee-yoo-tiful*!" … They had exploded on and near the strip. By now we were swinging round beside the Barat River. The planes ahead were diving at spots along the bank strafing. Then the first plane went in along the strip … We went back and strafed the strip again … every now and then a devastating stream of red trace[r] would be seen crashing into the trees, smoking and ricocheting, and behind that … a B-25, trailing twin streams of smoke and spent shells. No wonder the Nips were conspicuous by their absence.

During July 1944 combined operations with No. 18 Squadron, No. 31 Squadron Beaufighters and No. 24 Squadron Liberators were carried out against an increasing number of enemy vessels around Flores and Timor. On 19 July, No. 2 Squadron's incoming commanding officer, Wing Commander Dave Campbell, led six aircraft against a concentration of barges near Dili. Enemy anti-aircraft fire killed Warrant Officer Ian McCallum, the turret gunner in A47-15 and wounded the navigator and a waist gunner. However, all the Mitchells returned to base safely.

That evening another six Mitchells carried out an anti-shipping strike north of Dili. This was followed by a mast height attack on shipping in Dili harbour, during which a 500-ton vessel was bombed and sunk by Flight Sergeant Peter Hocking in A47-16. All aircraft returned to Hughes despite damage to two aircraft and a gunner wounded.

Flight Sergeant Joe Gleeson had joined No. 2 Squadron on 31 May 1944, with his first mission the 27 June strike on Lautem West strip. On the evening strike of 19 July he was the co-pilot to Flight Sergeant Lew Dinsdale on the mission, describing it succinctly as "Shipping Strike – Dilli." During July he flew a seaward search along the Heron route then the Dili mission, a seaward search along the Gull route on 21 July and a strike on Langgoer strip on 26 July. A night attack on Maumere on 31 July, rounded off the 29 hours and 10 minutes flying for the month. It was written up as:

> Strike – Maumere town & jetty 4 x 500 MC 12000' 8000 leaflets. Target afire.

During August Gleeson flew thirteen missions for the month including a strike from Truscott against an enemy camp five miles west of the Mina River bridge in Timor, a strafing exercise and a fighter cooperation flight with Spitfires. Then came three strikes on Langgoer, an anti-shipping sweep over the Leti-Romana-Wetar-Aloe Island area during which a 300-ton vessel was destroyed and his aircraft A47-1 holed by enemy fire. A formation anti-shipping sweep was carried out over the Banda Islands and another over the Jandena and Kai-Molo Islands area, along with practice attacks on a Fairmile launch for a total of 55 hours flying for the month.

August had also seen the first of the No. 2 Squadron Mitchells lost when A47-13 crashed during a practice bombing sortie over the Adelaide River range on 6 August. The aircraft was one of four engaged in medium level bombing practice when it experienced trouble releasing its bombs. The pilot advised the formation he was going the salvo the load – to release the bombs all together, as opposed to one by one – and as the aircraft neared the target the bomb doors opened and the bombs fell away but exploded 100 feet below the aircraft. The port engine and bomb bay caught fire and the aircraft went into a gentle dive while the pilot lowered the undercarriage and attempted a forced landing. The aircraft hit trees and exploded. While the pilots, Flying Officer S Davies and Flying Officer AK Buckland survived, the remaining crew and a passenger were killed. These were Pilot Officer DG Lane who later died in hospital; Warrant Officers JSM Campbell and AK Griesbach; Sergeant FH Conaghan and Flying Officer KJ Hadley (of No. 549 Squadron, RAF).

September saw Gleeson fly strikes on Saumlaki and Larat, and a search for missing Beaufighters A19-192 and A19-208 in the east Alligator area after they had disappeared following the completion of an escort operation for a Catalina over the Arafura Sea. Both had crossed the coast east of Darwin at nightfall and despite searches nothing further was found.

September also saw No. 2 Squadron lose two Mitchells. On 2 September A47-12 ditched in shallow water off Perron Island in Fog Bay when it ran short of fuel following a night attack on Toel in a combined operation with No. 18 Squadron. One of the Dutch Mitchells was shot down by a night fighter, while Flight Lieutenant Tige Carter's aircraft was hit in the wing by anti-aircraft fire, causing a fuel leak. With his instruments also gone Carter became lost and because of excessive fuel loss he considered he wouldn't make it to Hughes. However, Carter did make it to Australia and Fog Bay, where he elected to land on the beach opposite Perron Island.

Prior to dawn Flight Lieutenant Joe Simpson, the A Flight commander took off to search for the missing aircraft, and as he approached the search area at 400 feet he noticed a light. Turning in to investigate he was intent on the light rather than his altimeter, and in straightening out of the turn the aircraft crashed into the sea and broke in half. Conditions at the time were considered treacherous, with a full moon, a haze and a glassy ocean surface. An accompanying aircraft flew a search pattern while a vessel, the *George Post* took on survivors. Chaplain NC Easton and Warrant Officer CSJ King were killed in the crash.

The Mitchells also provided escort for a strike on Lingat village on Selaru Island by the three RAF Spitfire squadrons, Nos. 54, 548 and 549, remaining in the NWA. Flying Officer Les Ekert in A47-21 went in ahead of the fighters and dropped incendiaries before the Spitfires strafed the area. While enemy activity was fading in the latter months of 1944, armed reconnaissance missions, shipping sweeps and general harassing missions were carried out. On 22 September four Mitchells were on a shipping sweep along the north coast of Timor when A47-3 crashed into the sea killing Flying Officer Allan Slater and his crew – they had hit wires strung across the headlands of Manatuto harbour. Dying in the crash were Slater, along with Flying Officers MS Millett, JF Dagget and BA Wisniewski; Flight Sergeant KR Philipson and Sergeant DF Harberger.

On 26 September Wing Commander Dave Campbell led eight aircraft from Truscott for a sunset strike on shipping in Maumere harbour. However, no vessels were sighted and instead the port installations were bombed. During the return trip a *Sugar Baker* was spotted along the north coast of Flores and over the following days attacks were made from Truscott. The vessel managed to hide under Japanese defences in Wodong Bay; however, it was successfully attacked during October.

October, November and December 1944 saw No. 2 Squadron continue shipping strikes around Timor and the Wetar and Kai Islands, along with the usual seaward searches and searchlight and fighter cooperation flights. On 4 November Wing Commander Campbell led three aircraft in an attack on anti-aircraft positions at Goerita Bay in Dutch New Guinea. Flying Officer Jack Selway's A47-8 was hit by groundfire as it strafed barges and crashed into the sea killing all on board. Lost were Selway; Flying Officer AE Pott; Pilot Officer HB Worman; Warrant Officers JF Stormon and AE Hawkins; and Flight Sergeant RC Palfreyman.

Two days later four No. 2 Squadron Mitchells accompanied twelve No. 18 Squadron aircraft in an attack on Waingapoe harbour, after the Dutch reported seeing a 1,000-ton vessel leaving the wharf. The No. 18 Squadron aircraft attacked the enemy defences while No. 2 Squadron flew at low level and straddled a vessel which was estimated at 300 tons in size. The tail gunner in Flight Lieutenant Tige Carter's A47-17, Sergeant Alf Batten, recalled the run in to the target:

> We had to go in single file … we flew up the valley, at zero feet, and you could look up at the fields. Our number 4 tucked himself into our starboard side … and when we did get through to the other side, he stayed tucked in while we did the raid, down onto the deck to strafe and skip bomb the shipping. He was so low … and that close to us, it made it very difficult in the tail [for] shooting … in case the empty rounds flew out and hit his aircraft, or … I shot him down.

No. 2 Squadron B-25 Mitchells lined up along the runway at Hughes in 1945. The Mitchells were busy flying anti-shipping sweeps in the NEI during 1944-45. (AWM)

During November No. 2 Squadron continued to obtain excellent results in its anti-shipping operations in the Timor-Flores area, accounting for 32 vessels, including four small freighters and forcing the Japanese to use smaller native craft. A combination of the Mitchell harassing raids and Catalina minelaying operations meant that Japanese shipping was severely handicapped in getting supplies to its outlying NEI bases.

While November had been relatively quiet for Joe Gleeson, December was very busy. On 3 December he flew a shipping sweep from Truscott to bomb and strafe Cape Chater, followed three days later with a shipping sweep. On the 7 December a shipping sweep over the north coast of Flores Island was carried out, during which a lugger was strafed in Konger Bay and a *Sugar Dog* attacked in Maumere harbour in the face of heavy anti-aircraft fire. The following a day a further shipping sweep was carried out in heavy weather over Koepang and Dili. On 17 December a shipping sweep over the north coast of Soemba Island was carried out from Truscott, during which a *Sugar Dog* was destroyed at Waingapoe. Strafing runs on Sawoe island resulted in A47-22 being holed by groundfire. The following day Gleeson flew as co-pilot to Flying Officer Campbell on a shipping sweep over the Roti and Soemba Islands during which another *Sugar Dog* was destroyed at Waingapoe.

On 5 December A47-11 was leading a flight of four Mitchells on a shipping sweep around Lagar Island on Timor's north coast, when the aircraft, named *Petunia*, was hit by anti-aircraft fire while attacking a Japanese barge. The fuel feed system to the starboard engine was damaged resulting in fuel escaping and the engine was shut down to prevent fire. The failure of the port generator prevented fuel transfer and the port engine failed as the aircraft was over Bathurst Island, north of Darwin. The pilot, Flight Lieutenant J "Paddy" Norris, opted to force land the aircraft, putting it down on a clay pan. After skidding for 400 yards the aircraft came to rest in a tidal mangrove swamp.

On 20 December Gleeson was involved in a search for Mitchell A47-33 which had departed Hughes on a shipping reconnaissance of an area which took in Jandena island in the Tanimbars. Despite No. 105 Fighter Control Unit reporting the aircraft having been detected about 40 miles from Cape Hotham, no further news was heard. It was later discovered that the aircraft had been shot down 500 metres south of Saumlaki. There were no survivors from Flying Officer WFE "Elmo" Thompson's crew, which comprised Flying Officer LT Forsyth; Warrant Officers JES Thompson and FH Matthews; and Flight Sergeants JA Rolfe and TH Rowlands.

On 26 December Gleeson was flying as number four in A47-32 on a shipping sweep. Mitchell A47-9 was number three in the four aircraft flight when it crashed on take-off at Hughes. The navigator Brian Hawthorne recalled:

> Bob Avery opened the throttles and the plane surged forward. It seemed to wander from its straight course … and Bob had to kick the rudders violently to correct this … But passing the duty pilot's tower everything was OK … As we approached the end of the strip, Bob looked at Peter [Lee] who grasped the undercarriage lever ready to pull the wheels up. But when Bob eased the stick back, the plane came unstuck for a moment or two, but the wheels touched down again … At last lifted her off … and Pete moved the undercarriage to the "Up" position. Suddenly I saw Bob pull the throttles closed … and I felt the aircraft beginning to sink [when] we were only a few yards from the end of the strip and a solid wall of trees a few hundred yards ahead.
>
> We were only 10 feet or so above the ground … [and] a second later I felt the plane tearing through the tops of a few light saplings and bushes … and slithered and scaped and bumped through a blur of tall grass, bushes, stumps and light scrub. The left-hand side of the cabin opened up like a sardine can … [and] the plane came to a halt with a lurch and the nose dropped. I heard Bob say "Let's get out before she catches fire" I jumped to the ground … and saw that the plane looked fairly intact but a small red flame was licking about the nacelle of the port motor. I remember a strange silence, broken only by a faint sighing and hissing noise from the engines, and the crashing of the crew through the undergrowth. Our first thought was for the bombs, and we ran into the bush … I looked back, and saw an increasing spiral of black smoke.

A minute or so later the bombs exploded but much to the relief of all, the crew escaped unharmed.

Joe Gleeson was in A47-32 and as he flew over the scene the aircraft below blew up. He felt the thump of the shock wave as the remaining aircraft flew on to attack a *Sugar Charlie* in the Banda Sea. After strafing and bombing the vessel – during which A47-32 was holed by a ricochet – they landed back at Darwin as Hughes airfield remained closed following the crash of A47-9. As the aircraft returned they were advised by the leader, Flight Lieutenant ELE "Les" Ekert in A47-2 *Stormbird*, to land at Darwin, however he continued on to Hughes. With the weather rapidly deteriorating and with Ekert inbound, no warning message could be sent and a landing was attempted, however the aircraft dropped a wing, levelled out and hit the runway hard, shearing off the undercarriage. The crew managed to escape with cuts and bruises while the remaining aircraft landed at Darwin.

In early December 1944 the "bush telegraph" was working overtime with rumours that No. 2 Squadron was to move to a new destination. However, it was not until 11 December that Circular No. 232 announced that No. 79 Wing headquarters along with Nos. 2 and 18 Squadrons were to move to Jacquinot Bay in New Britain. No. 31 Squadron had been advised of a move in November and the movement of personnel began at the end of the month, followed by the Beaufighters on 1 December.

A gunner of a No. 2 Squadron B-25 in the tail turret position at Hughes in July 1945. He is protected by a plate of armour. (AWM)

A No. 2 Squadron crew discusses their mission beside their uncamouflaged aircraft after returning to Hughes in July 1945. (AWM)

While the tempo at No. 2 Squadron lessened with the news of the impending move, missions continued, including escorting the Spitfires of Nos. 452 and 457 Squadrons to Morotai via Merauke, shipping sweeps, army cooperation flights and bombing and strafing practice over local air weapons ranges. Joe Gleeson flew as co-pilot to Flight Lieutenant Ekert and Flying Officer Campbell while also flying as pilot in travel flights during February 1945. He flew shipping sweeps from Truscott on 4, 7 and 8 of February, the latter over Roti Island, the north coast of Timor, Lautem and Konger Island.

On 22 February a shipping sweep in A47-25 took him from Truscott to Roti Island, Sawoe, Soemba, Waingapoe and Ende where a barge was set afire and another damaged in the face of light shore-based anti-aircraft fire. From Ende they flew to Cape Goemah and back to Truscott. Completing his tour, Joe Gleeson had flown 371 hours and 10 minutes, with almost 31 hours of these at night. He recalled that on one anti-shipping mission:

> We had to circle the scene because the plane doing the bombing turned up too soon and rendered our role of giving cover to him dangerous. Of his four bombs, one had come off the bombing rack and fell out as soon as the bomb bay doors opened over the land. The remaining three were let go as a stick [and] the last one … [was] a direct hit.

On 8 March 1945 Flight Lieutenant Neil Sharpe led four Mitchells on a shipping sweep to Timor and an attack on bridges at Ende. The four split into two flights with Sharpe in A47-14 and Flying Officer Ted Westbury in A47-15 bombing a bridge at Nango Roro. Warrant Officer Bill White, the navigator, recalled:

> We approached through a misty shower of rain with F/L Sharpe the lead plane … I released the bombs at low level. As we passed over the bridge … my bombs fell alongside and destroyed the market gardens. F/O Westbury … was more fortunate as they blew it sky high.

The Mitchells of No. 2 Squadron were also involved in the attack on the Japanese cruiser *Isuzu* on 6 April when ten aircraft joined with ten of No. 18 Squadron, along with nine Liberators of No. 82 Wing. Unfortunately, the Liberators arrived twenty minutes late, and with the Mitchells at the limit of their range they attacked. The commanding officer of No. 2 Squadron, Wing Commander TS Ingledew, led four aircraft in from the starboard quarter at 10,000 feet, while Squadron Leader David Hannah lead his three in from the port beam at 11,000 feet. The last three aircraft under Squadron Leader John McMillan attacked from the port quarter at 10,000 feet. Sharpe's navigator, Pilot Officer WM "Bill" White, recalled:

> Our aircraft were in flights of three which attacked from different directions. The first flight made a hit on the stern [of *Isuzu*] after we had been attacked by 4 Oscar fighters. My bombs, unfortunately hung up.

Attacked by Ki-43 Oscars, the Mitchells came through unscathed; however, two Liberators were lost.[1]

The attack on *Isuzu* was essentially the last for the Mitchells of No. 2 Squadron, though a number of shipping sweeps and cooperation flights were flown for the remainder of the month. With news that preparation works on the airfield at Jacquinot Bay were delayed, both Nos. 2 and 18 Squadrons retained maintenance personnel and spares for 400 hours of operations to 21 April. Meanwhile advance parties departed, the first of which left on 25 February. By mid-

---

1 These losses are described in Chapter 13.

Outdoor servicing of a No. 24 Squadron Liberator at Manbullo, near Katherine, in July 1944. (AWM)

March 40 per cent of the ground staff and ground support equipment had left Hughes.

On 14 May 1945 the commanding officer of No. 79 Wing, Group Captain John Ryland issued a movement instruction:

> No. 79 Wing is now required to move to MOROTAI for subsequent employment in the BORNEO area. The move to JACQUINOT BAY, now in progress, is cancelled.

The main party of No. 2 Squadron departed Darwin for Port Moresby and Biak on 12 June and arrived at Morotai two weeks later.

With the departure of No. 79 Wing only the Liberator Squadrons of No. 82 Wing and the Catalinas of No. 76 Wing and No. 112 Air Sea Rescue Flight remained in the Darwin area. The Spitfires of Nos. 54, 548 and 549 Squadrons, RAF, were also there, basically waiting for something to happen following the cessation of enemy activity. The last enemy reconnaissance flight over Darwin occurred twelve months earlier in June 1944.

Meanwhile, No. 24 Squadron had moved into Fenton on 1 September 1944 and had flown a number of missions with the 380th BG, although these early operations were mainly seaward searches. But these were busy enough. As an example, over the four months to year's end Dick Overheu flew:

- armed reconnaissance and strike missions to Cape Chater, Menado, Laha, the North coast of Timor, Manatuto, Ambon, Macassar, Koepang, Pare Pare, Ambesia, the Celebes and Soemba
- a reconnaissance of the Bali-Lombok-Soembawa area
- a strike on the Maniang Island nickel mines
- a strike on Boro Boro
- a shipping sweep over southeast Borneo during which a convoy was attacked, with Squadron Leader McCombe sinking one vessel and Overheu damaging a 1,500-ton vessel and a barge with his six 500-pound bombs.

Flight Sergeant Lindsay McDonald, Overheu's flight engineer, reflected in his logbook entries in more detail, describing the 10 September mission to Laha airfield:

> 10.9.44 … 24 ship formation STRIKE, 15,200 ft. Laha A/drome. Bombs landed on dispersal bays & runway starting large fires, No interception – heavy Ack-Ack.

On 21 October he recorded an eighteen aircraft mission from Truscott to Pare Pare, during which:

> Bombs landed in shipping & wharf area. Three S. S. [single seat] fighters sighted going – away.

On 22 November McDonald wrote up the strike on Maniang as:

> STRIKE 10,000 ft. Maniang nickel mines. Bombs on target area & wharf starting fires etc. Heavy Ack Ack from Pomelaa on return track. Straffed [sic] two mast lugger.

While Dick Overheu and his crew were engaged in missions over enemy territory, Flight Lieutenant Roger Court was posted into No. 24 Squadron following conversion to B-24s at Nadzab in early December 1944. He was thrown in at the deep end. On 10 December he flew A72-77:

> … with a full crew, 31,000 gallons of fuel and 9 x 500 lb. bombs … to Manuto … to bomb Japanese positions. Flight time was 13 hours.

Three days later Court flew A72-67 to bomb Japanese positions at "Atapoepoe" and then shipping sweeps over:

> … the three plotted areas that covered the Band, Flores and Java Seas, they each had a letter of the alphabet … G. H. and I. They extended from Timor through to Borneo … covering a wide area … each one was 50 miles wide, so that gave the observer an area 25 Miles either side of the track to cover.[2]

On 12 January 1945 during a search to destroy any enemy shipping over area "G" (the Flores and Java Seas), Court and his crew sighted a heavily camouflaged *Sugar Dog* vessel. Flying at 1,000 feet, the bomb aimer set up the Norden bomb sight before the bombing run commenced. However, the vessel violently changed course as the bombing run commenced. Court instead descended to 100 feet and told the crew to strafe the vessel with their 0.50-inch calibre guns. The load of fuel drums and sullies were set alight, forcing the crew to jump overboard as Court turned for home. He later landed after a twelve-hour 30 minute flight – four hours of which were flown on instruments in cloud and two hours 30 minutes at night.

During late January 1945 twin-engine Mosquitos – the "wooden wonder" – of No. 87 (Photographic Reconnaissance) Squadron flew missions over Java selecting targets for the B-24s. On 26 January, No. 24 Squadron Liberators flew to Truscott for a strike against hydroelectric power houses in Java. For a few days prior several crews had been practising low level bombing techniques. The targets were to be the Siman and Mendalan power houses on Java.

On 28 January the Court crew took off in A72-57 as number three for the low-level formation attack. Each aircraft carried six 500-pound bombs and after battling poor weather they found the target blanketed by cloud. The lead bomb aimer recorded:

> Ceiling zero ft. at target … bombs jettisoned at sea.

All of the aircraft returned to Truscott after a thirteen-hour 30-minute flight.

Two B-24s had taken off earlier and had made it through, including that flown by the commanding officer of No. 82 Wing, Group Captain Kingwell. Although the power houses remained operational, the media was not deterred with the 15 May edition of *Wings* reporting:

---

2   Single letters had replaced the earlier code names for the search areas, so Gull and Heron became "G" and "H", etc.

A No. 24 Squadron B-24 returning to Fenton after attacking power stations in Java. (AWM)

The commanding officer of No. 82 Wing, Group Captain Kingwell, on return to Fenton after attacking power stations in Java in late January 1945. In a mission marred by low cloud, Kingwell was one of two pilots to carry out the attack. (AWM)

Climbing as they neared the target area, the two … picked up their targets. Twenty minutes later South East Java's electric light and power supply had been blacked out by … the RAAF.

On 5 February the crews of Wing Commander Russ E Bell, Squadron Leader AW Nichols, Flight Lieutenant Roger Court and Flight Lieutenant EV Ford made the trip to Java during which Court at 1,200 feet in *Cock O' The North*, recalled he could see:

> … billowing smoke from bombs dropped by the aircraft ahead … our bombs [went] right through the target and into the penstocks [with] a large fountain of water gushing out.

After evading a Japanese aircraft which dropped a phosphorous bomb over the formation, the Liberators returned safely to Truscott and then on to Fenton.

With the power houses still generating power, a final attempt at destroying them was carried out on 8 February. While the Bell and Ford crew hit the Siman powerhouse, Nichols and Court went after the Mendalan site. This time the destruction was complete with both targets put out of action. Russ Brooks in A72-84 recorded the action as:

> Truscott-Mendalan-Truscott. Bombing at 1200' - 6 x 500 lb bombs – Destroyed transformers

and workshop – intercepted by 2 Oscars – two phosphorous bombs dropped by Oscar – 3 … attacks made – no damage.

The aircraft all returned safely and without the fanfare claimed by the Kingwell mission – one which has been a contentious issue with No. 24 Squadron members for many years.

While the weather had caused the aborting of the first mission against the power houses it also became a factor in the seaward searches and shipping sweeps. On 3 February, Flight Lieutenant Arthur Cambridge encountered the vagaries of the cyclone season on return from a shipping strike on a 7,000-ton vessel by six Liberators. Each aircraft carried twelve 500-pound bombs and flew from Fenton to Waingapoe to Lintah Strait to Sangeang Island and then to Flores, although the ship was not sighted. Instead, they successfully bombed and strafed a number of other vessels, including one from which a boat was seen pulling away with approximately 40 personnel diving overboard.

On the return to Fenton in cyclonic weather, Cambridge in A72-88 missed the flare path and crashed through trees a mile west of the airfield. The impact ruptured the auxiliary power unit fuel tank and the aircraft caught fire, trapping Flight Lieutenant JR Parkinson and Flying Officer JM Pitt in the nose area. Neither had a chance of escaping and were killed while the remaining crew members incurred varying injuries.

Following its arrival at Fenton on 28 December 1944, No. 21 Squadron became operational on 11 January 1945, when the squadron's Liberators attacked targets at Laga and a radio station on Moena Island, while carrying out seaward searches and shipping sweeps. During the first two months of operations the unit flew more than a hundred missions against Japanese targets, including Koepang. On 6 April four of the unit's aircraft joined up with No. 24 Squadron in an attack on a Japanese convoy evacuating troops from Timor.

While the Japanese forces were depleted by the constant harassment of Allied aircraft, they were still capable of hitting back as a number of crews learned the hard way. While shipping strikes on vessels extracting troops from the island increased so too did the anti-aircraft defences. On 22 March 1945, Group Captain Kingwell and two crew members in A72-59 were injured when they were intercepted by what they identified as a Zeke and an Oscar during an attack on two *Sugar Dogs* at Sumbawa Island. Over 40 minutes, the B-24 was attacked with gunfire, while in a final act of desperation a length of chain was dropped, which crashed into the nose and turret, the port tailplane and vertical fin. The B-24 limped home and landed safely despite one undercarriage leg not locking.

The following day saw the loss of B-24L A72-80 *Old Nick* which crashed into Vansittart Bay shortly after take-off from Truscott on a shipping sweep. Unable to gain height, Squadron Leader Nathaniel "Fanny" Straus remained in contact with Truscott tower for 23 minutes before crashing. Flying Officer Russ Brooks was made the Adjusting Officer for Straus's personal belongings, recalling that it:

> … was a bloody tough job as everybody knew everyone and (I) had formed friendships with them.

Killed in the crash were Straus; Flight Lieutenant CD Parry-Okeden; Flying Officers RA Whiting and JW Hursthouse; Warrant Officers Boyd, WR Flanagan and HG Parker; Flight Sergeants RM Morris, AJ Rogers and JR Ryan; Sergeant AD Whitehead and a passenger,

Corporal DW Madden of No. 42 Squadron. Only the bodies of Straus, Parry-Okeden and Rogers were recovered.[3]

Throughout March and into April the Liberators maintained the shipping sweeps, along with a number of harassing raids. Sergeant Rod McDonald, a bomb aimer, flew shipping sweeps during the period February to April, along with attacks on Kalabahi, Kendari and Ambesia. He flew a nine-hour 40 minute strike on Kendari on 5 April, however they were forced to bomb the secondary target, Kairotoe strip. McDonald recorded:

> Bombed secondary tgt Kairotoe strip … 48 x 100 lb demos. All bombs in strip area – nil sightings – 2 bursts of A-A from Village near strip.

RAAF Liberator A72-61, identified as part of No. 21 Squadron because of the "MJ" fuselage code. No. 21 Squadron became operational at Fenton in January 1945. (Bob Livingstone)

A camouflaged Japanese Sugar Dog transport, as photographed from a No. 24 Squadron Liberator near Lombok. The vessel is ringed by splashes from machine gun fire. (AWM)

---

3   The story of A72-80 made the news decades later when the lost wreck was found by a local scuba diver, Jim Miles.

The crew of B-24L A72-80 Old Nick seen shortly before they were killed when their aircraft crashed into Vansittart Bay shortly after take-off from Truscott on 23 March 1945. The cause of the crash has never been determined. Squadron Leader Nathaniel "Fanny" Straus is the first on the left, standing. (AWM)

Boredom was a major problem for those serving in the isolated NWA during their free time. This RAAF mobile cinema unit at Gove was an example of official efforts to provide recreation for NWA personnel. (AWM)

CHAPTER 13

THE RAAF HEAVIES MOVE FORWARD

In early April 1945 an Allied submarine reported a Japanese convoy in the Flores Sea heading for Timor in an attempt to evacuate troops and equipment. The move was seen as an open challenge to Allied air strength in the NWA. Fighter cover for the convoy was to be provided by aircraft of the JAAF's 33rd and 54th *Sentai* from bases it had remaining around Sumatra along with the IJN's No. 902 *Ku* at Koepang.

At this time nineteen Mitchells of Nos. 2 and 18 Squadrons were busy attacking targets in the Tanimbar Islands and were unable to divert to the convoy. Instead, the commanding officer of the NWA, Air Commodore AM Charlesworth, ordered a strike for the following day when the convoy was expected to be departing from Koepang. All available aircraft from both Nos. 79 and 82 Wings were to make the attack.

In the meantime, the convoy was monitored by Mosquitos flying photographic runs at 21,000 feet during the daylight hours. Three Catalinas of No. 43 Squadron took over late in the day and shadowed the convoy that night. At 0100 on 6 April a Catalina reported that the convoy, including the 5,800-ton Natori Class cruiser, *Isuzu*, had left Koepang.

Early on 6 April ten Mitchells from each squadron along with nine Liberators (four from No. 21 Squadron and five from No. 24 Squadron) departed Truscott. Those from No. 21 Squadron were flown by Group Captain Peter Parker, Flight Lieutenant Hurst, Flight Lieutenant Rule and Squadron Leader White. The No. 24 Squadron contribution consisted of Wing Commander Russ Bell, Flight Lieutenant Roger Court, Flight Lieutenant Kirkwood and Squadron Leader Sid McDonald.

Each of the Liberators carried 3,100 gallons of fuel, extra ammunition and eight 500-pound bombs. The Mitchells arrived over the convoy first and made a number of attacks before having to turn back. This was not coordinated as intended because the Liberators then arrived twenty minutes late. Led by the commanding officer of No. 21 Squadron, Group Captain Peter Parker, the Liberators bombed from 21,000 feet but missed and encountered very accurate anti-aircraft

Liberator A72-81 in flames after being shot down by JAAF Oscars while attacking the Isuzu convoy on 6 April 1945. (Bob Livingstone)

fire and interception by Ki-43 Oscar fighters. One fighter closed in to within twenty feet of Roger Court's A72-106, while another attacked Flight Lieutenant Sid McDonald's A72-81, with the fighter's 12.7 mm machine guns starting a fire in the nose area.

McDonald ordered the crew to bale out. The aircraft dived vertically before appearing to pull out, only to stall in a climb and dive again. The machine then exploded as it headed towards the ships. The only survivor from A72-81 was Warrant Officer Keith Shilling. Those killed were Squadron Leader McDonald; Flying Officers PA Mouatt and AG Worley; Pilot Officer KA Brown; Flight Sergeants LK Walmsley, JA Thomas, RJ Banks, TE Bowen, and A Davis; and Sergeant WJ Wignall.

Parker then led the Liberators on a second run over the convoy, something Kingwell was adamant should never be done. He later told historian Alan Powell:

> You only make one pass at a target like that ... you never come back a second time ... and he did it because they missed. By this time the cruiser had got its altitude and its speed and the fighters were there and they lost an aircraft.

Roger Court's bomb aimer, Russ Brooks was more succinct:

> It was sheer bloody madness, you just don't do that!

The aircraft lost on the second run was Flight Lieutenant Eric Ford's A72-77. With one engine gone and the nose area on fire he ordered the crew to bale out of the stricken aircraft. Five crew members managed to bale out as Ford held the aircraft steady before the aircraft rolled on its back and exploded on impact with the water. Killed were Ford, along with Flight Lieutenants W Laing and Flight Lieutenant LD Crowther; Flying Officer RT Jordon; and Flight Sergeants L Raine and JM Waddell.

Roger Court recalled the attacks by the Japanese fighters as he commenced his bombing run:

> They sorted our formation out ... one of them closed in on us from slightly below the 11 o'clock position ... his tracer ... racing for the nose of our aircraft. I could see that if he held his present course he would pass between our port wing and the ... aircraft on our port side ...

With what seemed an inevitable collision, the Japanese banked and flew though the gap between the aircraft. With all his bombs gone, Court then:

> ... ordered the remaining aircraft to get down to sea level to try and sight any of the downed airmen. We saw a number of them floating with their Mae West inflated ... [the Liberators] also carried an eight man dinghy ... [and] I instructed them to ... throw these out to them, together with a smoke bomb ... making it easier for the air sea rescue Catalina to locate them ... We were now getting low on fuel and most of the aircraft had left the scene and were heading back to base ... the Air Sea Rescue Catalina was not sighted ... but it must have been close ... We landed at night [after] 12 hours and 30 minutes.

A Catalina, A24-54, captained by Flight Lieutenant CR "Ralph" Bulman had departed Darwin along with a No. 21 Squadron B-24 as escort under Flight Lieutenant Eldin Moore. Both arrived shortly after the Liberators had departed the scene. No sooner had the Catalina landed and its crew pulled aboard four of the survivors, it was strafed by an Oscar fighter, severing fuel lines and holing the fuselage. Burning fuel sprayed over Warrant Officer Keith Shilling's back before it was extinguished by a fellow survivor, Sergeant Sayer. The survivors and Catalina crew

RAAF ground crews prepare a variety of bombs for loading on a Liberator, giving an idea of the scope of the work to prepare for each mission. The smaller bombs in the foreground are probably incendiaries. (Bob Livingstone)

escaped the burning aircraft through the flames as Flight Lieutenant Eldin Moore flew over and dropped two dinghies and a supply cannister.

A second Catalina, A24-58, under Flight Lieutenant Robin Corrie was directed to the downed crew. After a 30-minute battle with heavy seas it was able to land. The subsequent report stated:

> All survivors were picked up via the bow except Sergeant Jones and Flight Sergeant Faichnie of whom we had lost sight. Flight Lieutenant Bulman took the second pilot's seat and explained the position as briefly as possible ... and gave an estimate of the position of the other two men.

Eldin Moore in the circling Liberator was diving over the two men to indicate their position when an Irving twin engine night fighter was sighted. With the laden Catalina commencing its take-off run, Moore turned the Liberator towards the Irving and a 30-minute stand-off ensued during which:

> ... maximum protection was given by the ASR [Air Sea Rescue] Liberator (A72-72) covering our tail.

Corrie and his cargo headed for Darwin. A second Liberator, A72-74, under Flight Lieutenant Noel Byfield was also on the scene and searched until darkness before returning to Truscott. No trace of Faichnie or Jones was ever found.

The same day, 6 April 1945, saw a boost to No. 82 Wing when its third squadron, No. 23, became operational. The squadron had moved from Leyburn in Queensland to Long airfield east of Fenton on 10 March. However, it was a further three weeks before all of its aircraft had arrived. On 7 April the squadron commenced operations with shipping sweeps. Sergeant Dave

Sieber flew in the Squadron Leader John "Mickey" Finlayson crew in A72-91 on an armed reconnaissance over the Flores Sea area. Armed with eight 500-pound bombs, no sightings were made during the eleven-hour 50 minute mission. It was a reflection of what was happening across the Pacific theatres as the Japanese command concentrated on its strategy to save the home islands. Outclassed, outgunned and outnumbered, many Japanese pilots remaining in outlying areas such as the NEI deliberately avoided combat.

Following the *Isuzu* mission, other targets attacked by the Liberators of No. 21 Squadron included troop areas at Tawo and fuel tanks in Tarakan, Borneo. No. 24 Squadron was confined to shipping sweeps and the occasional harassing raid for the remainder of the month and throughout May. On 28 April Roger Court flew in a nine aircraft strike on Bingkalapa airfield in the Celebes, with 85% of the seven 500-pound bombs each aircraft carried landing on the runway and adjacent areas. From 1 May a majority of No. 24 Squadron's aircraft, aircrews and ground personnel moved to Morotai while a detachment remained at Fenton.[1] From Morotai they were able to attack targets at Balikpapan, Labuan Island and enemy bases on Borneo along with undertaking intelligence gathering flights.

Moves by the other Liberator squadrons were also afoot. On 1 May 1945 No. 12 Squadron (another former Vengeance operator) moved to Darwin from Cecil Plains in Queensland after receiving its first two Liberators on 5 February. By the end of the month ten aircraft were on squadron strength. After working up the unit moved to the former 380th BG camp site on McMillans Road east of the RAAF base. From there it operated in conjunction with Nos. 21 and 24 Squadrons in attacks on enemy installations and shipping in the Timor, Banda and Arafura Seas, before No. 24 Squadron moved its remaining assets to Morotai on 6 June.

The first loss for No. 12 Squadron came in the early hours of 20 May when A72-160 crashed on take-off from Truscott. After becoming airborne the aircraft dropped, dug a wing into the runway and crashed. The load of depth charges detonated leaving the crew of Flying Officer Frank L Sismey no chance of escape. Killed were Sismey; Flying Officer WS Bell; Warrant Officers TN Rust and BL Cox; and Flight Sergeants L Duncanson, LM Bailey, INL Easton, TW Allan, DD Benson, JA Hollis and JRW Herps.

No. 23 Squadron, under Wing Commander RA "Arch" Dunne, had also moved. On 6 June the unit moved from Long airfield to the McMillans Road camp adjacent to No. 12 Squadron. From there they carried out strikes on Borneo using Morotai as a staging base. Sergeant Dave Sieber flew a harassing raid on the Boeloedoang and Limboeng strips on 12 June, and on 25 June a strike on Kendari was met with heavy anti-aircraft fire. The following month saw him fly on two strikes against Ambesia; a reconnaissance of the Flores area (during which he dropped ten demolition bombs and strafed a lugger and bombed and strafed two barges) along with an armed reconnaissance of the Kendari-Banda Sea area. None of the flights were intercepted by enemy aircraft.

On 10 June 1945, an opening air strike on Labuan in Borneo was carried out in support of the Australian 9th Division landing. Of the eight squadrons involved in the strikes, two were RAAF, and of those seven aircraft were from No. 23 Squadron. Each aircraft flew with an all-up weight of 68,000 pounds – a record for RAAF Liberators. On 17 June personnel of No. 23 Squadron

---

1   Mortai was an island in the Halmahera group in the northern NEI. Lying roughly midway between Dutch New Guinea and the Philippines. After it was recaptured by Allied forces in September 1944 it became an important base to support a war moving northwards.

departed Darwin for Morotai, where they arrived on 1 July. From there they played an important role in bombing Balikpapan, dropping some 119 tons of bombs over a six-day period from 19 June. Meanwhile some operations continued from a detachment remaining in Darwin.

By June 1945 the enemy's aircraft strength in the NEI was all but depleted. Headquarters RAAF Intelligence Command released *Intelligence Summary Issue No. 19* of 9 June 1945, which provided details of the aircraft available to the Japanese. By 6 June a total of only 64 aircraft were thought to have been available to cover the entirety of the NEI. Whether or not the figures were accurate it was a sure indication of the enemy's diminishing strength in the region:

HQ RAAF Intelligence Command. Intelligence Summary. Issue No. 19. 9 June 1945

Area	Fighter	Bomber	Fighter bomber	Floatplane	Reserves	Total 6 June	Total 30 May
Borneo	3	2		4	4	13	11
Celebes: Kendari-Macassar	7			3	2		
Bali-Java- Lombok	7	14	2	17	8	48	49
Flores-Timor					1	1	
Ambon-Ceram-Boeroe				2		2	2
	17	16	2	26	15	64	61

No. 21 Squadron continued operations from Fenton. On 1 July A72-61 was badly damaged by anti-aircraft fire over Balikpapan. At the time Roger Court recalled:

> … low level flights at 1,000 feet were being carried out in the Liberators over Balikpapan … [and] Australian and Dutch Army Intelligence Officers would be aboard to collect intelligence data.

It was during one of these flights that the commanding officer of No. 21 Squadron, Group Captain D McLean (who had taken over from Group Captain Parker on 24 April) was lost. McLean was captain of the aircraft and ordered the crew to bale out, however he and three crew members did not make it. Killed were McLean; Flight Lieutenant JA Roy – an Intelligence Officer; Warrant Officer HR Bardwell and Sergeant DL Martin. The remainder of the crew parachuted to safety and were rescued by a patrol boat and taken to the No. 82 Wing detachment at Morotai.

Squadron Leader Ivor Black took over as commanding officer while the entire squadron began its move to Morotai the following day, 2 July. A short time later, on 24 July, a detachment moved to Balikpapan. By August 1945 only No. 12 Squadron, and a detachment of No. 23 Squadron, remained at Darwin, along with the Catalinas of No. 76 Wing, which was by then confined to flying armed reconnaissance and shipping sweeps.

Sergeant JD "Jack" Fox, a gunner with No. 12 Squadron, flew in a six aircraft a strike on an enemy barracks at Badjo, dropping demolition, fragmentation and incendiary bombs totalling 6,000 pounds. On 15 August, the day the Japanese surrendered, he flew a return travel flight to Tennant Creek, 600 miles south of Darwin.

For Dave Sieber it was just another month. On 6 August he flew in A72-103 on an armed reconnaissance to the Flores area. Armed with ten 100-pound demolition bombs a barge was strafed and left burning fiercely. On 10 August he flew on a navigational exercise along the route Darwin-Wyndham-Truscott-Perron Island-Cape Fourcroy and back to Darwin, while on the 15 August (Victory over Japan Day) he flew on a practice bombing flight in A72-90.

While the Japanese had enjoyed victory after victory in the early stages of the war, the effectiveness of the Liberators in the NWA was one of continued harassment, strikes on installations, armed reconnaissance and shipping sweeps. This had denied the Japanese the freedom to move and build up or supply their depleted forces. In his work *Zero*, Masatake Okumiya wrote that:

> With the Liberators thundering constantly over our ships, airfields and staging areas, the situation was reversed. We were in the position of the traditional enemy … and handicapped by the same limitations we had always regarded as the opponent's weakness … we were compelled to discard plans long prepared and resort to the application of mass strength in battle.

It was a fitting summary as the war drew to a close.

An RAAF Liberator on the apron at RAAF Darwin, circa 1945, with many others in the background. The iconic water tower doubled as a control tower and survived the bombing of the base in 1942. Today it is preserved at the Darwin Aviation Museum. (NT Library via Bob Livingstone)

No. 23 Squadron Liberators overfly Darwin township, circa 1945. A line of "Black Cats" can be seen moored in the harbour, centre left. (Bob Livingstone)

CHAPTER 14

THE CATS FLY TO CHINA, AND THE WAR'S END

By mid-1944 the Catalinas had kept the Japanese defences busy as they continued their minelaying and harassing raids. But while they were bottling up the enemy in the harbours, they also lost men and machines in the process.

Catalina A24-78 was part of a three aircraft operation to mine Soerabaya harbour. Using Shecat in Yampi Sound as a forward base, on the night of 20 May 1944 they were met with intense anti-aircraft fire as they reached Soerabaya. They were able to release their mines, but Wing Commander HG "Harry" Havyatt later radioed that his aircraft had been holed in both fuel tanks, and he would use an escape point on the northeast coast of Bali. No further word was heard and despite post-war searches and the possibility of some crew members having been captured none were located. Missing, presumed killed were Havyatt; Flight Lieutenant FW Jeffrey; Flying Officers NB Gill, JAG Maslin and CR Whincup; Flight Sergeants L Dellitt and FH Russell; and Sergeants KHA Clarke, JD Cowley and HW Hall.

The effectiveness of the Catalinas over Soerabaya had seen an increase in the anti-aircraft defences of the harbour. Fifty-six heavy guns featured along with 27 medium and 68 light weapons. This was in addition to the weapons aboard the vessels in the harbour at any one time. The figures in a RAAF report on minelaying operations between 22 April 1943 and 21 July 1945 gave credit to the Japanese for dispersing:

> … merchant shipping in such a manner as to give maximum protection against minelaying aeroplanes.

Flying against such targets was a dangerous job for the Catalina crews, as Wing Commander Brett Hilder wrote. Hilder flew as second pilot to Flight Lieutenant Len Froud on a May 1944 minelaying operation to Soerabaya in A24-61. Six aircraft staged through Shecat before setting out with the:

> … setting sun [marking] the direction of our goal, Java. The last daylight is fading and … As darkness descends … We pass close to an island and in a few minutes we are off into the inky blackness … We pass other islands, rising to sufficient height to clear the trees and hills … and … as we get closer, hour by hour, to our target, we see pinpricks of light, which come from enemy rifles. To them we are a black shadow zooming close over their heads. We show no light, fire no gun, as our mission requires stealth. The night is especially chosen; no tropic moon will rise to … light up the clouds … to silhouette us … We bypass beautiful Bali … [and] time begins to drag … [then] With only ten minutes to go we suddenly arrive at the east coast of Java and turn north along it, close over trees, beaches and rivers … to us, speeding the last few miles to target, the massive land appears to be slumbering.

> At last we are coming up to our datum point, which has to be well identified – we can't afford a mistake. We turn over it on our first run, the navigator with his stopwatch counting the seconds aloud … Then the signal is given, I pull the release, and the blister reports, "Port mine gone," as the wing is relieved of its heavy load. Counting the seconds again, for the

second minedrop, [sic] when a clattering series of explosions and sparks comes from the port engine – "We've been hit!" – as the engine continues to backfire violently its power is lost and the wing droops. The engineer put the mixture into full rich, the pilot jettisons the starboard mine, and opens up the starboard engine to maintain height. By now we are very close to the water ... as we circle slowly around. The port engine at last begins to run smoothly at intervals. We increase power and climb away ... and begin to realise our danger, when, bang goes the starboard engine.

As we turn away to sea, other Catalinas are arriving over distant parts of the harbour; we can see searchlights and gun-flashes where the local committee of welcome is hard at work. We have recurrent visions of being captured if we are forced down. We are now flying east, climbing steadily, and the engines are both running well, but the port oil tank is leaking badly, and will only last another hour ... At last the oil runs out and the engine has to be stopped before it seizes up. The [air]screw is feathered to reduce drag. With one engine stopped, fuel consumption rising and the aircraft losing height, all excess equipment but for the dinghies was jettisoned. As we near home our speed slowly increases and we are fortunate in having only a slight head-wind. Finally, the shore of Australia comes into sight and we make good landfall with little fuel left. After over twenty hours flying it is a very good landing.

A post flight inspection revealed the cause of the problem was not enemy action, but a broken engine rocker arm.

On 1 June 1944, No. 42 Squadron formed at Darwin under the temporary command of Flight Lieutenant AM McMullin. Joining Nos. 20 and 43 Squadrons as part of No. 76 Wing, the main role of the new unit was minelaying, and the disruption of the enemy's shipping and sea lanes. In the meantime, No. 20 Squadron moved to Darwin's East Arm flying boat base.

An aerial photograph of Soerabaya naval base taken from 31,000 feet by a No.1 Photographic Reconnaissance Unit Mosquito on 25 June 1944. The availability of such detailed photos enabled the minelaying campaign to be planned with precision. (AWM)

Later that month No. 11 Squadron, which had operated alongside No. 20 Squadron from early in the Pacific war, and in operations from Darwin and Groote Eylandt, was advised that it was to move. In accordance with RAAF Command Operation Instruction No 68 of 1944, the move:

> … to RAAF Station Rathmines [in New South Wales], commencing on 28 June 1944 … be completed by 6 July 1944. The squadron will then come under the control of Headquarters Eastern Area.

Throughout the months to December 1944 the Catalina squadrons continued their minelaying missions to harbours in the NEI along with rescues and torpedo attacks. On 25 June four No. 43 Squadron aircraft took off to attack shipping in Bima Bay, Soembawa. One turned back with engine trouble, however the remaining Catalinas reached their target, led by Squadron Leader Lin Hurt, whose aircraft A24-45 was armed with torpedoes. Arriving at Bima Bay, Hurt sighted a 4,000–5,000-ton vessel and despite heavy anti-aircraft fire, successfully released a torpedo at a range of 1,000 yards. The results were not observed, as:

> … almost immediately, [A24-45] received hits from the intense light and medium ack-ack put up by the ship.

With Hurt wounded, Flying Officer Ben Titshall took over the controls and managed to straighten the aircraft enough to fire the second torpedo at a range of 700 yards. The torpedo was observed passing astern of the enemy vessel and Titshall turned the damaged Catalina for Darwin.

Over the period 26, 28 and 30 June No. 43 Squadron laid mines in Tioro Strait as part of its main function, while also carrying out special missions to Seroea Island and the rescue of a Spitfire pilot. Flying Officer Colin O'Loughlin had scrambled from Sattler airstrip on 12 June in a three aircraft flight to intercept a Ki-46 Dinah. During the attacks, in which the Dinah was shot down, O'Loughlin's aircraft suffered engine problems, losing oil and glycol coolant. Concerned the aircraft might catch fire O'Loughlin baled out and landed in the sea close to shore near Point Blaze. He was picked up by Catalina A24-40 later that day.

On 11 July No. 42 Squadron moved to Melville Bay in far east Arnhem Land, mooring its Catalinas off Drimmie Head. Wing Commander JP Costello took command of the unit nine days later. With all the moves of the Catalina units during this period, No. 43 Squadron bore the brunt of operations during the month.

On 20 July two No. 43 Squadron aircraft, one of them A24-45 flown by Flying Officer Don Temperley, took off from Darwin on a shipping search of Namlea harbour. Poor weather prevented Flying Officer Armand Etienne in A24-82 from locating the target, while Temperley and his crew failed to return. Nothing further was heard from the aircraft and it was not until December 1993 that two native timber cutters found wreckage on a mountain on Buru Island in Indonesia. Subsequent RAAF investigations confirmed it as A24-45. The remains of the crew were laid to rest at the Australian War Cemetery on Ambon on 7 October 1994: Temperley, Flying Officers LJ Blackwell and RM Harsley; Warrant Officer J Storer; Flight Sergeants HL Coggin and GIH Neate; together with Sergeants RJ Robinson, A Thompson and RSK Wheatland.

Following No. 42 Squadron's arrival in the NWA the unit's first operation was a shipping sweep by three Catalinas on 27 August. One aircraft was forced to return with engine problems. While no enemy vessels were sighted, the alternative target of Dili was bombed. Minelaying operations during September saw the Catalinas mining the Bankor, Lambeth, Tiworo,

Boetoeng and Wowoni Straits and in doing so sealing the southern and northern ends of the Celebes from the Japanese coastal vessels.

By September 1944 the Catalina minelaying missions had become so effective that RAAF command directed Nos. 20, 42 and 43 Squadrons to undertake the task as a priority. With each unit capable of flying 830 hours a month and with each mission lasting up to 24 hours, it was calculated that each squadron could carry out 100 sorties per month – in contrast to the 20 per month flown in the first six months of operations. It was also directed that No. 76 Wing headquarters then based at Cairns move to Darwin to take control of the three squadrons. By October the wing was established at Doctors Gully under the command of Wing Commander RE "Reg" Burrage.

By September 25 ships had been claimed as sunk or damaged by the minelaying activities of the Catalinas. No. 42 Squadron contributed with missions to the Bangka Straits, Boeton, Tiworo and Wowoni. On 24 September A24-94 was forced to land near Sermata Island with engine trouble whilst *en route* to minelaying Tiworo Strait. The crew was rescued the next day by Flight Lieutenant RT "Nobby" Clark in A24-91, following which A24-94 was strafed – by Clark's aircraft, to prevent its capture – before catching fire and sinking.

Mines were laid at Soerabaya, Liangkan Bay, Pare Pare, Balikpapan, Tarakan and Macassar during October. Four missions were flown against Macassar, with each being met by anti-aircraft fire. On 12 October, Flying Officer JM Kane's A24-96 was holed, and A24-102 flown by Flight Lieutenant Robert Kagi had most of its tailplane shot away by 25mm cannon fire from the shore batteries.

A further aircraft was lost two days later when A24-90 and A24-93 returned to Macassar. While A24-93 released its mines and met no opposition, its captain, Squadron Leader Ken Grant, noticed anti-aircraft gun activity which likely set his companion aircraft ablaze. Grant turned back to investigate, but nothing was sighted. A24-90 failed to return to Melville Bay and its crew were posted missing, presumed killed: Flight Lieutenant CA Williams; Flying Officers RLL Bodie and MG Sloman; Warrant Officers CS Billington and JR Cleworth; Sergeants JS Brown, AR Jones, GJ Ernst, DP Ryan and JI Vetter.

The Catalinas returned to Macassar at least twice during November, while Morotai, captured in September, was providing a stepping stone to the Philippines. Detachments of Catalinas from Nos. 20, 42 and 43 Squadrons were able to mine Balikpapan, Brunei Bay, Tarakan, Sandakan, Samaninda, Cape Selatan and the Balabac Strait via the seaplane tender USS *Tangier*, which had been positioned off Moratai. The 2,400-ton *Seeto Maru* and 3,000-ton *Kokko Maru* were sunk at Balikpapan while twelve ships were reported as being bottled up in Brunei Bay – all as a result of visits by the Catalina squadrons.

A No. 43 Squadron Catalina taxis in Darwin harbour in May 1945. (AWM)

Flight Sergeant Howard Davis flew with No. 43 Squadron from July 1944 to June 1945, succinctly recording a number of these missions as "Minelaying", "Minelaying in enemy waters Celebes", "Air Sea Rescue patrol", "Minelaying – Panaroekan", "Minelaying – Macassar" and "Minelaying – Laoet (Borneo)". While Davis' logbook entries provide sparse detail on the missions flown, *Wings* magazine provided a commentary on a minelaying mission in an article titled "Catalina Mine Shoot":

> …the navigator found the [datum] point. Down went the aircraft and the run into the harbour began. The few lights of the port seemed to rush toward [us]. The navigator was calculating … [and] the Catalina shuddered as one mine slipped into the water. "Ship dead ahead," called the wireless operator … the Jap vessel's machine guns went into action [and] pale pink tracers came up a few yards outside the port wing … already three or four searchlights were … probing for the aircraft … Trevor Arnold at one of the blister guns said … "That ship. We've still got another mine. Got to make another run."

> The Catalina circled the harbour again. More searchlights were sweeping across the sky … We raced along close to the surface … once more the craft shuddered as the mine went down. The task was finished, but the Catalina had to get out … The flying boat was still low down – to go higher meant being caught by the searchlights. Then the shore batteries would have some easy shooting. [We] turned and headed out to sea in a violent rush. Just too late the ground defences opened up. The bursts seemed about a hundred yard behind us … [Then] we were out …The flying boat gained altitude and I started to relax.

The expertise of the Catalina crew was soon to be tested in the largest single RAAF minelaying operation of the war – the laying of mines in Manila Bay. On 7 December 1944 Headquarters Eastern Area Operations Order No. 9 ordered six No. 11 Squadron aircraft to Darwin's East Arm for "courting" operations, as minelaying missions were named.

At East Arm they joined Nos. 20 and 43 Squadrons under the direct control of No. 76 Wing and mines were loaded under the wings of the flying boats. On 11 December twelve aircraft from Nos. 11 and 43 Squadrons departed for Woendi Island near Biak. The next day six aircraft of No. 20 Squadron and seven from No. 42 Squadron, including a spare, departed Darwin and Melville Bay for Woendi. In all 25 aircraft from the four squadrons took part in the mission.

Staging through Woendi the aircraft flew on to Jinamoc Island in San Sedro Bay, Leyte, the Philippines, an American base under development which, although having refuelling facilities:

> … proved somewhat unsatisfactory from several points of view … the squadrons … were tended by USS *Heron* … quite inadequate for the job. The Seventh fleet and USAAF were unable to provide … intelligence which it [was] hoped would be available.

Over the next two days No. 76 Wing officers attempted to obtain information on the target they were to risk their lives attacking. Unsuccessful, they:

> … took off with very little reliable information as to the defences of Manila or the amount and disposition of shipping in the harbour.

Despite their failings, the Americans assisted with airborne countermeasures and harassing raids on enemy aerodromes. The operation took place on 14 December, with the aircraft departing Jinamoc at dusk in two-minute intervals, maintaining an airspeed of 90 knots and all following the same route.

One aircraft each of Nos. 11 and 20 Squadrons failed to locate the datum points and jettisoned their mines, while a No. 11 Squadron aircraft failed to release one of its mines and returned to San Pedro Bay with it hung up. Other aircraft released their mines with little opposition, with some reports that the lights of Manila were still turned on. While the mission was successful, A24-64 flown by Flight Lieutenant Herbert C Roberts failed to return after missing a planned rendezvous over Cape Calavite and was presumed to have flown into a hill.

It was not until March 2019 that the RAAF investigated a crash site:

> … south-east of Cape Calavite on the north-west end of Mindoro Island, after they became aware of several artefacts at this location in 2014. These artefacts consisted of a small metal tube engraved with the aircraft manufacturer's logo, a brass crown identified by the RAAF Museum as part of an early RAAF officer's cap badge, and .303 ammunition. Although little remained of the aircraft, a number of small items of wreckage were found with metal detectors on this recent visit. Several items were subsequently identified as unique to the Catalina, which when combined with other evidence, confirmed the wreck site was the missing aircraft.

Killed in the crash of A24-64 were Roberts; Flight Lieutenants Frank W Silvester and James H Cox; Flying Officer Robert C Barbour and Raymond H Bradstreet; Flight Sergeant David J Albert; and Sergeants John C MacDonald, James R Robinson and Harold S Goodchild.

Meanwhile a further Catalina unit had formed at Darwin on 10 December, with the establishment of No. 112 Air Sea Rescue Flight under the command of Squadron Leader K Crisp. The first mission was flown on 27 December when Crisp borrowed a No. 20 Squadron Catalina. It was flown back from the Philippines following the Manila Bay mission, to the Semoes and Nila Islands to rescue an Allied meteorological party. The unit received its first dedicated aircraft, A24-56, on Boxing Day.

Soerabaya continued to be a prime target during January 1945 despite the monsoon creating difficulties for the Catalina crews. A24-204 was lost during one mission on 27 January during a minelaying mission in Laoet Strait. Other aircraft on the operation reported cyclonic weather over the Timor Sea. No trace of Flight Lieutenant Jim Seage's crew was found. Also missing was Pilot Officers P Laney and PM Brown; Warrant Officers VM Browness and HR Wickham; Flight Sergeant RL Warne; and Sergeants ASR Martin, RC Preston and JK Thomson.

Meanwhile on 14 January A24-96 was on its way to Soerabaya when it experienced engine failure. The aircraft captain, Flight Lieutenant Ron Harrigan, jettisoned his mines however height could

No. 42 Squadron Catalina A24-96 on 15 January 1945 after making a night landing near Soemba following an engine failure during a minelaying operation. The crew have taken to their inflatable dinghies and are moving across to Catalina A24-60 which had landed to rescue them. (AWM)

not be maintained, and a forced water landing was made south of Soemba, a large island to the east of Java. The engineers worked on the engine all night but were unable to fix it. Fortunately, Harrigan had radioed his position and A24-60 under Flight Lieutenant Brian Ortlepp arrived the next morning. With Harrigan's crew aboard, the overloaded aircraft failed to take off until all ammunition and excess equipment was dumped. Following take off A24-96 was strafed and sunk while a Liberator, A72-57, flown by Flight Lieutenant Roger Court circled the scene.

The Catalina squadrons were also operating detachments at Jinamoc from February 1945, when 67 successful mine drops were flown in the South China Sea following an advance party arranging accommodation and facilities for eight Catalinas, their crews and ground support personnel.

Missions were flown from the West Bay moorings at Truscott to Cape Seletan in southwest Borneo. These constituted supply drops to Allied intelligence parties as stand-by for B-24 Liberator operations. No. 76 Wing was requested to lay mines in ports throughout the South China Sea to dislocate Japanese convoys passing through from Takao to Singapore. Catalina A24-203 was lost when it failed to return from a night minelaying mission to the Pescadore Islands off Taiwan on 7 March, thought to have been as a result of poor weather. No trace of the aircraft or crew was located. Lost were Flying Officer K McCauley; Pilot Officers MO Merrett and RW Schulz; Warrant Officers WV Bates and JR Cleworth; Flight Sergeants AR Jones and WA Rowe; and Sergeants WD Scott and DK Storrie.

During March the No. 76 Wing flew 69 mining sorties, dropping a total of 169 mines. Sixty sorties were carried out from Jinamoc. Howard Davis flew a number of these with the Pilot Officer Milford Spaulding crew, recording:

> 11.3.45. 1730. A24-82 P/O Spaulding. Flight Engineer. Darwin-Jinamoc – Ops travel
>
> 13.3.45. 1000. A24-82 P/O Spaulding. Flight Engineer. Trip scrubbed – U/S. weather
>
> 13.3.45. 1145. A24-82 P/O Spaulding. Flight Engineer. Jinamoc – Lingayen Gulf.
>
> 13.3.45. 1830. A24-82 P/O Spaulding. Flight Engineer. Lingayen Gulf – Hong Kong – mine drop
>
> 16.2.45. 1000. A24-82 P/O Spaulding. Flight Engineer. Jinamoc – Lingayen Gulf
>
> 16.3.45. 1720. A24-82 P/O Spaulding. Flight Engineer. Lingayen Gulf – Amoy
>
> 19.3.45. 1000. A24-82 P/O Spaulding. Flight Engineer. Jinamoc – Lingayen Gulf
>
> 19.3.45. 1650. A24-82 P/O Spaulding. Flight Engineer. Lingayen Gulf – Amoy – Mine drop

Two days later the Spaulding crew flew back to Darwin. With the end of Davis's tour in mid-April he flew with the Spaulding crew to Bowen, Queensland, in A24-54 on 16 April. He had flown a total of 592 hours 25 minutes, with almost half of the time on night missions. The missions from Jinamoc and Lingayen Gulf had accounted for 96 hours 30 minutes of his recorded 100 hours 20 minutes flying time for March.

April 1945 saw the cruiser *Isuzu* appear off Timor, and on 6 April the Catalinas played a role in shadowing the Japanese convoy and rescuing survivors. Operations continued from Jinamoc against targets off China, Hong Kong, Amoy and Taiwan, contributing to 72 successful sorties and the release of 193 mines by the No. 76 Wing Catalina crews. Flying via Lingayen Gulf they were refuelled by the American seaplane tender USS *Orca* before setting out for their targets. These now included the Hainan Strait which, once closed to shipping, would force vessels to the south and east of Hainan Island where they were vulnerable to attack by both submarines and Philippine-based B-24 Liberators.

While operations far afield were carried out, so too were continued operations on Soerabaya and the Loet Islands among other targets using West Bay as a staging point. While the minelaying operations made the headlines the Catalinas made a dozen rescues during April 1945 – one by No. 20 Squadron, four by No. 43 squadron and seven by No. 112 ASRF.

During May 1945 minelaying operations were carried out at Amoy, Hong Kong, Wenchow, Swatow and Yulinkah Bay dropping 136 mines in 68 sorties. No. 20 Squadron flew nineteen of these while No. 42 Squadron flew 26 and No. 43 Squadron flew 23 sorties. The only opposition faced by the crew was rifle fire and on 10 May over Amoy:

A No. 42 Squadron Catalina on a slipway at an American base in Leyte, the Philippines, in June 1945. Using such forward bases the RAAF Catalinas were able to lay mines at ports on the Chinese Coast. (AWM)

> ...determined but inaccurate fire from an enemy night fighter.

In June No. 76 Wing carried out 108 sorties, and while minelaying remained a priority, harassing raids were carried out on enemy airfields in eastern Java and in the southern Celebes over 21-30 June. These necessitated 40 sorties in an effort to neutralise the airfields in support of landings on Balikpapan. Propaganda leaflets were also distributed over the wide area on the NEI, and in one case a Catalina sighted the Japanese hospital ship *Tachibana Maru* near the Kai Islands. An American destroyer stopped and boarded the vessel and finding guns and ammunition aboard, escorted it to Morotai. To assist with the effort placed on the wing, five No. 11 Squadron aircraft were detached to Darwin, while anti-submarine patrols, rescue duties, supply drops and special missions added to the workload.

The last minelaying operation was flown on 31 July when three No. 20 Squadron aircraft set out from Darwin's East Arm for the Banka Strait. After successfully dropping their mines the three returned safely, while supplies were delivered by Catalinas to Allied Intelligence Bureau groups in the NEI on 11 and 14 August.

On 14 August the following message was sent:

> Secret. Offensive operations against enemy cities land communications and other land targets except direct support for Allied ground forces in contact with the enemy will cease until further orders. Reconnaissance and photo missions anti-shipping strikes and fighter attacks against airborne enemy aeroplanes will continue. Forces charged with air defences will be especially alert.

The Japanese surrendered the following day, 15 August 1945, and it was declared Victory

After the end of the war on 15 August 1945 a key task was to identify POW camps and drop supplies to the (former) prisoners. This camp at Menado was photographed by a No. 24 Squadron Liberator. Note the "P.W" sign (upside down) visible in the centre of the camp. (AWM)

over Japan or Victory in the Pacific Day.[1] Despite the war being over there was still work to do. Aircraft from the NWA were engaged in a range of duties in coming weeks including the transport of POWs from the islands; supply dropping to POWs and Allied troops; searches for enemy shipping, land forces and POWs; support and transport services for occupation forces; and leaflet dropping.

Machines of war were now transformed into machines of peace. With the cessation of hostilities, the effectiveness of the Catalinas in their multi-role activities over the war years was assessed. While the missions were considered as mundane, exciting or just moments of sheer terror by their crews, they were considered an outstanding success in bottling up the Japanese at ports throughout the NEI and along the Chinese coast.

To the Japanese, however, they were a menace, and the success of the "Cats" flying out of Darwin was best expressed by Rear Admiral Akira Matzusaki, the Chief of Staff of the Second Expeditionary Force at Soerabaya from 1943 to 1945:

> … By the end of 1943 mines became of serious consequence … a radar warning net was established as well as [using] watchers. By tracking planes with radar an effort was made to establish the dropping point. Night fighters were employed but proved quite ineffective. Beginning in 1944 mining had a considerable effect on the exploitation of the vast resources of the [NEI]. Not only were ships and cargoes destroyed but convoys were delayed and unloading areas were jammed at Soerabaya and Balikpapan pending [mine] sweeping operations. The destruction of oil tankers and the delay in oil shipments were particularly serious … about 40 per cent of all vessels over 1,000 tons … were either sunk or damaged by mines. In many cases ships were salvaged only to be sunk a second time … After February 1945 no attempt was made to sail large ships and only smaller vessels, schooners and wooden barges were employed.

---

1 The Australian government, with the state governments following, gazetted a public holiday as "VP" Day, and most newspapers reported it as so. However, the governments of Britain, the United States and New Zealand preferred "VJ" Day, resulting in much confusion ever since.

CONCLUSION

It had been a long hard war for the bombers, but a necessary one. If the attacks and invasions of the Imperial Japanese Empire were to be stopped, and then turned around, attacks on their strength had to be made. Airpower was one of the only ways to start what would have to followed up by attacks from warships, and finally landings by troops to take the enemy's land away from him.

Northern Australia offered a platform to do this. For months, then years, the north of the continent served as a base for aircraft which became more and more sophisticated in their missions to deliver high explosives against the enemy. While the Allies were seeking to carry out this mission, of course, the Japanese were seeking to do it to them. As this book has pointed out, what has been outlined is only half the story. So apart from the occasional mention, the reader has been left to imagine that happening. The Japanese bomber assaults were vast. Over Australian territory alone they operated over 200 combined missions with nearly 1,900 individual aircraft flights.

What has also only occasionally been hinted at in this work is the vast infrastructure which underpinned the Allied bomber missions, a result of millions of man-hours of construction effort. The associated logistical support of everything from fuel and ammunition to rations and personnel, required thousands of workers in a continuous operation that never stopped, for war is a seven day a week business, 24 hours a day. Much of the war material used within Australia was provided by the efforts of the United States; that giant of industrial production which, when it turned its effort to war, would produce an inevitable result – victory for the Allies.

As the war closed in on what in military terms is known as "the centre of gravity" – Japan's sacred home islands – the bombing effort from Australia lessened. The effort was concentrating further north. The Battle of Leyte Gulf, the largest naval battle of World War II, finished off the IJN's ambitions, and in the background, unknown except to a chosen few, the atomic experiments and build process continued. Meanwhile, the airpower armadas drew closer to Japan in two ways: from island airbases and from aircraft carriers, and behind them gathered the amphibious assault.

Another aspect of airpower came to the fore: the relentless missions of the B-29s. These pressurised, heated, high-flying Boeing aircraft delivered a new type of weapon too: the firestorm raids. The largely wooden towns and cities of the Japanese were burnt, along with their engineering capacities, usually embedded in with the houses. In one raid alone, that of 10 March 1945, some historians say that up to 100,000 people died. But it took the two atomic blasts to bring the Japanese war machine to a halt. The mission of the bombers that went north from Australia had been finalised.

In closing, it is timely to reflect on the nature of the Allied bomber fleets. They had brought, in less than six years of war, aircraft capable of flying hundreds of miles and dropping tons of explosives onto the enemy's presence. Their technological advances would pave the way for an airline industry that changed the face of human travel forever. But at the same time, like so many weapons of war, the nature of this special machine came into being and was soon itself obsolete: the all-conquering fleets of B-29s would quickly give way to the jet age.

The time of the WWII-era bomber was a fascinating one, but it was quickly over.

APPENDIX 1

NO.18 NEI SQUADRON AND ITS AUSTRALIAN ROOTS

By Elmer Mesman

Prior to WWII present day Indonesia was a vast Dutch colonial possession: the Netherlands East Indies. When the Japanese forces began to push south after Pearl Harbor, they drove out many thousands of people whose entire lives had been bound up with Holland's far-flung possessions. Some of this ended disastrously: the attack on Broome in early March 1942 was the second-biggest air raid in terms of fatalities in Australia's history, killing many Dutch refugees who had just arrived on flights from Java. But the Dutch forces regrouped and came back. The story of No. 18 (NEI) Squadron and its operations from the Northern Territory was a unique one and bound up with these roots.

RAAF FAIRBAIRN, CANBERRA

After the Dutch colony of the Netherlands East Indies capitulated to the Japanese on 8 March 1942, thousands of Dutch and Indonesians working for the Dutch fled to Australia. They included many military personnel, formerly members of the KNIL (Koninklijk Nederlands Indie Leger – Royal Netherlands East Indies Army). Already on 4 April 1942, not even a month after the capitulation, No.18 (NEI) Squadron was formed at RAAF Fairbairn in Canberra.

Major General van Hoyen, Operating Commander NEI Forces in Australia and Air Chief Marshal Sir Charles Burnett, RAAF Chief of Air Staff, agreed to form a Dutch Squadron of eighteen B-25 Mitchell twin-engine bombers. This squadron would be under the operational control of the RAAF but its personnel and aircraft would be provided by the NEI authorities. In case of insufficient NEI staff the RAAF would provide further personnel to ensure the squadron was maintained at its proper strength. When formed in April 1942, No.18 Squadron consisted of 80 NEI staff in Canberra and 50 at the NEI Commission for Australia in Melbourne.

An agreed eighteen B-25 Mitchell bombers were originally assigned to No. 18 Squadron in mid-March 1942. But due to immediate need by the USAAF for use in New Guinea, it would take another month before the first five B-25s arrived at Fairbairn. The Dutch NEI base in Canberra primarily had a training role. NEI Rear Admiral Coster made it clear that as soon as No.18 Squadron was ready for action both tactically and operationally, it would be placed under the control of the USA supreme commander General Douglas MacArthur in the same way as all the other forces. When establishing and setting up the squadron's base in Canberra, it would remain under Dutch command until the NEI headquarters in Melbourne would declare it operationally fit to hand over to RAAF control.

Although the time No. 18 Squadron spent in Canberra was intended to be for training and for crews to get acquainted with their new bomber, it did not take long before the unit was deployed to good use in anti-submarine and patrol operations. Its first operational success was on 5 June 1942 when sinking a small Japanese submarine off the eastern coast of Australia.[1]

On 6 July 1942, No. 18 Squadron was declared a Netherlands unit and no longer an RAAF one although the Australian personnel assigned to keep it at its strength would be available as long

---

[1] Dutch records are mistaken here. There was no Japanese submarine lost around that time off the east coast – as the IJN records show – although there were plenty of attacks made on possible contacts.

as necessary. In fact, this would remain the case throughout the entire period on Australian soil during World War II.

Meanwhile eighteen new B-25 Mitchell bombers arrived from the US and brought No. 18 Squadron to its full operational strength. Modification to the new factory aircraft had to be made but with the lack of proper spare parts and equipment being universal to all squadrons, priority was given to units in combat rather than training units. The need for larger fuel tanks would later result in dangerous and even catastrophic situations.

The need to move away from the cold climate during the winter in Canberra became imperative. Most NEI personnel had come from warmer and more tropical climates and had a rough time getting used to local conditions, not to mention the primitive tent housing provided.

Finally in October 1942, No. 18 Squadron was declared ready for operational service. As moving a squadron that grew to 40 NEI officers, 210 NEI airmen, eight RAAF officers and 300 RAAF airmen would take quite some time and effort, Admiral Coster requested the unit be put under RAAF control until 1 December. This gave the time to set up base at the allocated aerodrome at McDonald, south of Darwin, to become the first wartime operational Dutch base in the Northern Territory.

MCDONALD FIELD

McDonald airstrip was constructed in the second half of 1942 as a basic runway with taxiways in two loops at one side for positioning aircraft. It was first known as Burkholder Field and was situated some 10 miles northwest of Pine Creek. It was not up to standard to accommodate No. 18 Squadron with its medium range B-25 bombers. The airstrip was made out of gravel and too short for fully loaded and heavily armed bombers. Formation landing was impossible as the airstrip was also too narrow and the shoulders of the airstrip too soft with the risk of getting bogged upon landing. The airstrip was basically the only part of the aerodrome, and a campsite to house its personnel was non-existent.

Everything from extending the strip and setting up a camp to include kitchens, waterholes, tents, toilet facilities, operation huts, etc. had to be erected by the Advance Party arriving on 11 December 1942. Upon arrival disappointment amongst the officers and airmen was all too obvious. Some quotes from the officers clearly show their feelings:

> "A bigger mess than here in McDonald is almost unthinkable."
>
> "McDonald Airbase was nothing. The crews had to make everything on their own. Initially it didn't even have a proper airstrip."
>
> "At start we didn't even have tents, no officers' mess and hardly any food. We went out hunting to shoot caribou's[2] to get meat for food. Morale was not as good as we hoped."

Needless to say No. 18 Squadron's first commanding officer Major Fiedeldij had a hard time getting his airbase and squadron up and running in the shortest possible time. Hence no operational sorties other than familiarisation flights over surrounding areas would be carried out in December 1942. Finally on 18 January 1943 No. 18 Squadron's move to McDonald was officially completed, more than a month after the first advance party arrived. It needs to be mentioned though that these harsh conditions and circumstances weren't isolated to No. 18

---

[2] It is unclear what is meant by this, but presumably a Dutch officer's perception of a buffalo, then present in the NT in large numbers before being shot out half a century later, might have been confused with a Canadian caribou.

Squadron alone. RAAF and US squadrons and units arriving to the Northern Territory around the same time between July 1942 and early 1943 experienced similar difficulties.

No.18 Squadron had a diverse role in activities being assigned to it when operating from the North-Western Area, as it was called during wartime operations:

a. Sea reconnaissance flights of between six and seven hours over occupied territory mainly the former NEI islands. These operations were primarily to scout for potential Japanese attacks and enemy shipping between the islands.

b. Day and night bombing of Japanese targets

c. Low level "mast height" attacks on Japanese shipping

d. Reconnaissance and photography of special targets

e. Special assignments like leaflet dropping with propaganda over enemy territory

f. Friendly shipping protection between Torres Strait and Melville Island all the way to Darwin

g. Dusk to dawn stand-by patrol

h. Target practice and training together with other (fighter) squadrons in the same area

The operational range of the Mitchell B-25 bomber would be at the centre of a bitter debate and negotiations between Fiedeldij; his NEI headquarters in Melbourne, and RAAF Headquarters NWA. RAAF command pushed the operational range to the maximum limit as indicated by the B-25's designer's specification, ignoring a maximum bombload, extra ammunition for protection and enough fuel for evasive action.

It took Fiedeldij until 27 April 1943 to convince both RAAF, NWA Command and the NEI headquarters to limit the operational range requirement from 1,700 to 1,200 statute miles. This came only after yet another loss of one of his aircraft due to fuel shortage. The B-25 made a forced landing on the beach of Melville Island (B-25 N5-133 recovered and salvaged in 1982) after a mission of 1,250 miles, during which it was attacked by three Japanese fighter aircraft, and damaged. The NEI headquarters was convinced only after a trial reconnaissance mission with a B-25 in New Guinea of 1,375 miles. The aircraft returned with only 120 US gallons of fuel left in its tanks, well below its safety limit.

No. 18 Squadron operated in the NWA focussing on East Timor plus the Tanimbar, Kai and Aru Islands. The Japanese Navy Marine Base in Ambon and the south west coast of New Guinea was a major target for the bomb loads of No NEI Squadron from Batchelor. Most missions could only be accomplished by refuelling and loading of bomb ordnance in Darwin, to the north, on the way to and from the target area, making it time consuming, inefficient and exhausting for the crew.

Coinciding with this were difficulties such as that Darwin was insufficiently equipped with only British bombs (not fitting in the American B-25 bomb racks), and fuel bowsers made to accommodate British aircraft types like the Hudson, Beaufort and Beaufighter. Such aspects made the position of McDonald less and less desirable for No.18 Squadron. The solution was improved aircraft with better armament for defence while in flight, and relocation of the entire No. 18 Squadron to a base closer to the coastline.

BATCHELOR AIRFIELD

On 12 and 13 April 1943 the squadron finally made the move to the newly assigned airfield based in Batchelor. This airfield was closer to Darwin and much better equipped as it had housed both USAAF and RAAF squadrons operating both small and large, British and American aircraft including B-17 long range bombers.

Improvement of maintenance and service levels compared to McDonald were encouraging for both officers and airmen. The move to Batchelor brought more than the necessary operational advantages. On the personal level it brought a camp site with all the facilities the personnel had missed in previous camps in Canberra and McDonald. Electricity in every tent, telecom between internal sites, an open-air cinema, sporting facilities and swimming areas, local camp broadcasting with music, bus services, hospital and church services, and last but not least hot and cold water. No wonder that Batchelor would remain the base for No.18 Squadron until almost the end of the war.

During September 1943 replacement crews from the Dutch Flying School at Jackson, Mississippi, arrived at Batchelor and brought their own better equipped B-25s, replacing the older ones with heavier nose armament and longer-range fuel tanks. The arrival of the new recruits, new aircraft, better facilities and joint operations on Batchelor airfield with the USAAF and RAAF gave a well needed boost to the NEI personnel which had grown to an average of 82 officers and 492 other ranks by the end of 1944.

In 1944 the squadron flew a total of 1,240 operational sorties ranging from leaflet dropping, low level strafing and bombing of strategic targets well into enemy territory. The end of 1944 also meant an end of No.18 Squadron at Batchelor as No. 79 Wing (including Nos. 2 and 18 Squadrons) was being assigned to Jacquinot Bay in New Britain, New Guinea.

No.18 Squadron operations from Batchelor ended from 1 May 1945 altogether and all staff and equipment were relocated. Already in June the same year, No. 79 Wing had moved further out to Morotai, one of the eastern Indonesian larger islands strategically positioned closer to Japan. Movement of No. 79 Wing was so rapid that some personal, still including both RAAF and NEI staff, did not even have the chance to get ashore in Jacquinot Bay but had to stay for a total of eight weeks pending a decision to move on to Balikpapan, Borneo. Finally, when the decision was made, No. 79 Wing including No.18 Squadron arrived at Balikpapan on 17 July 1945. This base would be the last where No.18 Squadron was a combined RAAF and NEI entity, as from 25 November 1945, the RAAF component was disbanded ending a four-year association.

On 15 January 1946, No. 18 Squadron became a total Dutch squadron but following pressure from the US and UN the Netherlands began co-operating with the Indonesian Nationalists who fought for independence from the Dutch. All occupied airfields were returned to the Indonesians and the Dutch squadrons disbanded or transferred to the now free Republic of Indonesia. No.18 Squadron was the last Dutch squadron to be transferred to the Indonesians and finally disbanded on 25 June 1950. Most personnel returned to the Netherlands or took their discharge in America or Australia.

In total 4,000 men of 38 nationalities served in No.18 Squadron during the eight years of its operational life. While fighting the Japanese No.18 Squadron lost nineteen B-25 Mitchell bombers and 102 of its crew with 21 of them being RAAF personnel assigned to the unit. Lest we forget.

APPENDIX 1

Elmer Mesman is the Commercial Manager Benelux (Belgium, Netherlands, Luxembourg) for Qantas Airways, based in Amsterdam, the Netherlands. Besides his professional career with Qantas he is a freelance journalist travelling the world for several local magazines ranging from sports to historical publications. His fascination with aviation, WWII and Australia brought him to the Northern Territory in September 2015 to explore all the sites and traces of Dutch wartime influences, with No.18 (NEI) Squadron being the main topic. With emphasis on 70 years of liberation in Europe he thinks it is time to put the forgotten role and sacrifices of fellow countrymen on the other side of the world in the spotlight.

Elmer Mesman

Sources:

De Militaire Luchtvaart van het KNIL in de Jaren 1942-1945, OG Ward

Up in Darwin with the Dutch, Gordon Wallace 1983

Australian Air Force since 1911, NM Parnell & CA Lynch

No.18 NEI Squadron archive Australian War Memorial, Canberra

The No. 18 Squadron badge, featuring a woman cleaning up, modelled on a popular Dutch cleaning product sold in Australia at the time.

A group shot of No. 18 Squadron at Batchelor on 31 August 1944 in celebration of the Dutch Queen Wilhelmina's birthday. (Elmer Mesman)

APPENDIX 2

FLYING IN RAAF BOMBERS – BRIAN WINSPEAR'S STORY

Brian Winspear has been a friend of the author's for over 20 years. He routinely attended the 19 February commemoration in Darwin, partly because it was where he was based for some of the war, and partly because it was where so many comrades fell. He started off though in Tasmania, and after the war, set down these words.

When war was declared in Europe in 1939, like many other 19-year-olds, I thought it would be an interesting adventure to join the air force. I was sure that the blue uniform would impress my girlfriends, and it seemed the right thing to do. From the start, I decided that if my feet were to leave the ground, I wanted to be in the driver's seat so, being assured by the recruiting officer that I could sign on as "pilot only", I took the plunge.

Brian Winspear checks out a bomber gun turret – he flew as a gunner in Hudson bombers in the first months of the Pacific War. (Great Southern Rail)

After a wait of nearly 12 months in the RAAF Reserve, on 5th December 1940 I became an AC2 [Aircraftman, Second Class], and did the usual training at the Initial Training School in Victoria, on No. 9 Course. There my hopes of being a pilot were dashed, and I became a trainee wireless air gunner [WAG]. After six months at Ballarat and one month at Evans Head, we were promoted to flight sergeants and judged ready to go to war.

In July 1941, I was posted to No. 2 Squadron at Laverton with three other WAGs from No. 9 course. I discovered that I was the only Tasmanian in the air crew. We started flying in the squadron's Lockheed Hudsons in August, sometimes as radio operators and other times as gunners, in the hydraulically controlled turrets with two .303 Browning machineguns. The RAAF had bought 247 of these planes from the USA.

In October 1941 a flight of four Hudsons flew to Hobart from Laverton, landing at Cambridge, taking two and a quarter hours to travel what jets now do in one hour. We did several flights around Hobart on photographic and army cooperative missions during our 15 days, boarding 'in luxury' at the Cambridge Hotel.

As I was the only Tasmanian in the squadron, one Sunday the CO – Squadron Leader John Ryland – said, "Let's go for a burn to the west coast." It was a beautiful day and we flew around the coast at low level to Port Davey and Bathurst Harbour, exploring the waterways at about six metres before flying back over the mountains to Hobart. We were in the air for about two and a half hours. At that time the liners *Queen Elizabeth* and the *Queen Mary*, both converted to troop carriers, were in Hobart. When the *Queen Elizabeth* left at 4 a.m. we did an anti-submarine patrol for her lasting four and a half hours.

Being a keen photographer and using a little black and white camera I took some lovely photos of the ship from the rear gun turret. I made one of my many mistakes of having the film developed at Kodak in Hobart, and when we arrived back at Laverton the next day, I was surprised to see half a dozen MPs waiting for our plane. Smelling a rat, I sent most of the negatives down the spent cartridge chutes to be retrieved later. I was severely reprimanded and had leave cancelled for two weeks. My camera and some photos were confiscated.

OFF TO WAR

By early December 1941 we were issued with tropical gear, and the whole squadron of 12 Hudsons took off from Laverton on December 8th to Darwin via Oodnadatta and Alice Springs. I fiddled the wireless tuning onto the civil stations and heard the news the Japs had bombed Pearl Harbor. At our refuelling stop at Oodnadatta I told the mob but no one believed me. By the time we arrived in Darwin after 12 hours in the air, the panic was on. Instead of going to bed we had to belt up ammunition for our machineguns all night in soul-destroying heat of around 35 degrees and 97% humidity.

The day after arriving in Darwin the whole squadron moved 100km south to Batchelor, because it was expected that Darwin would be attacked. We were even instructed to wear our Smith and Wesson revolvers at all times. For the next few weeks the weather was so hot that I lived under a "cold" or luke-warm shower whenever possible and did the least amount of work. It was a shock after Tassy's kind climate. However, near the Batchelor camp was a lovely natural swimming hole which we often used when not on radio duty.

Soon after our arrival in Darwin we were issued with tracer ammunition for our Browning machineguns, which made aiming a lot easier. They were pretty to watch, so I called up the captain to tell him to watch for a burst over the front of the aircraft, and cleverly shot away our front aerial mast...

 At short notice on December 12th we were roused early, told to pack and set off to Koepang in West Timor, a Dutch colony. With seven other Hudsons we refuelled at Darwin and did the four-hour crossing of the Timor Sea. We would repeat the flight often during the next few months, sometimes at night.

We arrived at Penfui airport at 730 pm. The natives and the surrounding jungle were strange, but the tent camp wasn't too bad. The 2/40 Tasmanian Battalion was camped nearby, and I soon made contact with several ex-Scotch College Launceston boys; also Geoff Richards of EE Richards Real Estate who was engaged to my sister Rae.

The 2/40 Battalion Timor story is one of the black spots in Australian military history. The all-Tasmanian Battalion of about 1,000 men had been in the NT for seven months in 1941 and were tired and bored and ready for the six weeks of leave in Tasmania which had been promised. The *Zealandia* was in Darwin ready to take them home. However, as a consequence of the Jap advance towards Australia, their leave was cancelled and they were sent to Koepang to protect the Penfui airport there.

Apparently their Commanding Officer Colonel Geoff Youl refused the assignment because his troops were under-equipped and would have no naval or air support. It would have been a suicide mission and because of his protests he was replaced by Lieutenant-Colonel Leggatt, who also argued against the mission.

Nevertheless, despite these protests, on 8 December 766 troops embarked onto a transport ship at Darwin, hampered by go-slow bloody-minded wharfies, who would not touch ammunition and purposely dropped fragile boxes of radio equipment.

The troops landed at Koepang on December 12th and set up camp near Penfui aerodrome. The battalion had 24 trucks, six Bren gun carriers and six Bofors anti-aircraft guns. In February they received 100 reinforcements, but they arrived with no rifles. On our many Koepang-Darwin flights I would carry their mail and bring back some luxuries such as condensed milk, beer etc.

After the Japs landed 3,850 troops on 20 February 20th, many of the battalion took to the hills with 40 Timor ponies that they had commandeered, but most surrendered after killing 439 enemy paratroops and many ground troops. The final 2/40 casualty list was 50 killed in action, 42 died later, 70 wounded and finally 150 missing when a US submarine torpedoed a ship transporting 1,200 POWs to Japan. Some of my friends were amongst those drowned. Seventy men were later rescued by a US submarine after being in the water for four days.

We also flew long patrol flights without any significant sightings. On December 17th we flew for six and a half hours giving air cover for a landing at Dili by 270 men from the Tasmanian 2/40 battalion and 500 Dutch native troops, as the Portuguese settlement was considered to be unable to defend itself. We arrived back at Koepang with all tanks showing empty.

Soon after arriving I developed symptoms of malaria with a high temperature, but managed to continue flying. In between the flying programme we went into the town; very primitive with few shops and no hotels. We got to like the plentiful Dutch beer, and had no option but to eat water buffalo, black and tough, served with boiled buffalo grass (similar to a coarse spinach), interspersed with meals of rock-hard biscuits and bully beef.

The main objection I developed to air force life was the fact that all the flying days commenced with breakfast at 2-3am, so that we could take off at first light, often when one had a hangover. I vowed that when and if I returned to civvies I would not have an alarm clock in the house and would never get up early!

After the usual early take-off on December 14th, and a patrol right around Timor, we were back in Darwin doing patrols almost to New Guinea. Then we were back to Koepang again. On Christmas Day we had a Christmas Dinner of sorts in Darwin and later, tea in Koepang.

During the rest of December we spent days digging "fox holes" or trenches and flying more patrols. I had lost a stone in weight since Laverton, due no doubt to the climate and food. Boarding an uninsulated plane standing in the sun the inside temperature would be over 60 degrees, and you could fry an egg on the wing. We would fly in nothing but shorts and the sweat would run down our bodies in rivers to make the shorts sopping wet. After take-off and climbing up to 4,000m everything froze. We often took beer up to cool it down.

New Year's Eve saw me on guard duty at the aircraft which were camouflaged and dispersed in the jungle. When I sat down for five minutes a scorpion about the size of a king prawn bit my bum and it hurt like hell. I went to the medical officer, but he wasn't much help. He said "I haven't struck this problem before. Sit there a while to see what happens."

By the end of January the health of the Timor squadron had deteriorated. Thirty percent were on sick parade with malaria, dengue fever, dysentery, tropical sores etc. The weather in January is hot and wet, with regular storms. On one night trip from Darwin flying at 3000m we ran into an invisible solid wall of water, causing the engine temperatures to drop to the point where they lost power. We were forced down to 250m before coming out of the storm.

Up to the time of the invasion of Timor on 20 February my life was full of long reconnaissance flights north of Koepang. When not flying we worked hard at trench digging and road and track marking. The aerodrome was protected by two six-inch guns pointing seawards. As the Jap invasion was from the opposite direction, the big guns were never fired.

It was a period of devastating losses of aircraft and aircrew for Nos. 2 and 13 Squadrons. Most of the enemy action losses were at Ambon. Koepang had more than its share of accidents. On January 20th I was detailed to go to Ambon with three relief crews and had packed all my gear, but was replaced at the last moment by the CO by a more senior WAG.

At the time my job was to sit at the top of a radio tower with an Aldis lamp to send and receive messages to and from an American cruiser one kilometre away in the harbour. After unpacking my kit I went back to the tower, 100 metres from the airstrip. I watched aircraft A16-79 take off, obviously tail-heavy, as it became airborne and went straight up to about 70m. Halfway up I heard the pilot put the throttles "through the gate", and the engines screamed. The plane flicked over and crashed vertically at the end of the strip. No one could get near the burning plane because of the exploding bullets ricocheting everywhere, and with a full load of petrol on board all that was left was 12 charred bodies. The thought that I was nearly on that plane gave me a mighty uncomfortable feeling, and I became a great believer in the power of fate. Then in February Flying Officer Mitchell, with whom I often flew, struck a hill coming into land on one engine in a heavy rainstorm with very poor visibility. All the crew were killed.

At that stage, out of the four Wireless Air Gunners who had been posted to No. 2 squadron, I was the only survivor. I was either lucky or had a guardian angel. On 6 February we were on patrol for six hours to the Celebes, north of Timor, and we later learnt that we had just missed running into a flight of 24 Zeros and 18 bombers. On another occasion I was down to go to Ambon again when another WAG, Jack Maudsley, jumped the queue in front of me. He was killed three days later.

Earlier in January we were landing at Darwin after a night flight when we hit 44-gallon drums on the strip, put there to prevent enemy landings. The duty pilot was very drunk and not capable of guiding us into land.

"Friendly fire" caused problems on other occasions. On one patrol our plane was fired on by American anti-aircraft gunners, and on another occasion one of our planes bombed an American cruiser USS *Perry*, killing two sailors.[1]

Penfui was becoming too dangerous in daylight by the end of January, so we flew to a concealed jungle strip half an hour away. Kim Bonython of Adelaide was pilot on my aircraft, and he always carried with him an old wind-up gramophone with lots of jazz records which he played till late at night in the jungle camp.

On one flight, for the first time in my life I took with me a packet of nine State Express cigarettes and smoked the whole packet in my gun turret to calm my nerves. It didn't work, so I have not smoked since.

Having watched a dozen mates burn and waited in vain for another dozen to return from missions, I felt that my time was well overdue and that the prospects for me reaching old age were zilch. So on 18 February I made a will and left it with the squadron adjutant – not that I had anything of value to bequeath.

---

1   This is the USS *Peary*, a destroyer, not a cruiser, later sunk in Darwin harbour.

Next day with two other repaired Hudsons, overloaded with 23 men each, we evacuated most of our ground staff from Koepang to Darwin, leaving at 3am to dodge the Jap air raids. The aircraft was so heavy it took over half an hour to reach cruising height and five hours to reach Darwin. Shortly after we left the Penfui drome, it was attacked by a dozen Jap bombers and dive-bombers.

Relieved to get back to Darwin safely, we had just had breakfast when the air raid siren sounded. I was in a slit trench 150m from the hangers which were one of their main targets.

I was wandering around the destruction after the raid, when half an hour later 54 bombers arrived from the south at 4500m in beautiful formation. At first they were thought to be US planes from Brisbane, but as I watched them I saw what looked like confetti coming down as the sun reflected off the bombs. I lost no time in jumping into the nearest trench with a cork in my mouth to stop concussion. All hell broke loose as bombs burst all over the RAAF station. My tin hat blew off and I got a hot metal splinter in a finger when I tried to hold it on.

At dawn the next day my crew took off in the only Hudson, dodging the bomb craters in the runway, for our last trip to Koepang to bring back the remaining ground staff. The plane was stripped of everything including parachutes to minimise weight to enable maximum loading from Koepang.

We arrived at the south-west coast of Timor at 11am to meet the Japanese invasion fleet of an aircraft carrier, four heavy cruisers, three destroyers and five transports. Being a solitary aircraft having no bombs and no radio we could do nothing but fly around them at low level. Luckily all the 63 aircraft from the carrier were away attacking Koepang. When all the ships began to use their anti-aircraft guns against us, we headed back to Darwin. We had nowhere enough petrol to reach home, so we headed at the most economical cruising speed to Bathurst Island, landing there with no petrol left after nearly seven hours in the air.

The only habitation on Bathurst Island apart from natives was a mission station run by Father McGrath. Fortunately there were a few drums of aircraft fuel hidden in the bush, so we rolled these to the plane and hand-pumped the petrol into the wing tanks. We had not had a meal for two days due to bomb damage to the mess at Darwin and also to the fact that the cooks had "gone bush", so I still remember how good a tin of pineapple tasted which was given to us by the mission staff. We finally arrived back in Darwin at dusk. The ground personnel whom we had been unable to pick up became prisoners of war.

At the RAAF station we slept in the old married quarters, some of which had survived the bombing. The standard routine when a crew did not return was to sort out their personal things and give them to the adjutant, then put all their clothes in a heap in a spare bedroom. By that time the heap was one metre high and we all delved into it to save washing our own shirts and shorts.

That night I had just gone to sleep when we were roused with orders to fly to Daly Waters. As I was totally exhausted I said to the captain, Flying Officer Lamb, "As it's only a travel flight you don't need two WAGs. I'll stay here." He agreed.

They took off with 14 passengers, got lost and did not arrive at Daly Waters. We were just about to put their clothes on the deceased pile several days later when news arrived that they had crash-landed at 250kph out of fuel at night in four foot deep Lake Woods, 250km south of Daly Waters – the only lake for thousands of kilometres. They were found by a boundary rider on his annual inspection of fences, hungry and hot, but alive.

Darwin was bombed 58 times over the following few months, so on February 23rd, to get away from the air raids, we flew to Daly Waters in a DC-2, a two-and-a-half-hour flight. I was not impressed with Daly Waters. The Yanks had taken over the only pub which was a prohibited area to us. Dust and flies were horrific and water scarce. After a shower of rain I sometimes drank from puddles in the road. We slept in tents on the ground, and one morning I discovered a five-foot snake coiled up under my legs.

It was so hot that we regularly grabbed a plane and flew up to 3,000 metres just to cool off. One day I watched a Yank in a P-40 single-seater fighter as he climbed to about 3,000m and then started a series of loops all the way down. Half-way through the last one he hit the ground vertically at about 400kph. He and the motor were buried ten feet underground.

For the next month from February 26th onwards, after receiving some replacement Hudsons, we carried out dozens of reconnaissance flights from Daly Waters and Darwin looking for submarines and signs of an invasion force heading to Australia. We saw evidence of ships from both sides sinking or sunk, but no submarines or carriers. Returning from patrol on February 28th we hit trees when landing, putting a few dents in the wings. In between our flying we had to work hard clearing dispersal areas for the planes, burning out the pit toilets (always waiting for them to be occupied!) and digging trenches.

A trickle of American planes began to arrive, but many were lost due to inexperienced pilots. On March 11th a Flying Fortress crashed killing one crew member, and on the 18th we spent five and a half hours in the air searching without success for a lost Kittyhawk pilot.

Without any warning we were instructed on 20th March to fly an unserviceable Hudson A16-36 to Laverton for repairs. It had been stripped of everything including gauges not vital to keep it airborne, and on the way we had to land often to top up the engine oil. Our first stop was Alice Springs, which we found after much searching. You have no idea how beautiful it was to sleep in a hotel bed, drink lots of cold beer and eat some decent food after four months of roughing it.

Next day we got as far as Oodnadatta where we had to land with engine magneto trouble. The hotel there was fantastic, the people hospitable and the food and beer wonderful. We had to stay several days waiting for parts for the engines. After a short test flight we flew off to Adelaide, landing at Parafield. Here we had another very pleasant night in a city hotel, where we were very conspicuous in our worn-out tropical gear. It was great to arrive at Laverton, although the cold weather was a shock.

We were granted five days sick leave, so I made the most of wining and dining at all my favourite Melbourne restaurants. The first one was Russell Collins where they wouldn't let me pay because I was "returned" from the war. My pilot Flying Officer Lamb kept on getting extensions to sick leave and I had to stay around Melbourne ready to go north when he was fit. I was never able to find out what his problem was.

There is no doubt that if we had returned to Darwin we would have joined the casualty ranks, as I estimate that fatalities for air crew in No. 2 Squadron at that time were around 100% every six months. Nos. 2 and 13 Squadrons received a Citation by the US War Department for their outstanding action in the Darwin, Koepang and Ambon areas.

In the meantime I enjoyed the three weeks living it up in Melbourne. As I was having trouble with a sore eye, I reported sick and they fished out a piece of steel that had been there since the Darwin raid. I passed out while they were digging for it. On April 9th I disobeyed orders and hopped on the *Nairana* for Launceston, where I had a few days re-uniting with family and friends. Everyone remarked on how thin and how yellow I was, due to the anti-malarial tablets we had to consume.

In Melbourne I saw a lot of John Smith who had lost an eye flying in Singapore. He wore a big black patch to cover the gory mess where his eye had been, and when passers-by in the street made rude remarks about the patch he would horrify them by lifting the patch. Later when he was fitted with a glass eye he would pop it out into his beer as a party trick.

By May 17th the RAAF became tired of granting me leave as my pilot was still on sick leave, and they posted me to Parkes, where for six weeks I did a crash course on navigation together with 30 other wireless air gunners.

We flew in old Avro Ansons all over NSW as navigation training, and whenever I became lost, which was quite often, I would ask the pilot to find the nearest railway station and fly low over it to read the name of the town. We all qualified and could now wear the "N" for navigator half wing, but as Phil had spent most of the whole six weeks drinking with the instructors his navigation skills were very limited.

WESTERN JUNCTION INTERLUDE; THEN TO NO. 12 SQUADRON VULTEE VENGEANCES

In July I was surprised to get a posting to No. 7 Elementary Flying Training School at Western Junction near Launceston, my hometown. For the next seven months I was attached to civil aviation to advise of all aircraft movements in and out of Tasmania by land line and radio. It was a terrific job. Two of us had to man the radio 24 hours of the day and sleep on the job.

Phil Corney and I gained our commissions on 28 December, 1942, back dated to 1 October, so from Flight-Sergeants we became Pilot Officers, and moved up to the officers' mess. Our pay was the equivalent of $1.75 a day, plus 30c deferred pay, less 25c income tax.

The seven-month period there was one long holiday, with parties, fishing at St Helens, swimming, climbing Cradle Mountain and more. By February '43 the long party was over, and we were posted to No. 4 Operational Training Unit at Williamtown for an eight-week course of navigation, radio and gunnery in preparation for posting to a Vultee Vengeance dive bombing squadron.

After 12 hours flying Wirraways we were judged fit to upgrade to the Vultee. Most of the flying was done in low level formation a few centimetres above the water of the many lakes in the area. The leader of the formation of four or five Wirraways would fly about 300 mm lower than the others and would try to roughen the water with his propeller.

In April we had our first Vultee flight. They were quite a unique two-seater vertical dive bomber. The RAAF ordered 342 of them from the US where they had been designed to be better than the successful German Stukas.

The big advantage of diving vertically was that the pilot could corkscrew the plane around to get the target on-line. To prevent the aircraft from exceeding the speed of sound on the way down, it had dive brakes on the wings. Sometimes the pilot would retract the dive brakes too soon, and the speed would increase to the point where servicing flaps and other bits would blow off.

An obvious problem was that as the aircraft did a vertical dive, the bombs wouldn't come out of the bomb bay, and if they did they could fall into the propeller. To fix this, the bombs were thrown clear by pivoting arms.

Another difficulty was that because the pilot could only see ahead and not vertically down, he could not know when he was directly over the target to commence the dive. So he had a small trap door in the floor between his legs which, when it and the bomb doors were open, gave him limited vision straight down. During the dive he could fire his four wing guns and if the tracer bullets hit the target, he knew that his bombs also would.

The attack procedure was for the squadron of 12 planes to fly in echelon to the target at 3,500m, roll over in turn and all be in the vertical dive together, pulling out at 40m and leaving the area at a very low level. Both the crew members would black out for several seconds during pull out, and amongst other things the rapid change in pressure during the dive gave me a stabbing headache between the eyes. Needless to say, there were many casualties. As time went on their reputation in action was not good, so the squadrons I was associated with were used mostly for anti-submarine patrols.

On April 15th I was posted to No. 12 Squadron of Vultee Vengeances at Batchelor, south of Darwin. The camp was much better than the ones I had been in 12 months ago. Being in the officers' mess helped, and there was a lovely swimming hole not far from camp.

My first patrol was on May 6th watching over a six-ship convoy off Melville Island for over four hours, flying with a rookie pilot just out of training school. We did several more patrols and two flights searching for a lost Beaufighter around Daly River.

Several aircraft and pilots were lost at that time:

- On 13 May a Hudson dropped a load of bombs on a 3,000-ton ship in Ambon harbour at very low level. The ship exploded, but so did the Hudson. No survivors.
- On 21 May a B-25 crashed when taking off, and next day one Vultee did not return from a flight of 15 off Darwin.
- Phil Corney could not be found on 30 May when his plane was due to go off on a job, and I was about to fill in for him when he turned up. I watched them crash on take-off. They were OK, but the Vultee was a write-off, and the pilot was sent south for further training.

On June 18th 12 Vultees took off from Batchelor, landed at Bathurst Island to refuel, and dive-bombed an airstrip on the island of Selaru. It was the first Vultee action in the war. All returned and all bombs hit the target. For some unknown reason they were ordered not to fire their guns. I could never understand why Vultees were not used more in action, as their bombing accuracy was unbelievable.

In May RAAF Command in Melbourne decided No. 12 Squadron should go to Merauke, the last Dutch outpost in New Guinea. For some crazy reason, possibly my seniority, I was put in charge of a working party of ground staff to go there by ship.

At Darwin, in between air raids, we had to load 32 truckloads of supplies and 17 trucks of men and baggage onto an 8,000-ton US Liberty ship *Charles P Steinartz*. With 500 on board we departed Darwin on June 29th for Thursday Island escorted by two corvettes. We slept on stretchers in the hold and were fed from army cookers on the deck. We organised a few concerts and played cards to fill in time.

On July 4th we sailed into the Merauke River to unload the tons of supplies, all in heavy rain. Merauke has often been described as the arsehole of the world. Before the war it was a Dutch penal settlement. It was all flat, swampy, always raining and only two metres above high tide level, while the mosquitoes were the biggest in the world and in infinite numbers. In addition, big green frogs, scorpions and snakes were everywhere.

The RAAF station was all tents, which had to have split coconut palm logs for floors to avoid the soggy ground. For the next few weeks, with my group, I worked on making roads and building a camp for the whole squadron to occupy. Conditions were horrific as it rained every day. The mud was bottomless, so that some of the roads had to be corduroyed with split coconut palm logs, while the landing strip was special steel sheeting. We also constructed miles of foot tracks over the sodden ground using split coconut palm logs set up on round cross logs.

I had at my disposal an Indian motorcycle and side car, an old Triumph motor cycle and a 30 hundredweight Chev truck, which had such a lovely gear box that you could change gears without the clutch. At 22 years of age I became a fast learner on road and bridge construction. The men had four 6-wheel drive trucks plus loading equipment and worked well.

Within a few weeks I had a comfortable two bed tent and a garden with lettuces, cucumbers, tomatoes and coconut palms. I also adopted a skinny native dog I named "Clockwork", which travelled everywhere with me, either on the roof of the truck or on the motor bikes.

The officers' mess gradually grew into shape and the food improved. There was a limited supply of grog which we would occasionally supplement with proof spirit from the hospital. The toilets were pit types, on a mound of earth two metres high, to be above the water table. One day I was doing my "job" and peacefully reading the toilet paper – a two-year old women's magazine – when there was a loud crack as the rotten superstructure collapsed and I fell with it into the hole.

The squadron of 12 Vultees arrived in October '43, as the camp was ready, and remained there until July '44. There was also an American Kittyhawk squadron based on the Merauke strip, so the Japs only tried a few ineffectual air raids. There were the usual crash casualties due to bad weather and bad flying by both the Vultees and the Kittyhawks.

While the squadron had been waiting for the Merauke camp to be ready the planes were based at Cooktown, where they did a lot of convoy patrol work. On July 4th A27-217 crash-landed on the beach at Port Douglas, and on August 4th A27-235 crashed on Ruby Reef, 45 miles east of Cooktown. The crew, including Tasmanian friend Dennis Holmes, was rescued by a Catalina from Cairns.

In September I was appointed squadron photographic officer, which gave me endless opportunities to take photos and do my own developing and enlarging. A few weeks later I was also appointed acting squadron signals officer.

By this time we had an outdoor picture theatre showing regular screenings, and when not there I played lots of bridge with the squadron medical officer and other air crew.

A trio of No. 12 Squadron Vultee Vengeance dive-bombers near Merauke in December 1943. (AWM)

During the nine months I was at Merauke I flew 20 sorties, mainly on patrol plus one trip to Horn Island for grog. Apart from a few dive-bombing practices, they were fairly uneventful except for one occasion flying with Squadron Leader Guthrie, the CO, when he practised his shooting by diving at white caps on the waves and forgot to pull up. I'll swear we flew through the spray of our own bullets.

My 23rd birthday was spent on patrol over the Arafura Sea. The only way we could top up our grog supply was to send a Vultee to Cooktown or Cairns for stocks. It was quite a work of art to load the bomb bay with cartons and shut the doors, then catch the cartons when the bomb doors were later opened. We got 70 dozen on October 28th and 64 dozen on January 1st – very important events.

On Christmas Day it is an air force custom for the officers to wait on the airmen. With grog supplies plentiful that day it was a long party. Someone detonated some dynamite, someone else let off smoke bombs in the mess, someone pinched all the Padre's port and someone crashed the CO's car into a tree. I was thrown down the well (our drinking water supply) because they caught me lacing the dwindling beer supply with medical alcohol while serving behind the bar.

One day Phil Corney, army officer Jim Leach, the CO Bill Guthrie and I went for a long trip up the Merauke River on the ketch *Sylvia,* calling at all the native villages. We shot crocodiles and bought bananas and bird of paradise feathers.

By January 1944 I had been in Merauke for six months, so I was granted a very welcome month of leave. The only way I could get south was to bum a ride in a Dutch B-25 going to Brisbane. It was a terrific trip. Sitting in the Perspex nose I could see everything, and after Cape York we flew at a low level following the coast all the way to Townsville where we had an overnight stop. Next day we flew on to Brisbane, and then I caught various flights to Tassie where I enjoyed a month of parties and a wonderful change from the Merauke living conditions.

February 10th saw me on the *Nairana* from Burnie to Melbourne, and then I took the train to Sydney and Brisbane, then a Lockheed Lodestar to Townsville-Cairns-Horn Island, and 'home' to Merauke and business as usual.

In early March two friends in a Vultee came out of a cloud going straight down for some unknown reason and crashed into the sea.

The next major event happened on March 13th when my dog "Clockwork" gave birth under my bed to five pups, four boys and a girl. They survived well on a diet of condensed milk and bully beef.

I was getting a bit fed up with the boring Merauke life after nine months of it, so I submitted an application to do a Signals Officer course at Point Cook near Melbourne. This was approved after I passed an adaptability test, so on March 29th 1944 I departed Merauke for good.

After another six weeks leave in Tasmania I commenced the six month radio course at Point Cook. It was tough in places, but I enjoyed the officers' mess, played plenty of squash and spent a lot of time in Melbourne and Ballarat. Moreover I did learn to design and build radio receivers and transmitters.

I was promoted to Flight Lieutenant in November, backdated to October 1st, and made a permanent squadron signals officer. My first posting in this capacity was to No. 14 Squadron of Beauforts at Pearce, just out of Perth, WA.

On November 22nd I caught a troop train to Perth. It took four days to get there, with stops for meals served from an army kitchen on a flat top wagon. There were nine carriages of men and one of service women, who were guarded by an MP at each end of their carriage. This did not stop some of the more enterprising male passengers from climbing out of their windows onto the roof and crawling along to the female carriage and in through their windows!

WEST AUSTRALIAN SOJOURN

The RAAF station at Pearce was a permanent camp and very comfortable. I took control of the 24 wireless air gunners and 24 ground staff and all the radio activities of the squadron and soon settled in. As I was not in a crew, I could pick and choose when I wanted to fly and rostered myself on all the interesting trips, sometimes as photographer.

The first trip was a seven-hour anti-sub patrol on Boxing Day, covering the Royal Navy cruiser *London.* Christmas day was spent on the traditional waiting on airmen for their Christmas dinner and drinking heavily.

Over the next six months I clocked up about 70 hours of Beaufort flying, mainly on submarine patrols and travel flights. The weather was uncomfortably hot, up to 42 degrees in Perth and 45 further north. One of my duties was to organise a mobile communication truck to go after dark to Applecross, a suburb of Perth, to liaise with an army searchlight company while one of our Beauforts flew overhead for their training. This exercise finished about nine pm, and there just happened to be excellent mud crabs just off the beach next door. We would light a fire on the beach, drink lots of beer and net lots of crabs which we cooked in a drum on the fire.

To make it a better party I arranged for several WAAAFs to come along (to practise radio operating with aircraft). Unfortunately, an MP saw a girl out of uniform getting into the radio truck in Perth and reported the incident. I was subsequently court-martialled and received a severe reprimand by the CO. He had his tongue in his cheek, as he was also fraternising with WAAAFs.

Brian Winspear served later on the northern coast of New Guinea, and was demobilised in late 1945. He went on to business opportunities following the war, which included starting Innkeepers, a chain of Tasmanian hotels which spread to the mainland, eventually becoming 20 establishments in five states. He married Shirley, later a successful painter, and was awarded an Order of Australia for services to the tourism industry and the community. A regular and much-loved attendee at the 19 February commemoration every year in Darwin, Brian still lives in Hobart, but spends several months in the winter annually in Bowen, Queensland.

MAIN SOURCES

Akasaka, Susumu. Pilot, 70th DCS IJAAF re activities of 70th DCS, 1942-44. Interview with Bob Alford, 1990.

Alford File AL/19th BG/1. Note extracted from microfilm held at the National Archives and Records Administration, USA.

Alford, Bob with Osamu Tagaya. *Minoru SUZUKI – IJNAF WWII – NWA. Biographical Notes Minoru Suzuki*. 2015.

Alford, Bob. *Darwin's Air War*. Aviation Historical Society of the Northern Territory. Revised Edition 2010.

Alford, Bob. General notes and files relating to Japanese aircraft, units, actions and individuals of the Japanese air forces in the NWA, 1941-45. 2009.

Atkinson, Wing Commander RA. *Most Secret. Report on Mine Laying Operations – Kavieng – April and May 1943*. Undated. Alford Collection.

Australian War Memorial. Series AWM 54 generally, AWM 86/5/1, AWM 423/2/13, AWM423/2/51, AWM 423/4/92, negative No. P02822.001.

Bell, Squadron Leader C. C. *Report of visit of B.17s to North Western Area 17.5.42 – 21.5.42*. RAAF Historical Section. 1988. Alford Collection.

Bennet, John. *Highest traditions. The History of No. 2 Squadron, RAAF*. AGPS. 1995.

Chowns, Pilot Officer NA. Log Book and in correspondence from Chowns' brother to Alford.

Claringbould, Michael. *IJN Floatplanes in the South Pacific*. Pacific Profiles Volume 8. Adelaide: Avonmore Books, 2022.

Combined Fleet website. http://www.combinedfleet.com

Craven, WF and Cate (Eds). *The Army Air Forces in World War II. The Pacific: Guadalcanal to Saipan August 1942 to July 1944*. Vol. IV. University of Chicago Press. 1960.

Crosbie JD. 436683. Extract of Log Book. Alford Collection.

Dakeyne Sergeant/Warrant Officer Richard. Extracts of RAAF Log Book. See also news clippings and correspondence, Dakeyne to Alford. 1991.

Dalkin, Bob. *Flying Fifty Years Ago and Other Experiences*. 1992. Manuscript held AHSNT Archives.

Davies, Dudley, Warrant Officer - Air Gunner, No 2 Squadron. Interview with Dr Peter Williams, Darwin. 24 April, 2005.

Davis, Harold D. and Evans, Jack. Extract of Log Book of Correspondent, *Wings* magazine. 12 June 1945.

Gaylor, W, Lieutenant. Historian 22nd Bomb. Group, in correspondence of 18 May 1989; Alford, Bob. *Timor Operations, 1942, North Western Area 22nd Bomb. Group, USAAF*; and Robert AG 'Bill"s Log Book extracts courtesy Mrs Mavis Roberts in correspondence to Alford, 1990.

Gill, G. Hermon. *Royal Australian Navy 1939-1942*. Melbourne: Collins, 1957.

Gill, G. Hermon. *Royal Australian Navy 1942-1945*. Melbourne: Collins, 1968.

Gillison, Douglas. *Royal Australian Air Force 1939-42*. AWM 1962.

Gleeson, Joe J. Extracts of Log Book. Alford Collection.

Glover, Ralph C. Lt. Col. *The History of the 808th Engineer Aviation Battalion 15 September 1941 to 12 January 1946*. Association of 808th Engineers, 1985.

Griffith, Owen. *Darwin Drama*. Bloxhall and Chambers. 1946.

Hata, Ikuhiko and Izawa, Yasuho. (Translation by Don C. Gorham) *Japanese Naval Aces and Fighter Units in World War II*. Airlife. 1989.

Hata, Ikuhiko, Izawa, Yasuho and Shores, Christopher. *Japanese Naval Air Force Fighter Units and their aces 1932-1945*. Grub Street. 2011.

Hilder, Wing Commander Brett. Night Flight to Sourabaya. *RAAF Saga*. Australian War Memorial, 1944.

Hill, Nelson. In correspondence to Alford. 28 June 1977. Copy held File Al/A16-/1 Lockheed Hudson. RAAF History and General.

Horton, Glenn. *The Best in the Southwest. The 380th Bomb Group in World War II*. Mosie Publications. 1995.

Ichimura, Hiroshi. *Ki-43 'Oscar' Aces of World War 2*. Osprey. 2009.

J-aircraft.com and Pacific Air War History Associates.

Japan Centre for Historical Records (JACAR) www.jacar.english/index.html.

Johnson, Paul. *Excerpts from the Diary of Paul E. Johnson. Pilot. 319th Sqdn. 90th Bomb Group. From Feb 2. 1943 to July 9, 1943*. Alford Collection.

Johnson, Sue, and Winspear, Brian. (Eds.) *Tasmanians at War in the Air 1939-1945*. Brian Winspear: Hobart, 2002.

Journal of the Australian War Memorial. Clayton, Mark. The North Australian Air War 1942-44. No 8, April 1986.

Journal of the Australian War Memorial. Hiromi, Tanaka. The Japanese Navy's operations against Australia in the Second World War, with a commentary on Japanese sources. Issue 30 - April 1997.

Lambert, Des. Correspondence to Alford, 10 December 2005 and 11 September 2009.

Lee, Arthur Gould. *No Parachute*. London: Jarrolds, 1968.

Lewis, Tom, *Eagles over Darwin – American Airmen Defending Northern Australia 1942*. Avonmore Books, 2021.

Lewis, Tom. *The Empire Strikes South – Japan's Air War Against Northern Australia 1942-45*. Avonmore Books, 2017.

Livingstone, Bob. *Under the Southern Cross. The B-24 Liberator in the South Pacific*. Turner Publishing. 1988.

MacDonald, Ron S. to RN Alford. 1990 and extract of Pilot's Log Book. Copies held AHSNT/Alford files.

Marks, Sergeant John. Extract of Log Book. Alford Collection.

McDonald, Lindsay. Extracts of Log Books. Alford Collection.

McLaren, Peter. Typed notes of his RAAF service for RN Alford. 1987. Copy held AHSNT/Alford Colln.

Military History Department of the National Institute for Defence Studies,Tokyo. *Kodochosho*.

Military History Department of the National Institute for Defence Studies,Tokyo. Ran'in Bengaru-wan hômen kaigun shinkô sakusen [The Dutch East Indies and Bengal Bay Area: Naval Advance Operations]. Senshi Sôsho vol. 26. Tokyo: Asagumo Shinbunsha, 1969. Translated by Haruki Yoshida.

Minty, AE. (Ed.) *Black Cats*. Point Cook: RAAF Museum, 1994.

National Archives and Records Administration. (USA). Item SQ-BOMB – 64 – HI. History of the 64th Bomb. Squadron, 15 January 1941 to April 1944. Copy held AHSNT Archives.

National Archives of Australia. various RAAF squadron records including Nos. 1, 2, 11, 12, 13, 18, 20, 21, 12, 24, 42, 43.

National Archives of Australia. Series CRS M431 Item 1; Series F1; Series 1196; Series 1980; Series 11093; Series 11231; Series A816 Item 14/301/14; Series A1564/1 Item 1/4/2 INTEL, A1564/1 Item 1/4/3 INTEL, A1564/1 Item 1/4/4 INTEL, A1564/1 Item 1/4/5 INTEL, A1564/1 Item 1/4/6 INTEL, A9186 (various unit records), A9696/1 Item 606 and A9696, Item 690;

National Archives of Australia. Series E72 Item D14873 and Series F1 Item 1968/1368

Nelmes, Michael V. *Tocumwal to Tarakan: Australians and the Consolidated B-24 Liberator*. ACT: Banner Books, 1994.

No. 18 Squadron NEI-RAAF Forces Association Newsletter. Osborne, Tom. "The Morning I Bombed Darwin". No 38, July 1992.

Odgers, George. *Air War Against Japan 1943-1945. Australia in the War of 1939–1945*. Series 3 – Air. Vol. 2. Canberra: Australian War Memorial, 1968.

Overheu, Richard F. Log Book extracts. Copy held AHSNT Archives.

Ozatwar.com website

Pacific Wrecks website

Packer, Group Captain G. Commanding Officer, Forward Echelon, RAAF Headquarters. *Aerodrome Requirements in Western and Northwestern Parts of Australia*. Minute of 5 June 1943. Alford Collection.

Powell, Alan. *The Shadow's Edge*. Melbourne University Press. 1988.

Riley, Harry. Extracts of Diary and Log Book in correspondence to Alford of 30 October 1992. Alford Collection.

Royal Australian Air Force. *North Western Area Campaign "Original Brief" May 1942 to April 1944*. Vol. II. Page 72.

Sakaida, Henry. *Imperial Japanese Navy Aces 1937-1945*. Osprey Publishing: Great Britain, 1998.

Sakaida, Henry. *Japanese Army Air Force Aces 1937-45*. Osprey. 1997.

Salecker, Gene Eric. *Fortress Against the Sun: The B-17 Flying Fortress in the Pacific*. USA: Da Capo Press, 2001.

Senshi Sosho. Chapter Nine of *Bôeichô Bôei Kenshûjo Senshishitsu* [Military history Department, National Institute of Defense Studies, the Defense Agency] ed. *Ran'in Bengaru-wan hômen kaigun shinkô sakusen* [The Dutch East Indies and Bengal Bay Area: Naval Advance Operations]. Vol. 26. Tokyo: Asagumo Shinbunsha, 1969. Translated by Haruki Yoshida with assistance by Darwin Military Museum historian Dr Peter Williams.

Sieber, Dave. Extract of Log Book. RAAF. 531st Squadron, 380th Bomb Group USAAF and 23 Squadron RAAF.

Stevens, Virgil H. 529th Squadron 380th Bomb Group USAAF. Extract of Log Book. Alford Collection.

Thompson, Tommy. Comments to Alford, during 380th Bomb Group reunion in Darwin. 1988.

Tipping, EW. "Venturas Strike From NWA". *Wings*. 7 August 1945.

United States Navy. Recognition book *Merchant Ship Shapes*. Lewis Collection.

Van Velzen, Marianne. *Bomber boys*: the extraordinary adventures of a group of airmen who escaped the Japanese and became the RAAF's celebrated 18th Squadron. Sydney: Griffin Press, 2017.

Venn, John. Correspondence to his mother dated 2nd 3rd, 4th, 5th February 1942. Alford Collection.

Vincent, David. *Catalina Chronicle. A History of RAAF Operations*. Catalina National Committee. 1981.

Vincent, David. *The RAAF Hudson Story. Book Two*. Vincent Aviation Publications. 2010.

Walker, Brian. In correspondence with Bob Alford of 22 March 1990.

Wallace, Gordon. *Up in Darwin With the Dutch*. Self-published. 1983.

Williams, Theodore J. and Gotham, Barbara J. *We Went to War Part XI: Our Opposition. Japanese Anti-aircraft Artillery and Fighter Units in the Southwest Pacific*. 380th Bomb. Group Assn. 2007.

Winckel, Gus. *The Forgotten Squadron' and Various Other Wonderful Reports*. 1991.

Wings. Official Magazine of the RAAF. Various wartime editions.

Yeaman, John. *Notes on Aerodrome Development Programme North Western Area as from 1st January 1942*. Alford Collection. (Also see R.A.A.F. H Q file 175/6/3)

INDEX OF NAMES

Abbey, Flight Sergeant Don 90, 91
Abeleven, Sergeant GF 44
Ackerman, Staff Sergeant Alanson S 95
Adamson, Flight Sergeant LG 62
Adkins, Lieutenant Kenneth R 57
Ahern, Flying Officer KJ 36
Aiani, Staff Sergeant Louis J 77
Albert, Flight Sergeant David J 128
Alcock, Flying Officer JE 37
Alford, Bob 9
Allan, Flight Sergeant TW 120
Allchin, Flying Officer GWC 29
Allen, Staff Sergeant Joseph T 75
Ames, Flight Sergeant Lloyd 102
Amess, Flying Officer JWB 63
Anderson, Lieutenant 45
Anderson, Flight Lieutenant G 102
Andrews, WAG Bill 39
Angel, Pilot Officer 29
Anstey, Sergeant Frederick W 95
Arnold, Trevor 127
Austin, Flight Lieutenant SJ "Bunny" 67
Avery, Bob 104, 108
Bacon, Flight Sergeant David BE 99
Badger, Flight Lieutenant Neil T 36, 81, 82
Bailey, Flight Sergeant LM 120
Baker, Corporal Bruce E 46
Baker, Lieutenant Dexter 60
Banks, Captain Jack 56, 76
Banks, Flight Sergeant RJ 118
Barbee, Staff Sergeant William F 77
Barber, Flight Sergeant William R 95
Barbour, Flying Officer Robert C 128
Barclay, Flight Sergeant Thomas H 99
Bardwell, Warrant Officer HR 121
Barnes, Corporal JH 89
Barnes, Sergeant JL 51
Bassen, Sergeant TW 51
Bates, Lieutenant Arthur A 80
Bates, Warrant Officer WV 129
Batten, Sergeant Alf 106
Batho, Flight Lieutenant Jack 102
Baumann, Lieutenant Frederick R 82
Beddoe, Pilot Officer Don C 83, 84
Beenken, Staff Sergeant Alvin W 95
Belcher, Lieutenant William 45
Bell, Wing Commander Russ E 113, 117
Bell, Flying Officer WS 120
Beller, Lieutenant Maurice 57
Belling, Sergeant Major F 72
Belshaw, Flight Sergeant AM 91
Bennett, Lieutenant Earl 77
Benshoff, Staff Sergeant William G 77
Benson, Flight Sergeant DD 120
Bevan, Pilot Officer Keith 57
Bilgrai, Sergeant S 71
Billington, Warrant Officer CS 126
Bird, Sergeant Walter J 95

Black, Squadron Leader Ivor 30, 121
Black, Pilot Officer RL 84
Blackwell, Flying Officer LJ 125
Bladin, Air Vice Marshal Frank 25, 30, 56, 64, 67
Blanchard, Flying Officer R 28
Boanas, Sergeant Jack 68
Bodie, Flying Officer RLL 126
Bonython, Kym 141
Bottiglio, Corporal Aldo A 60
Bouche, Lieutenant R 73
Bouwman, Sergeant A 55
Bowen, Flight Sergeant TE 118
Boyd, Warrant Officer 114
Boyd, Flying Officer AS 63
Boynton, Flying Officer GV 37
Bradley, LAC Roy Gordon 48
Bradstreet, Flying Officer Raymond H 128
Brereton, Major General Lewis 10
Brissey, Captain Forrest 59
Brockhurst, Pilot Officer CD 84
Brooks, Flight Lieutenant 64, 90
Brooks, Flying Officer PG 29
Brooks, Flying Officer Russ 113, 114, 118
Brough, Warrant Officer R 87
Brown, Sergeant JS 126
Brown, Pilot Officer KA 118
Brown, Pilot Officer PM 128
Browness, Warrant Officer VM 128
Buccia, Staff Sergeant Steve J 94
Buckland, Flying Officer AK 105
Bullis, Captain Harry J 44
Bulman, Flight Lieutenant CR "Ralph" 118, 119
Burke, Sergeant Glover 32
Burnett, Air Chief Marshal 133
Burns, Corporal A 63
Burns, Squadron Leader MC 51
Burrage, Wing Commander RE "Reg" 126
Burtis, Staff Sergeant Charles F 81
Butler, Sergeant JG 51
Byfield, Flight Lieutenant Noel 119
Caballero, Sergeant Francisco 97
Calder, Flight Lieutenant E 102
Calhoun, Staff Sergeant Charles R 60
Cambridge, Flight Lieutenant Arthur 40, 114
Cameron, Flying Officer John 52
Campbell, Flying Officer 107, 110
Campbell, Wing Commander Dave 71, 105, 106
Campbell, Pilot Officer DG 31
Campbell, Sergeant GA 38
Campbell, Warrant Officer JSM 105
Cannon, Staff Sergeant James 11
Cannon, Flying Officer Roy 97
Cantor, Pilot Officer CV 31
Carnell, Corporal SJ 89

Carr, Lieutenant Commander PE 89
Carter, Sergeant PC 91
Carter, Flight Lieutenant Tige 106
Cater, Technical Sergeant Clifford D 60
Cave, Private 1st Class Fred C 95
Charlesworth, Air Commodore AM 117
Chinnick, Flying Officer RL "Chick" 90
Chote, Sergeant KG 40
Chowns, Pilot Officer Nerdan 102
Churchek, Technical Sergeant Arnold W 7
Churchill, Prime Minister Winston 54
Clapinson, Sergeant HW 81
Clark, Sergeant 45
Clark, Sergeant BR 74
Clark, Sergeant RM 40
Clark, Flight Lieutenant RT "Nobby" 126
Clarke, Sergeant KHA 123
Clarkson, Flying Officer P 102
Cleworth, Warrant Officer JR 126, 129
Coates, Sergeant HJA 91
Cochrane, Lieutenant Kenneth M 60
Coedam, Lieutenant WAC 71
Coggin, Flight Sergeant HL 125
Cole, Air Vice Marshal Adrian "King" 67, 74
Cole, Technical Sergeant Robert F 48
Collett, Staff Sergeant Howard G 60
Collins, Russell 143
Combs, Captain Cecil 11
Conaghan, Sergeant FH 105
Cook, Flight Lieutenant HO 28
Cook, Sergeant James E 95
Cook, Flight Lieutenant John 97
Cooper, Sergeant Robert 45
Corbin, Technical Sergeant Richard W 94
Corney, Phil 144, 145, 147
Corrie, Flight Lieutenant Robin 119
Costello, Wing Commander JP 125
Coster, Rear Admiral 133, 134
Court, Flight Lieutenant Roger 112, 113, 117, 118, 120, 121, 129
Coventry, Squadron Leader GW 88, 89
Cowan, Pilot Officer WA 94
Cowey, Sergeant James 72
Cowley, Sergeant JD 123
Cox, Warrant Officer BL 120
Cox, Flight Lieutenant James H 128
Crabtree, Flight Lieutenant Ed 78
Craig, Captain Doug 80
Craig, Major Richard 60
Crawford, Pilot Officer GR 31
Crisp, Squadron Leader K 128
Cropley, Flying Officer Alan A 95
Crosbie, Sergeant David J 73
Cross, Technical Sergeant Charles W 95
Crough, LAC AH 63
Crowther, Flight Lieutenant LD 118
Cullen, Flight Sergeant JF 69
Currie, Lieutenant Aldan 46

INDEX OF NAMES

Cutten, Warrant Officer NE 51
Dagget, Flying Officer JF 106
Dakeyne, Sergeant Dick 56
Dalkin, Flight Lieutenant Bob 26, 28, 31, 33, 35, 37
Daniel, Lieutenant Howard Q 45
Daniel, Flying Officer KE 51
Danks-Brown, Sergeant KD 48
Darlington, Technical Sergeant Urban V 60
Davidson, Warrant Officer Stuart H 95
Davies, Dudley 85, 87
Davies, Flying Officer S 105
Davis, Flight Sergeant A 118
Davis, Lieutenant Everett "Stinky" 32
Davis, Flight Sergeant Howard 127, 129
de Eerens, Sergeant W 71
de Hoog, Sergeant HJ 65
de Jong, Sergeant AH 50
de Knecht, Lieutenant JBF 50
de la Porte, Captain PC Andre 98
de Putter, Sergeant W 65
de Roller, Lieutenant Colonel EJT 73
de Rozario, Sergeant R 99
Dean, Sergeant AA 51
Dellinger, Staff Sergeant Walter H 81
Dellitt, Flight Sergeant L 123
Dennis, Squadron Leader RS 102
Dewey, Staff Sergeant Vernon E 75
Diamed, Pilot Officer DG 89
Dias, Lieutenant Herman J 77
Dickinson, Flying Officer RF 89
Dienelt, Captain James H 56
Dinsdale, Flight Sergeant Lew 105
Dobbs, Sergeant GS 36
Donk, Lieutenant AE 99
Donovan, Lieutenant Joseph A 56
Draaier, Lieutenant JJ Th 98
Drake-Brockman, Sergeant RFN 69
Drean, Staff Sergeant Marvin L 77
Dreher, Lieutenant AA 99
Dunbar, Sergeant GP 40
Duncanson, Flight Sergeant L 120
Dunne, Wing Commander RA "Arch" 120
Dunning, Lieutenant Dan A 77
Dunning, Flight Sergeant RKR 37
Durkin, Lieutenant Thomas H 48
Dwyre, Pilot Officer NF 89
Easton, Flight Sergeant INL 120
Easton, Chaplain NC 106
Eaton, Group Captain Charles "Moth" 71
Eckert, Lieutenant Clarence "Bud" 45
Edeson, Sergeant WR 36
Edwards, Lieutenant Andrew B 60
Edwards, LAC KEG 48
Eggleston, Lieutenant John G 82
Eisenhower, Major General Dwight D 10
Ekert, Flying Officer ELE "Les" 106, 108, 110
Elkington, Flying Officer LA 62
Emery, Sergeant DA 52
Enders, Technical Sergeant Robert K 48
Engelsman, Sergeant F 99
Ernst, Sergeant GJ 126

Estes, Lieutenant Frederick J 75
Etienne, Flying Officer Armand 125
Eubank, Brigadier General Eugene L 96, 97
Evatt, Dr HV 77, 78
Faichnie, Flight Sergeant 119
Falconer, Pilot Officer 87
Farmer, Flight Sergeant DC 67
Farr, Technical Sergeant Bradley F 82
Farrington, Captain John 60
Faull, Pilot Officer SW 36
Fenton, Flight Lieutenant Clyde C 25, 37
Ferguson, Staff Sergeant Lee E 77
Fiedeldij, Major 134, 135
Fike, Technical Sergeant Monte L 77
Finck, Staff Sergeant Peter H 75
Finlayson, Squadron Leader John "Mickey" 97, 120
Fisk, Flying Officer JD 62
Flaherty, Flight Sergeant RJ 69
Flanagan, Staff Sergeant Henry P 81
Flanagan, Warrant Officer WR 114
Fleming, Lieutenant Bob 60
Fleming, Lieutenant Russell P 75
Flessert, Lieutenant William Q 45
Ford, Sergeant Bill 58
Ford, Flight Lieutenant EV 113, 118
Forsyth, Flying Officer LT 108
Fowler, Flight Lieutenant AM 67
Fox, Sergeant JD "Jack" 121
Francis, Sergeant DW 37
Francis, Technical Sergeant Harry T 60
Franken, Lieutenant WG 99
Fraser, Sergeant LHS 37
Freidman, Lieutenant Norman 20
French, Sergeant Robert 32
Frew, Flight Sergeant RG 84
Fritschy, Technical Sergeant Joseph A 95
Froud, Flight Lieutenant Len 123
Fruin, Lieutenant R 73
Gad, Lieutenant Howard E 75
Gallagher, Staff Sergeant William F 60
Gardner, Lieutenant James 75
Garrison, Staff Sergeant Charles W 75
Geerke, Lieutenant JH 72
Gerards, Sergeant LJ 65
Gill, Sergeant Edward J 94
Gill, Flying Officer NB 123
Gill, Pilot Officer RL 31
Gillies, Pilot Officer HJ 84
Gilmore, Lieutenant Raymond E 75
Gitsham, Sergeant D 28
Gleeson, Flight Sergeant Joe 105, 107, 108, 110
Gontha, Sergeant CB 71
Goodchild, Sergeant Harold S 128
Gordon, Squadron Leader "Butch" 71
Goudie, Flying Officer AG 101
Gould, Lieutenant Harry R 95
Gould, Sergeant WH 36
Gove, Sergeant WJ 51
Graham, Sergeant JA 29
Graham, Sergeant John A 48

Graham, Sergeant Maurice 68
Graham, Flying Officer TS 69
Grant, Squadron Leader Ken 126
Gray, Squadron Leader 100
Greene, Technical Sergeant Leonard R 60
Greenfield, Staff Sergeant Bernard 56
Grenfell, Lieutenant Wilfred L 6
Grey, Flight Lieutenant Robin 91
Griesbach, Warrant Officer AK 105
Grummels, Lieutenant BJQ 44
Guilfoyle, Sergeant Thomas E 75
Gunn, Paul 27
Gunson, Flying Officer PC 37
Guthrie, Squadron Leader Bill 147
Guy, Sergeant O 28
Hadley, Sergeant HH 51
Hadley, Flying Officer KJ 105
Haga, Staff Sergeant David L 82
Hagerty, Lieutenant James R 60
Haggerty, Bill 44, 47
Hagler, Lieutenant Curtiss 75
Hall, Sergeant HW 123
Halliday, Flight Lieutenant Lex 82
Hamby, Master Sergeant William 45
Hamilton, Flight Sergeant William J 86
Hammang, Lieutenant Daniel C 60
Hannah, Squadron Leader David 110
Harberger, Sergeant DF 106
Harrigan, Flight Lieutenant Ron 128, 129
Harrison, Flying Officer Alan L 95
Harsley, Flying officer RM 125
Hastings, Lieutenant Max 74, 75
Havener, Lieutenant Hal 45
Havyatt, Wing Commander HG "Harry" 123
Hawkins, Warrant Officer AE 106
Hawthorne, Flight Sergeant Brian 104, 108
Hawthorne, Staff Sergeant JD 94
Hay, Flying Officer 33
Haydon, Flight Lieutenant CW 62
Hayward, Sergeant LR 31
Hearle, Sergeant HF 28
Hedges, Lieutenant Ernest R 81
Heile, Sergeant L 44
Helsham, Flying Officer Mick 67, 69
Helzer, Staff Sergeant Harold H 47
Henderson, Warrant Officer Jim 85
Henschke, Lieutenant Colonel John 55, 96
Hepworth, Flying Officer WA 67
Herbert, Flight Sergeant Donald N 58, 59, 95
Herps, Flight Sergeant JRW 120
Herres, Flight Officer Francis E 60
Hesse, Lieutenant Charles 44-48
Heys, Sergeant LH 72
Hian, Lieutenant Lie Kok 8
Hicks, Flying Officer DR 52
Hien, Lieutenant Liem Yoe 73
Hilder, Wing Commander Brett 123
Hill, Flight Sergeant RJ 50
Hine Flight Sergeant AJ 91
Hinze, Lieutenant Frederick 60
Hitchcock, Lieutenant Charles 38
Hobbs, Sergeant RJ 63

Hocking, Flight Sergeant Peter 105
Hoffman, Flight Sergeant DG 91
Hollingsworth, Flying Officer 69
Hollingsworth, Private 1st Cl Clinton 82
Hollis, Flight Sergeant 120
Holmes, Dennis 146
Holohan, Joseph 56
Holswilder, Captain CM 71
Holt, Staff Sergeant James C 82
Honan, Flying Officer Bob 63, 64
Hootjij, Sergeant R 65
Horsburgh, Sergeant DJJ 26
Horseman, Sergeant JC 40
Hosie, Bernard 58
Hosie, George 59
Howe, Flying Officer EM 63
Howley, Sergeant Edward R 71
Hudspeth, Staff Sergeant Frank A 48
Hughes, Mr 25
Hurst, Flight Lieutenant 117
Hursthouse, Flying Officer JW 114
Hurt, Squadron Leader Lin 125
Hyde, Flight Lieutenant JR 89
Ichikawa, Flying Petty Officer 1st Cl Mitsugu 66
Ikeda, Lieutenant 68, 76
Ikin, Sergeant 68
Imada, Flying Petty Officer 2nd Cl Toshio 65
Ingledew, Wing Commander TS 110
Inglis, Sergeant SL 31
Jackman, Warrant Officer VL 52
Jackson, Sergeant M 68
Jacobs, Sergeant 28
Jacobs, Flying Officer ER 78
Jacques, Flight Lieutenant Mick 78
James, Flying Officer RR 36, 37, 51
Jamieson, Flight Sergeant 86
Jamieson, Sergeant Stuart H 95
Jansen, Lieutenant HJ 73
Janssen, Sergeant JJLM 44
Jeffrey, Flight Lieutenant FW 123
Jennings, LAC Charles Conroy 48
Jerge, Lieutenant Clarence F 75
John, Flying Officer RE 51
Johns, Flying Officer MWC 40
Johnson, Technical Sergeant Lincoln 57
Johnson, Captain Paul 44, 45, 55
Johnstone, Sergeant RJ 51
Jones, Sergeant 119
Jones, Sergeant AR 126
Jones, Flight Sergeant AR 129
Jones, Captain Charles E 44, 45
Jones, Sergeant Harry 91
Jones, Sergeant K 51
Jones, Lieutenant Thomas M 77
Jope, Pilot Officer LR 51
Jordon, Flying Officer RT 118
Kagi, Flight Lieutenant Robert 126
Kane, Flying Officer JM 126
Karbach, Lieutenant William C 94
Katz, Staff Sergeant Raymond 60
Kawaguchi, Warrant Officer Takeshi 52

Katayama, Sub-Lieutenant 84
Kay, Warrant Officer J 102
Keally, Sergeant LR 31
Keenan, Wing Commander William J 101, 103
Keesmaat, Sergeant Cornelis 70
Keiran, Private Raymond A 45
Kelly, Lieutenant Hugh S 77
Kelly, Staff Sergeant William J 56
Kemp, Sergeant FP 37
Kenihan, Sergeant ML 37
Kennedy, Lieutenant Brian J 81
Kennedy-Dwyer, Ray 102
Kenney, Lieutenant General George C 15, 63, 65-67, 77, 78
Keon, Warrant Officer Felix E 86
Kerns, Staff Sergeant Russell E 82
Kerr, Flying Officer 86
Kersten, Pilot Officer KI 29
Kessels, Sergeant Major NMW 44
Kilcheski, Lieutenant Eugene A 98
Killen, Warrant Officer Leonard 95
Kilpatrick, Sergeant BA 29
King, Warrant Officer CSJ 106
King, Flight Sergeant Robert 83
Kingwell, Group Captain Derek 94, 112-114, 118
Kino, Reserve Lieutenant Yuji 47
Kirkwood, Flight Lieutenant 117
Klemm, Warrant Officer KF 87
Knauer, Flying Officer IG 52
Knauer, Flying Officer GL 69
Knight, LAC Lindsay 73
Kosciuszek, Staff Sergeant Peter P 94
Kreahe Sergeant EH 91
Krech, Sergeant KD 51
Krist, Staff Sergeant John J 77
Laidlaw, Captain "Bull" 38
Laing, Flight Lieutenant W 118
Laman, Sergeant James E 33
Lamb, Flying Officer 142, 143
Lamb, Sergeant John 68
Lancaster, Flying Officer JG 62
Lane, Pilot Officer DG 105
Laney, Pilot Officer P 128
Latrelle, Major Roger 95
Laws, Flying Officer J 51
Lazarus, LAC PR 48
Leach, Jim 147
Lee, Peter 108
Leggatt, Lieutenant Colonel 139
Leithhead, Pilot Officer VC 28
Lemons, Technical Sergeant Harold J 98
Levandowski, SA 94
Lewallen, Staff Sergeant Boyd H 77
Lewis, Staff Sergeant Donald A 82
Lewis, Ted 42
Lindsay, Flying Officer RC 67
Lockley, Pilot Officer A 28
Lomas, Warrant Officer 86
Lonergan, Wing Commander CA 88
Long, Pilot Officer BE 31

Longfield, Technical Sergeant Bennett H 77
Lught, Lieutenant GJ 99
Maarschalkereerd, Sergeant A 44
MacAlister, Flight Lieutenant JL 26
MacArthur, General Douglas 9, 10, 67, 133
MacDonald, Sergeant John C 128
Madden, Corporal DW 115
Maddern, Sergeant JR 26
Manabe, Flying Petty Officer 2nd Cl Tsuruo 47
Markowitz, Staff Sergeant Harold B 60
Marks, Sergeant John 72
Marshall, General George C 10
Marshall, Lieutenant Howard K 75
Marshall, Technical Sergeant William A 75
Marsman, Sergeant RW 99
Martens, Lieutenant Otto 81
Martin, Sergeant ASR 128
Martin, Sergeant DL 121
Martin, Flying Officer Lynn 68
Maslaskas, Sergeant Alfonso W 46
Maslin, Flying Officer JAG 123
Mason, Flight Lieutenant John F 52, 69
Massin, Staff Sergeant Morris 95
Matthews, Warrant Officer FH 108
Matzusaki, Rear Admiral Akira 131
Maudsley, Jack 141
McCallum, Warrant Officer Ian 105
McCauley, Flying Officer K 129
McCombe, Squadron Leader 78, 111
McDaniel, Lieutenant Bill 97
McDonald, Flight Sergeant Lindsay 80, 93, 111
McDonald, Sergeant Rod 115
McDonald, Squadron Leader Sid 117, 118
McDonnell, Flying Officer KL 36
McDowell, Lieutenant Francis G 58
McFarlane, Squadron Leader AB "Tich" 29
McGarry, Frank 60
McGuire, Sergeant M 31
McHarris, Lieutenant Thomas J 45
McKenzie, Flying Officer 68
McKenzie, Flight Sergeant IW 52
McLay, Pilot Officer WC 29
McLean, Group Captain D 121
McLean, Sergeant N 68
McMahon, Sergeant T 89
McMillin, Lieutenant Douglas G 94
McMillin, Squadron Leader John 110
McMullin, Flight Lieutenant AM 124
McPherson, Sergeant David L 44
Meakin, Flying Officer AR 91
Meijer, Lieutenant FH 98
Merkel, Captain Howard 57
Merrett, Pilot Officer MO 129
Mesman, Elmer 42, 133, 137
Miles, Jim 115
Miller, Colonel Bill 55, 57, 74
Miller, Flight Lieutenant Damien 90
Miller, Staff Sergeant Glenn A 82
Miller, Flight Sergeant JB 91

INDEX OF NAMES

Miller, Staff Sergeant William E   75
Miller, Staff Sergeant William O   60
Miller, Staff Sergeant WR "Dub"   81
Millett, Flying Officer MS   106
Mills, Lieutenant Archibald S   60
Mills, Flying Officer KR   3, 51
Miners, Pilot Officer Lloyd M   33
Mirachi, Staff Sergeant Albert   60
Mitchell, Flying Officer   141
Mitchell, Staff Sergeant Mark A   60
Monisko, Technical Sergeant Jack C   75
Montgomerie, Sergeant LJ   29
Moore, Flight Lieutenant Eldin   118, 119
Moran, Squadron Leader RH   35, 37, 40
Morgan, Robert   13, 17
Morris, Sergeant NGW   50
Morris, Flight Sergeant RM   114
Morrison, Sergeant RL   55
Moshier, Technical Sergeant Francis L   75
Moss, Flying Officer AW   29
Moss, Flying Officer Frank S   33
Mouatt, Flying Officer PA   118
Muecke, Flying Officer Robert C   33
Mueller, Lieutenant Alvin J   11
Mueller, Staff Sergeant Jack S   45
Mulhollen, Lieutenant Harold S   75
Munker, Lieutenant George O   45
Murphy, Flight Sergeant HL   91
Muscato, Staff Sergeant Harold   48
Musson, Staff Sergeant Howard W   81
Nakano, Ensign Seiichi   66
Nango, Captain Shigeo   57
Napier, Flight Lieutenant John   78, 80
Neal, Lieutenant Bobby   97
Neate, Flight Sergeant GIH   125
Neville, Technical Sergeant Clarence E   56
Newbold, Staff Sergeant Ralph T   60
Nichols, Squadron Leader AW   113
Nigrini, Staff Sergeant Paul   57
Nixon, Pilot Officer JF   40
Norris, Flight Lieutenant J "Paddy"   107
Norris, Sergeant RE   51
O'Dea, Flying Officer Donald J   95
O'Donnell, Staff Sergeant Thomas J   77
O'Hea, Sergeant GA   50
O'Loughlin, Flying Officer Colin   125
O'Loughlin, Lieutenant John T   95
O'Neill, Lieutenant John T   95
O'Reilly, Sergeant FM   36
Ochala, Staff Sergeant Carl A   56
Odegaard, Lieutenant Clifford M   81
Odom, Staff Sergeant Dossie J   60
Okumiya, Masatake   122
Oldridge, Pilot Officer JP   69
Oliver, Flying Officer AJP   63
Olsen, Captain Roy W   47, 48
Olsen, Technical Sergeant Wallace M   95
Omsby, Sergeant LA   29
Oppy, Sergeant LN   62
Orchard, Sergeant K   28
Ortlepp, Flight Lieutenant Brian   129
Oudraad, Lieutenant AF   50

Overheu, Flight Lieutenant Dick   28, 29, 31, 32, 37, 51, 79, 80, 93, 111, 112
Owen, Sergeant Charles R   77
Owen, Lieutenant Jack W   98
Paalman, Lieutenant GH   65
Pafahl, Staff Sergeant Harold C   75
Palamountain, LAC Max T   42, 44
Palfreyman, Flight Sergeant RC   106
Palmer, Lieutenant John A   56
Parker, Lieutenant Benjamin G   57
Parker, Warrant Officer HG   114
Parker, Group Captain Peter   117, 121
Parker, Lieutenant Roy M   81, 82
Parkinson, Flight Lieutenant JR   114
Parks, Sergeant JT   77
Parris, Lieutenant Hugh B   60
Parry-Okeden, Flight Lieutenant CD   114, 115
Parsons, Lieutenant Laverne F   60
Patterson, Staff Sergeant Leonard G   75
Payne, Lieutenant John B   56
Peacock, Warrant Officer Eric C   102
Penrose, Corporal IL   63
Petch, Sergeant DJ   69
Peterson, Staff Sergeant Robert F   77
Philipson, Flight Sergeant KR   106
Philpot, Pilot Officer RJ   84
Pitt, Flying Officer JM   114
Pocknee, Flying Officer FR   91
Poole, Flying Officer B   102
Poor, Captain Samuel S   60
Pott, Flying Officer AE   106
Powell, Alan   118
Powell, Sergeant WS   37
Prest, Lieutenant Robert F   95
Preston, Sergeant RC   128
Pritchard, Sergeant FC   55
Pugh, LAC J   102
Quinn, Flight Sergeant E   52
Rabbitt, Technical Sergeant William T   81
Raine, Flight Sergeant L   118
Rakow, Staff Sergeant Floyd E   57
Ramsdell, Lieutenant Keith K   75
Reece, Sergeant WD   91
Reed, Staff Sergeant Harry H   94
Reedijk, Lieutenant W   73
Reen, Sergeant PS   37, 51
Rees, Captain AJ   71
Reilly, Sergeant H   37
Rhoads, Staff Sergeant Richard R   75
Richards, Geoff   139
Riding, Squadron Leader Doug   39
Riemens, Lieutenant Ch   98
Riley, Wireless Air Gunner Harry   30
Rivera, Staff Sergeant Ernest   57
Robert, Lieutenant   38
Roberts, Sergeant AG Bill   38
Roberts, Flight Lieutenant Herbert C   128
Roberts, Staff Sergeant James C   46
Robertson, Flight Lieutenant JW   40
Robertson, Sergeant William R   48
Robinson, Flying Officer FK   91

Robinson, Sergeant James R   128
Robinson, Lieutenant Marvin H   75
Robinson, Sergeant RJ   125
Rogers, Flight Sergeant AJ   114, 115
Rogier, Corporal L   71
Rolfe, Flight Sergeant JA   108
Roll, Sergeant PC   29
Roosevelt, President Franklin D   54, 77, 78
Root, Flight Officer Lee A   57
Rose, Warrant Officer Warwick   91
Ross, Sergeant K   40
Roubal, Staff Sergeant James F   60
Route, Lieutenant Hilary E   98
Rowe, Flight Sergeant WA   129
Rowland, Sergeant GR   52, 69
Rowlands, Flight Sergeant TH   108
Roxburgh, Squadron Leader   86
Roy, Flight Lieutenant JA   121
Royce, Brigadier General Ralph   27
Rubin, Lieutenant Max   94
Rudge, Flying Officer Richard "George"   101
Rule, Flight Lieutenant   117
Rumble, Flight Sergeant DN   69
Russell, Staff Sergeant Donald D   56
Russell, Flight Sergeant FH   123
Russell, Lieutenant Roland W   45
Rust, Warrant Officer TN   120
Ryan, Sergeant DP   126
Ryan, Flight Sergeant JR   114
Ryan, Sergeant RD   51
Ryland, Group Captain John   111, 138
Sacre, Sergeant Gerald D   97
Sahoer, Sergeant Arsil   71
Salemi, Sergeant John   46
Samalo, Sergeant M   98
Sandwell, Flight Sergeant William D   86
Sasaki, Ensign Kasuka   33
Sayer, Sergeant   118
Scanlan, Lieutenant Walter E   97
Schaetzel, Lieutenant George   11
Schalk, Lieutenant L   44
Schechtel, Sergeant Arthur J   81
Schell, Staff Sergeant Eugene O   75
Scholte, Lieutenant WJM   99
Schulte, Technical Sergeant Alvin J   56
Schulz, Pilot Officer RW   129
Scott, Wing Commander ED   77
Scott, Squadron Leader John L   70, 83, 84
Scott, Sergeant WD   129
Seage, Flight Lieutenant Jim   128
Selway, Flying Officer Jack   106
Setterblade, Lieutenant Russell R   48
Sharland, Corporal Darcy AJ   46
Sharp, Arthur   25
Sharpe, Flight Lieutenant Neil   110
Shaw, WAG John   39
Shek, Captain Bill   56
Shepardson, Staff Sergeant RF   60
Shepherd, Colonel Edward   60
Shilling, Warrant Officer Keith   118
Sieber, Sergeant Dave   97, 120, 121
Silvester, Flight Lieutenant Frank W   128

Simms, Sergeant John 38
Simon, Staff Sergeant William C 48
Simpson, Flight Lieutenant Joe 106
Siple, Flight Officer Raymond E 60
Sismey, Flying Officer Frank L 120
Skillman, Tom 25
Slater, Flying Officer Allan 106
Sloman, Flying Officer MG 126
Slunaker, Sergeant Robert W 45
Smead, Sergeant Lowell F 46
Smith, Flying Officer EC 63
Smith, Lieutenant Gorman 77
Smith, John 144
Smith, Pilot Officer Les 104
Smith, Captain Paul G 57
Smith, Captain Weldon 32
Smith, Captain Zed 55, 57
Soeterik, Sergeant E 71
Soute, Lieutenant 72
Sowa, Captain Charles 57
Spaulding, Pilot Officer Milford 129
Speet, Flight Lieutenant TWJ 87
Spink, Master Sergeant Thomas N 45
Spoel, Lieutenant HJ 98
Stacy, Flight Lieutenant Brian 91
Stacy, Flying Officer Ted 67
Stauffer, Technical Sergeant Gaylord N 75
Stevens, Lieutenant Lawrence 93
Stevens, Captain Virgil H 76-78, 93, 94
Stevenson, Staff Sergeant John C 75
Stewart, Sergeant 45
Stewart, Sergeant Rex 75
Stilling, Wing Commander SG 89
Storer, Warrant Officer J 125
Storrie, Sergeant DK 129
Stormon, Warrant Officer JF 106
Straus, Squadron Leader Nathaniel "Fanny" 114-116
Stringer, Flight Sergeant LW 91
Strong, Lieutenant Kenneth F 48
Suzuki, Lieutenant Commander Minoru 60
Sverdrup, Colonel 25
Swan, Warrant Officer RA 91
Swane, Lieutenant Rudy 49
Swann, Flying Officer TW 52, 69
Takahashi, Flying Chief Petty Officer Takeshi 60
Taylor, Pilot Officer PG 28
Temperley, Flying Officer Don 125
Templeton, Sergeant Billie R 77
Thame, Sergeant Gordon J 40
Thoen, Staff Sergeant Kenneth R 94
Thomas, Flying Officer Don 66
Thomas, Flight Sergeant JA 118
Thomas, Private William M 57
Thompson, Sergeant A 125
Thompson, Sergeant DJ 28
Thompson Lieutenant Forrest "Tommy" 95
Thompson, Warrant Officer JES 108
Thompson, Sergeant KE 91
Thompson, Flying Officer PG 40
Thompson, Lieutenant Tommy 78

Thompson, Flying Officer WFE "Elmo" 108
Thomson, Sergeant FH 89
Thomson, Sergeant JK 128
Thornton, Flying Officer Harold A 94
Tijmons, Sergeant Major G 50
Titshall, Flying Officer Ben 125
Tjoe, Sergeant Kwee Wan 71
Todd, Squadron Leader John 91
Topperwein, Captain Clifton 80
Treloar, Flying Officer V 36
Trewren, Flight Lieutenant Lindsay 31, 35, 37
Trexler, Lieutenant John W 57
Trimnell, Sergeant Maurice E 98
Tucker, Technical Sergeant Raymond L 98
Tyler, Sergeant DK 40
Tyler, Sergeant RG "Tim" 44
Tyrell, Sergeant MB 63
Van Bremen, Major 100
Van Bremen, Sergeant K 50
Van Burg, Sergeant J 65
Van Buuren, Captain Paul 73
Van Den Berg, Lieutenant H 55
Van Der Coevering, Sergeant WF 65
Van der Linden, Sergeant BJ 98
Van Hoyen, Major General 133
Van Kan, Sergeant MP 65
Van Lier, Lieutenant Th W 73
Van Polanen Petel, Sergeant JC
Van Renesse, Lieutenant HJ 99
Van Straalen, Lieutenant P 98
Van Wormer, Lieutenant Harold 77
Van Wylick, Sergeant Major FJM 50
Van Yperen, Sergeant RH 65
Vanek, Staff Sergeant Emil F 56
Venn, Pilot Officer John 25, 26, 29
Vercoe, Sergeant EA 29
Vetter, Sergeant JI 126
Vicks, Lieutenant Joe 75
Visser, Lieutenant A 73
Visser, Sergeant C 65
Vogler, Lieutenant KG 99
Vromen, Lieutenant B 71
Waddell, Flight Sergeant JM 118
Wadey, Flying Officer Sid 36
Wadham, Sergeant AHB 91
Wallaart, Sergeant P 72
Wallace, Flight Sergeant Bruce 69, 70, 83
Wallace, Staff Sergeant John H 45
Wallace, Flight Sergeant Terrence 86
Walmsley, Flight Sergeant LK 118
Walsh, Lieutenant Ricard W 97
Walton, Sergeant Harold O 42, 44
Ward, Lieutenant William G 97
Wards-Smit, Sergeant G 36
Warne, Flight Sergeant RL 128
Watts, Flying Officer C 102
Webley, Flight Sergeant Douglas V 98
Welch, Staff Sergeant Robert W 77
Weller, Sergeant GB 50
Wertzler, Staff Sergeant George L 75
West, Sergeant Bryson 32

West, Sergeant RM 40
Westbury, Flying Officer Ted 110
Wettenhall, Pilot Officer MC 68
Wheatland, Sergeant RSK 125
Whincup, Flying Officer CR 123
Whitacre, Technical Sergeant William G 75
White, Squadron Leader 117
White, Warrant Officer Bill 110
White, Pilot Officer WM "Bill" 110
Whitehead, Sergeant AD 114
Whiting, Flying Officer RA 114
Whitlam, Gough 103
Whitley, Sergeant GW 91
Whyte, Squadron Leader Jock 67
Wickham, Warrant Officer HR 128
Wignall, Sergeant WJ 118
Wilken, Flight Sergeant Charles L 95
Wilkinson, Lieutenant Bob 96
Willems, Sergeant G Th 73
Willer, Staff Sergeant Arthur N 75
Willesden, Flight Sergeant JW 91
Williams, Flight Lieutenant CA 126
Williams, Squadron Leader Cyril 67
Williams, Major Howard C 95, 96
Williams, Staff Sergeant Lloyd E 95
Williams, Pilot Officer RH 68
Williams, Air Marshal Sir Richard 77, 78
Williams, Flight Sergeant TEW 55
Wilson, Lieutenant John 45
Wilson, Sergeant TW 51
Winckel, Lieutenant Gus 42, 49, 55
Winspear, Brian 9, 138, 139
Winterbon, Flight Sergeant BK 91
Wisniewski, Flying Officer BA 106
Witham, Sergeant WD 28
Wolf, Staff Sergeant Robert R 60
Wood, Flight Lieutenant JR 52, 69
Wood, Flying Officer KWH 87
Woodhouse, Sergeant ND 91
Woodnutt, Corporal Bill 41
Woods, Sergeant D 28
Woods, Flight Sergeant RD 69
Woolley, Sergeant Fred 91
Worley, Flying Officer AG 118
Worman, Pilot Officer HB 106
Wright, Flight Sergeant Keith 83
Wright, Sergeant JL 26
Wynnands, Sergeant G 53
Yeaman, Flight Lieutenant John 25
Yokota, Flying Chief Petty Officer Sadayoshi 75, 77
Youl, Geoff 139
Young, Lieutenant Bob 78, 94
Zelby, Staff Sergeant Samuel 77
Zeydel, Lieutenant PL 65

BOMBERS NORTH

Allied bomber operations from Northern Australia 1942-1945

DR TOM LEWIS

AVONMORE BOOKS

Bombers North

Allied bomber operations from Northern Australia 1942-1945

Dr Tom Lewis OAM

ISBN: 978-0-6452469-9-5

First published 2023 by Avonmore Books

Avonmore Books
PO Box 217
Kent Town
South Australia 5071
Australia

Phone: (61 8) 8431 9780
avonmorebooks.com.au

A catalogue record for this book is available from the National Library of Australia

Cover design & layout by Diane Bricknell

© 2023 Avonmore Books.

No part of this book may be reproduced or transmitted in any form or by any means, electronic or mechanical, including photocopying or recording, or by any information storage and retrieval system, without permission in writing from the publisher.

Cover artwork captions:

Front cover: A 319th Bombardment Squadron B-24 fights off a No. 202 Ku Zero during a 1943 mission over the Netherlands East Indies.

Back Cover: A Lockheed Hudson of No. 2 Squadron, RAAF, is prepared for a bombing mission from Batchelor. The Hudsons were the main offensive strength of the Allied air forces in the Darwin region in 1942, and often targeted their former base of Penfui in Timor. (AWM)